HASTINGS & ST LEONARDS

THROUGH TIME

Nathan Dylan Goodwin

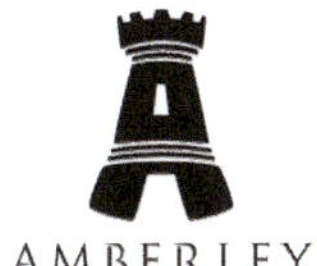

AMBERLEY

I would like to dedicate this book to
Darren, Ainsley, Hannah, George, Oliver, Henry and Daisy

First published 2010

Amberley Publishing
Cirencester Road, Chalford,
Stroud, Gloucestershire GL6 8PE

www.amberleybooks.com

Copyright © Nathan Dylan Goodwin, 2010

The right of Nathan Dylan Goodwin to be
identified as the Author of this work has been
asserted in accordance with the Copyrights,
Designs and Patents Act 1988.

ISBN 978-1-4456-0052-9

British Library Cataloguing in Publication Data.
A catalogue record for this book is available from
the British Library.

Typeset in 9.5pt on 12pt Celeste.
Typesetting by Amberley Publishing.
Printed in the UK.

Appointed GPSR EU Representative: Easy Access
System Europe Oü, 16879218
Address: Mustamäe tee 50, 10621, Tallinn, Estonia
Contact Details: gpsr.requests@easproject.com,
+358 40 500 3575

Contents

Acknowledgements

I am especially grateful to David Padgham for allowing me access to his vast postcard collection; he has graciously allowed me to pick my way through the images in order to choose the best for *Hastings & St Leonards Through Time*. He has also provided additional information and pointed out a few inaccuracies! I would also like to thank Mark Edwards for stepping into the breach and taking photographs of the Blessing of the Sea and Hastings Carnival while I was busy on holiday. Many thanks are also due to Andy Gunton for allowing me to use his photograph of the pier on fire. Other images used in the book were supplied by the *Hastings & St Leonards Observer*, for which I am grateful. Also my thanks for photos are extended to Norman Stanley Dengate, Eveline Florence Edwards and, although I 'inherited' the pictures after her death, my great aunt, Elsie Dorothy Glazier. Hastings Library staff have been very helpful in the completion of this book, in particular Zoë Edwards. Finally, my gratitude goes to Robert John Bristow: for everything, as always.

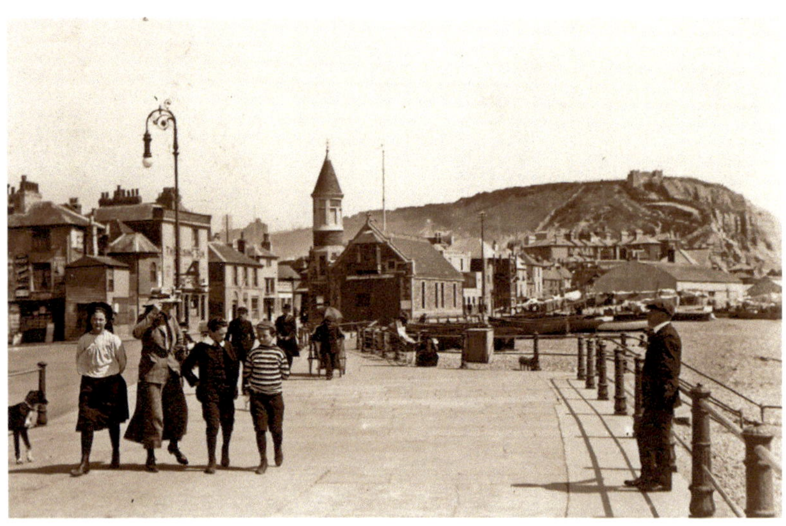

Introduction

Is there room for yet another collection of photographs of Hastings? That was the question I asked myself when considering the potential merits of writing *Hastings & St Leonards Through Time*; 'yes' was the unequivocal answer! Although a number of photo books exist of the town, this collection is unique in a number of ways. Firstly, the vast majority of the images selected have never before been published, thereby giving a fresh glimpse into Hastings' past. Secondly, this volume does not set out to be strictly 'then and now', which very much works in its favour; if, for example, the modern view of a fantastic old image is dreary and unimaginative then an alternative view or an entirely different angle has been used. In this way, only the best photographs are shown. Some of the pictures are compared geographically, showing a comparative view of the same street, while others are linked thematically by the event featured in the old image. This has given me a wide scope in writing and an opportunity to reveal a new window on the history of Hastings.

For the most part, the sepia images were taken in the Edwardian era and the majority of these old photographs were taken by the maestros of Edwardian photography – Frederick Broderick and Fred Judge. Frederick Broderick began taking photos of the town around 1902, Fred Judge the following year. Both of these men were renowned locally for their professional photographs. Frederick Broderick hailed from Ryde on the Isle of Wight, so his photographs tended to capture evocative everyday scenes taken during his visits to Hastings. In contrast, Fred Judge was a Hastings resident who was able to quickly take his camera to dramatic events that occurred without notice, such as fires, storms or visiting dignitaries. Indeed, it was not uncommon to be able to purchase one of Judge's postcards the day after a significant blaze or flood. Several of the photographs in the 'Fire and Flood' chapter of this book were taken by Fred Judge and were available for locals to buy the day after the event had taken place.

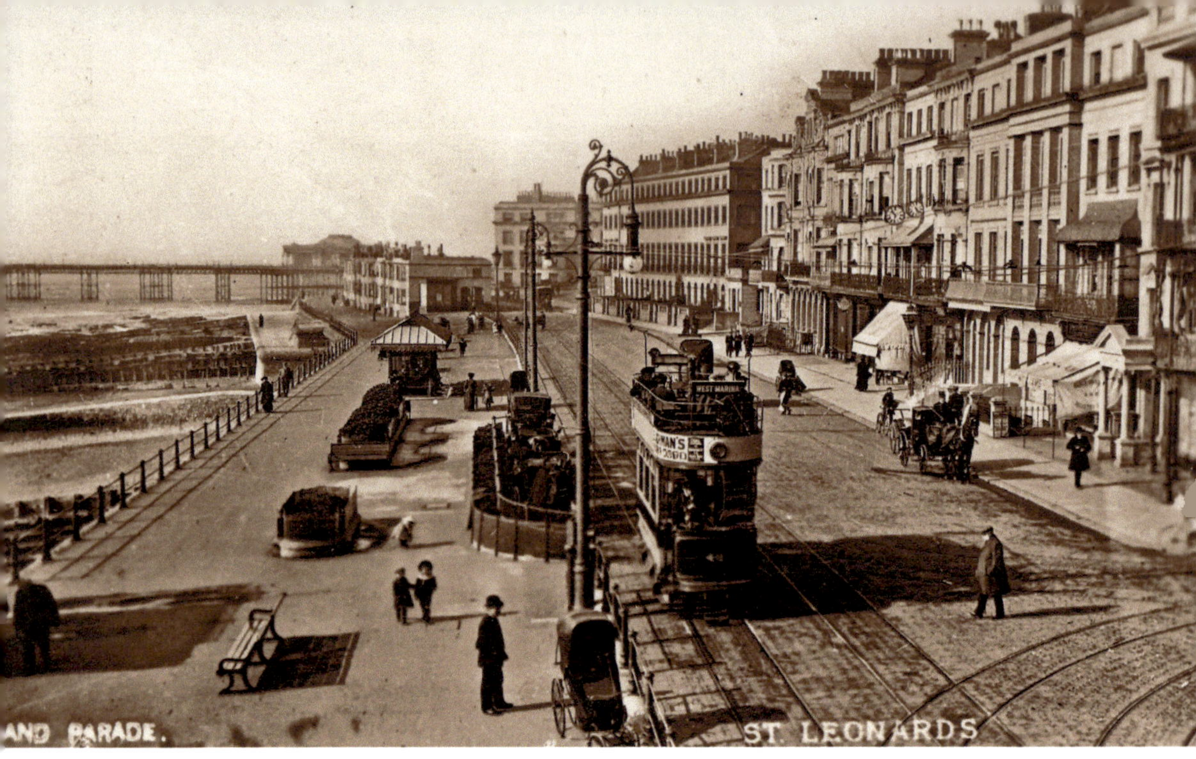

Hastings, like many seaside towns, has experienced a veritable rollercoaster of change. This book goes some way to show how these changes have affected the town, arguably not always in a good way! With the help of various government grants and private investment, Hastings has been undergoing a series of large-scale building developments in and around the town, among them the University Centre, the Priory Quarter development, the Jerwood Art Gallery and Asda supermarket. Also scheduled for major redevelopment was Hastings pier. This, however, suffered a tragic setback when, in the early hours of 5 October 2010, a huge blaze ripped through the Victorian structure, destroying 95 per cent of the once 'peerless pier'. Ironically, the fire occurred just hours after architects were invited to submit plans for its refurbishment. Many of these developments have not been without their share of controversy and many of them will change the architectural landscape of the town for ever. Only time will tell whether these buildings will help propel Hastings back towards a new golden era as a fashionable seaside destination.

With one or two exceptions, the majority of the modern images were taken in the summer of 2010. I very much hope that in the future the modern images in this book will have stood the test of time and be of use as a record of the town during such historic change.

Nathan Dylan Goodwin BA MA
October 2010

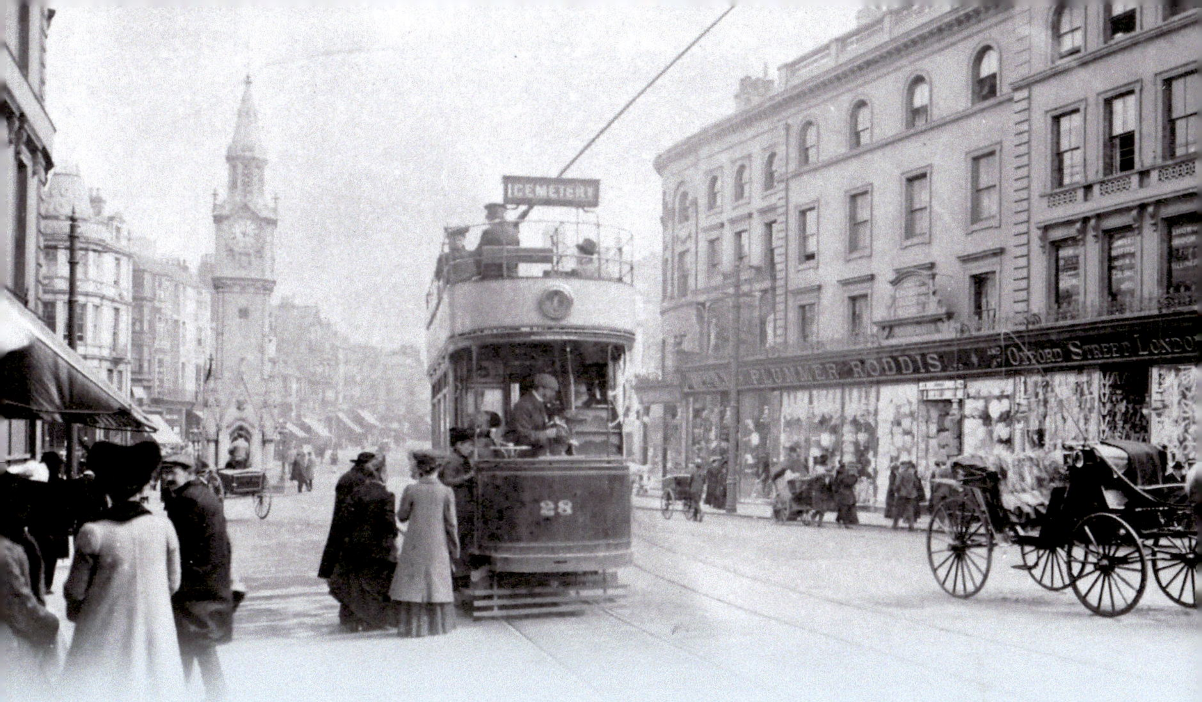

CHAPTER 1

Town Centre

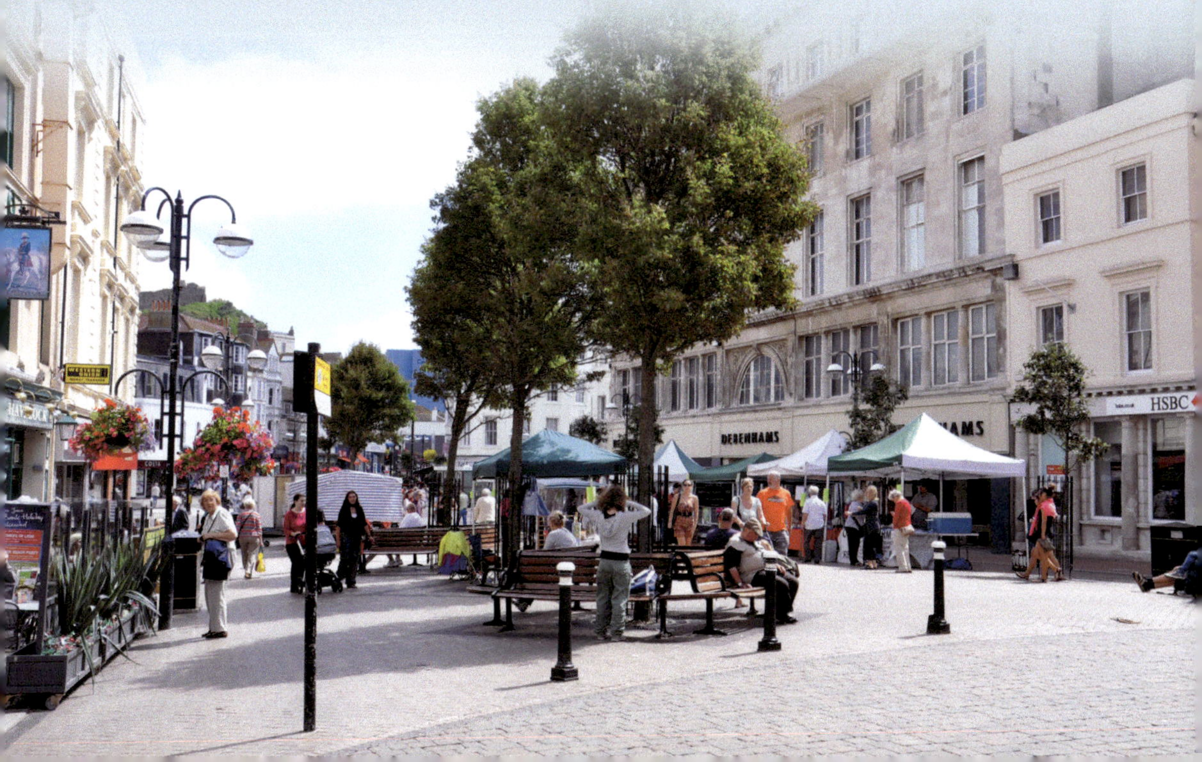

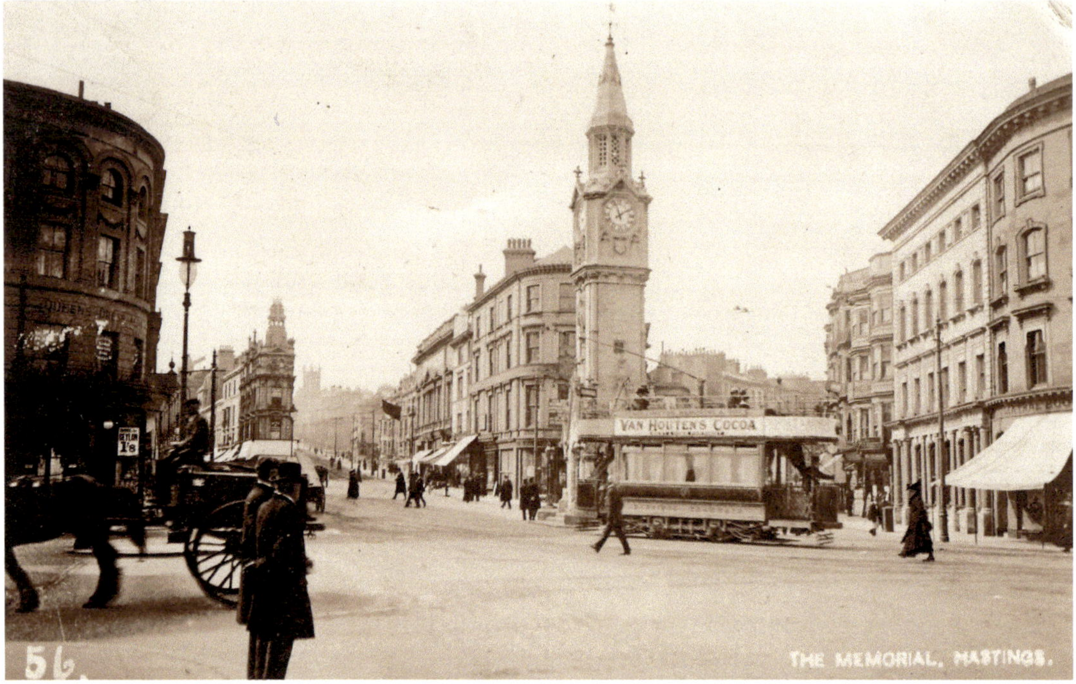

The Memorial

The Albert Memorial has long been a cause of controversy; many lament its loss and continue to campaign to have it reinstated. The 65-feet-high tower was completed in 1863 on the site of the old Priory Bridge, a clock being added the following year. In 1973, having captured the hearts of several generations in the town, the tower had its top partly damaged in a fire and, in November of that year, the council ordered that it be demolished.

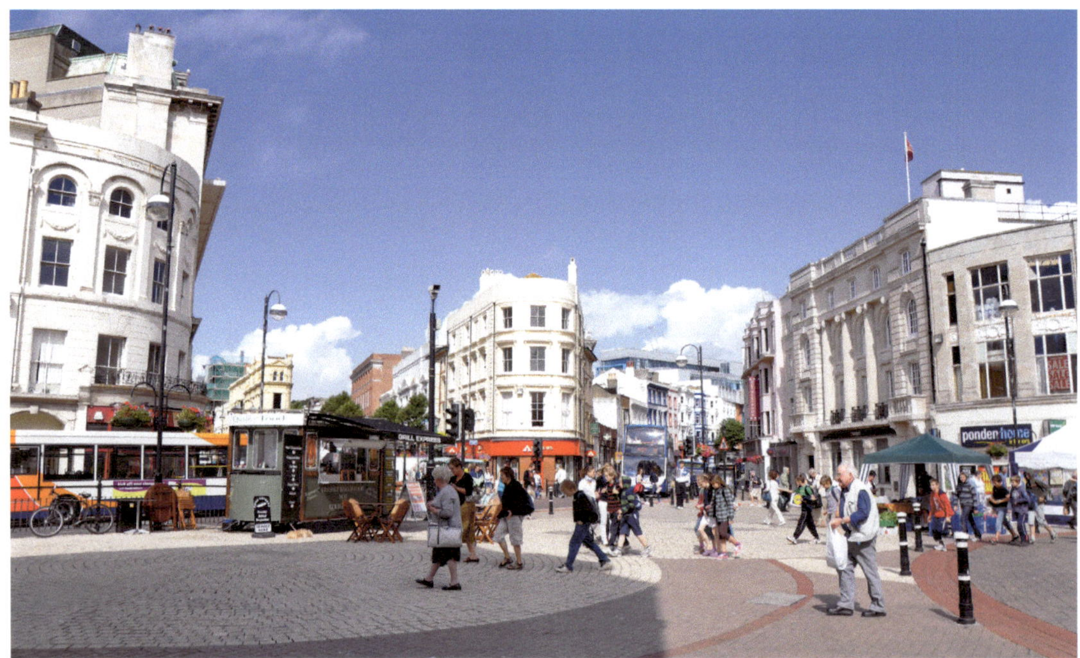

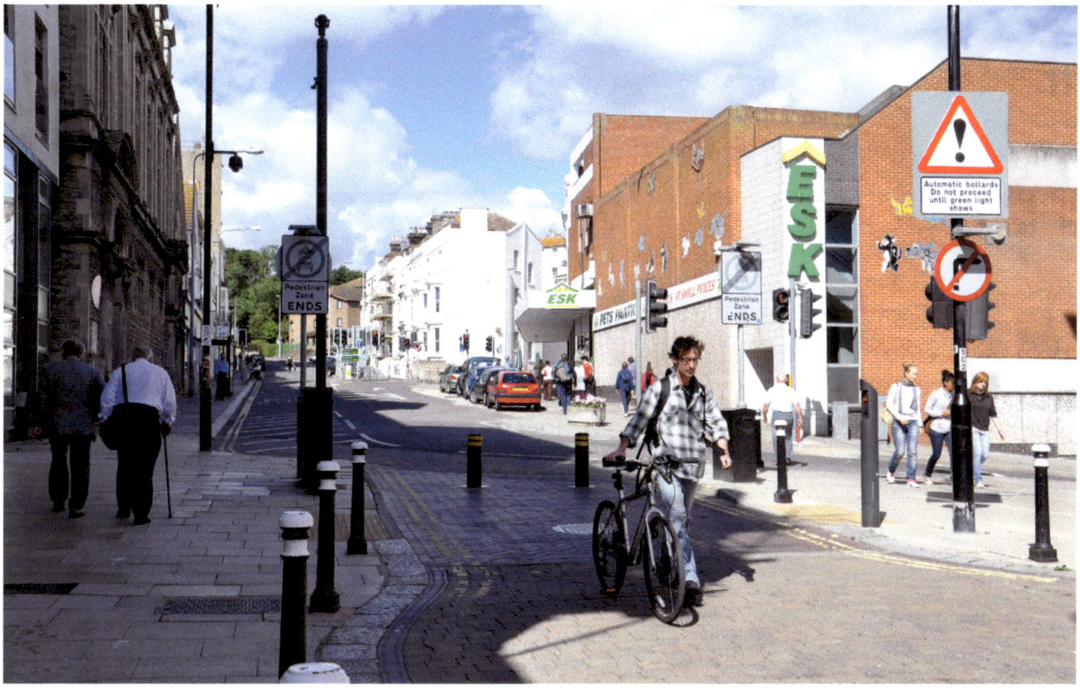

Cambridge Road

Many of the buildings in the earlier photo have long since been demolished, redeveloped and changed hands several times since it was taken in 1904. The large ESK store on the right in the modern photo served for many years as a Sainsbury's supermarket until the company moved to its current location at John Macadam Way. The church in the distance was the Central Methodist church, which opened on 14 July 1876. It was demolished in 1980, replaced by a block of flats.

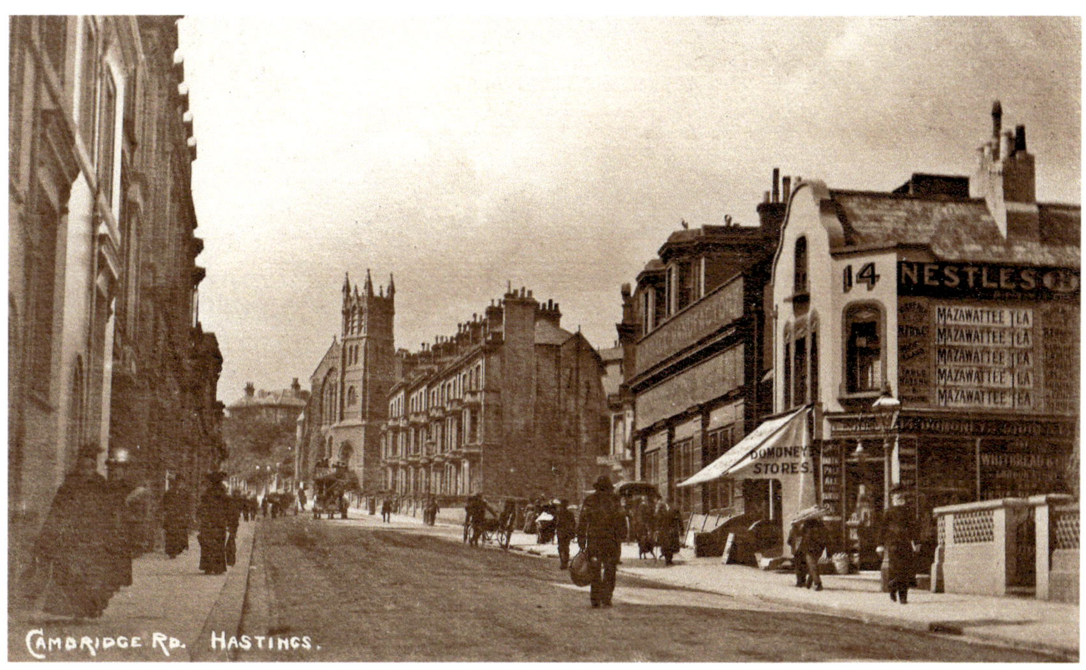

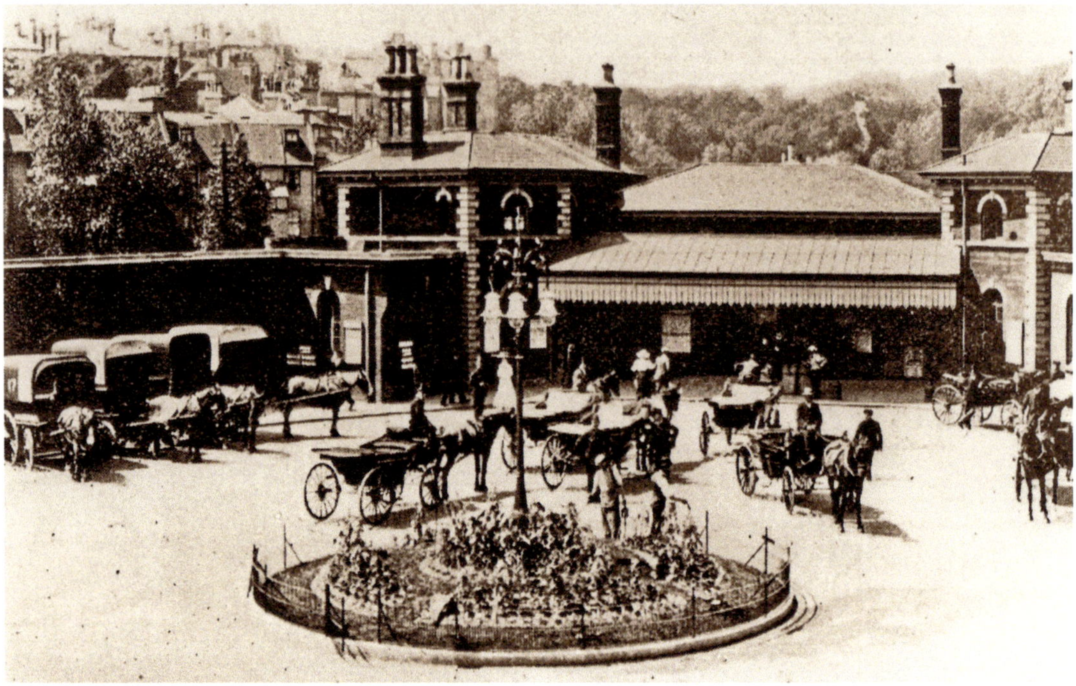

Station Plaza

There have been three station buildings on this site. The current one was officially opened on 14 October 2004 (the anniversary of the Battle of Hastings) by Lord Rooker, Minister of State for Regeneration. Behind the hoarding on the right in the modern photo is the new development of the Priory Quarter – a complex comprising apartments, shops, a doctors' surgery, Sussex Coast College Hastings and the Creative Media Centre.

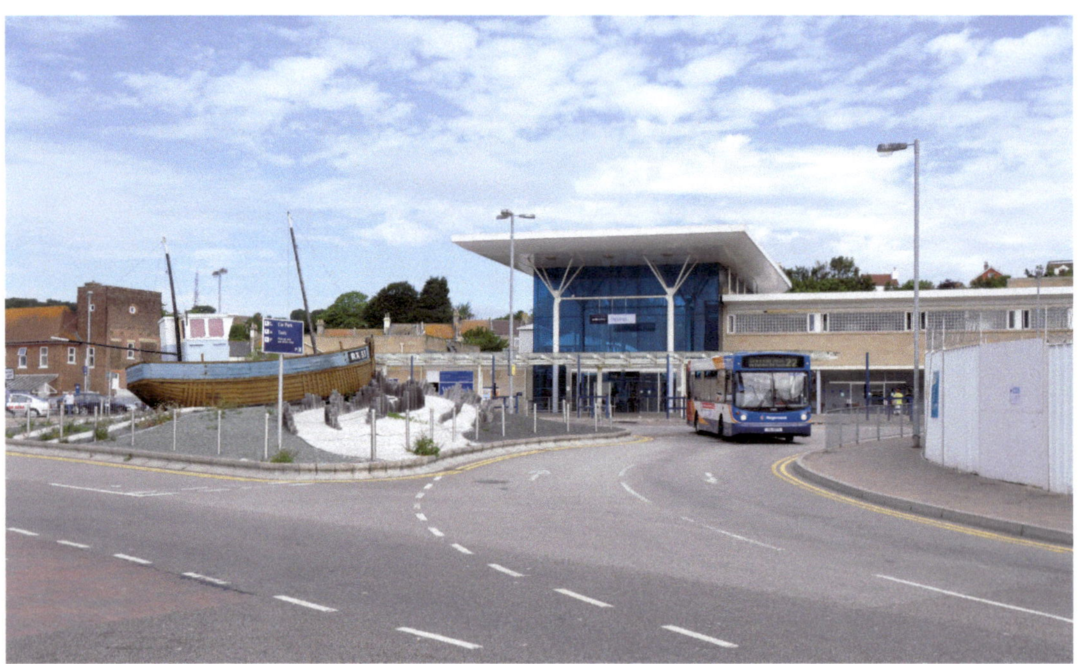

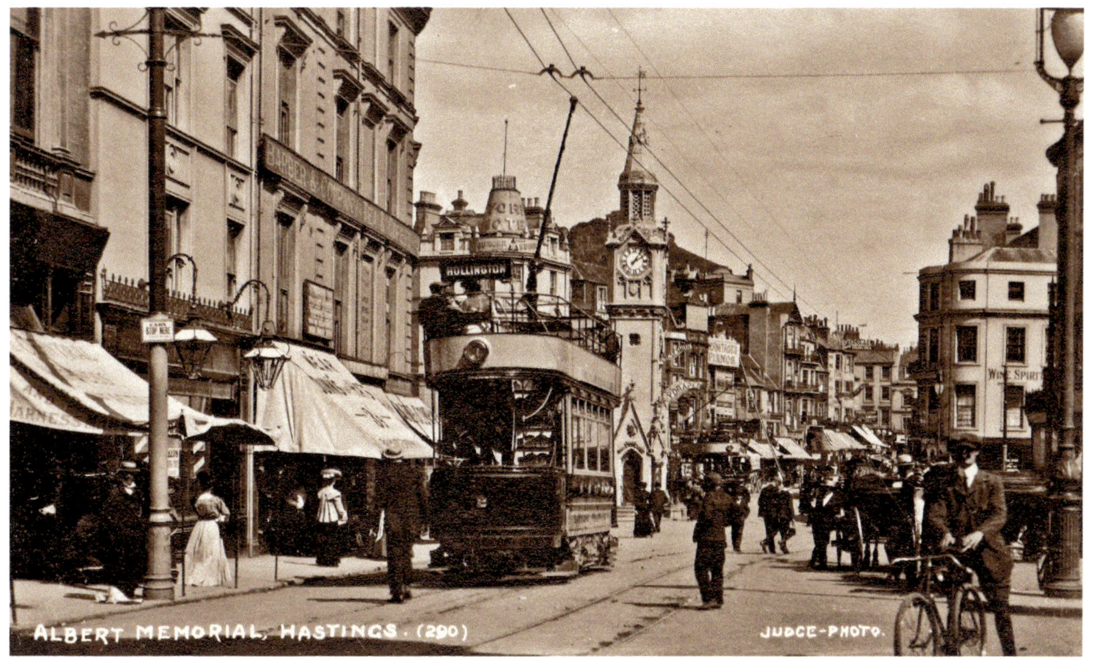

Robertson Street

Robertson Street was named after Patrick Francis Robertson, a wealthy London merchant and later MP for Hastings. Robertson took a 99-year lease on the road that now bears his name when, in 1834, the Crown repossessed an area of land dubbed the America Ground. An impromptu community numbering around 1,000 people had been living there in ramshackle huts and shacks, moving around on a series of ropewalks and declaring themselves to be the twenty-fourth American state!

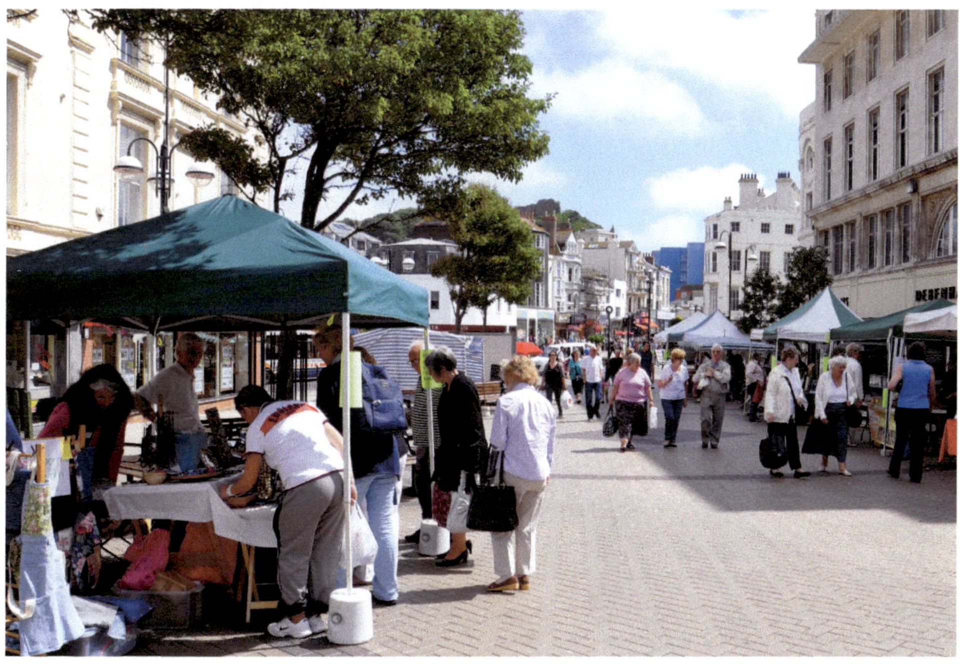

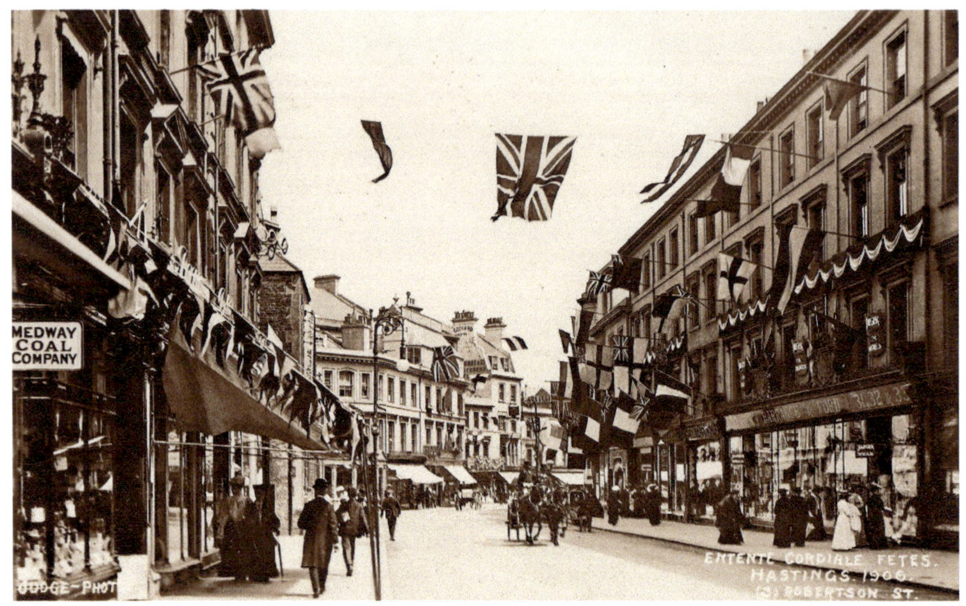

Entente Cordiale

On 26 June 1906 a gathering of dignitaries from Rouen, France, arrived in Hastings to take part in the Entente Cordiale celebrations. The Entente Cordiale was a pact made in April 1904 between France and England in an attempt to end historical animosity over colonial countries. The French visitors were greeted to a reception by the Mayor at the Town Hall followed by a luncheon at the Albany Hotel. The festivities continued in Alexandra Park with a demonstration by the fire brigade, a military tattoo and a concert on Hastings pier. At the Memorial a large banner had been erected bearing the words, 'Vive La Normandie!' The *Hastings & St Leonards Weekly Mail & Times* reported, 'There can be no doubt that Robertston Street afforded the most brilliant display in the town.'

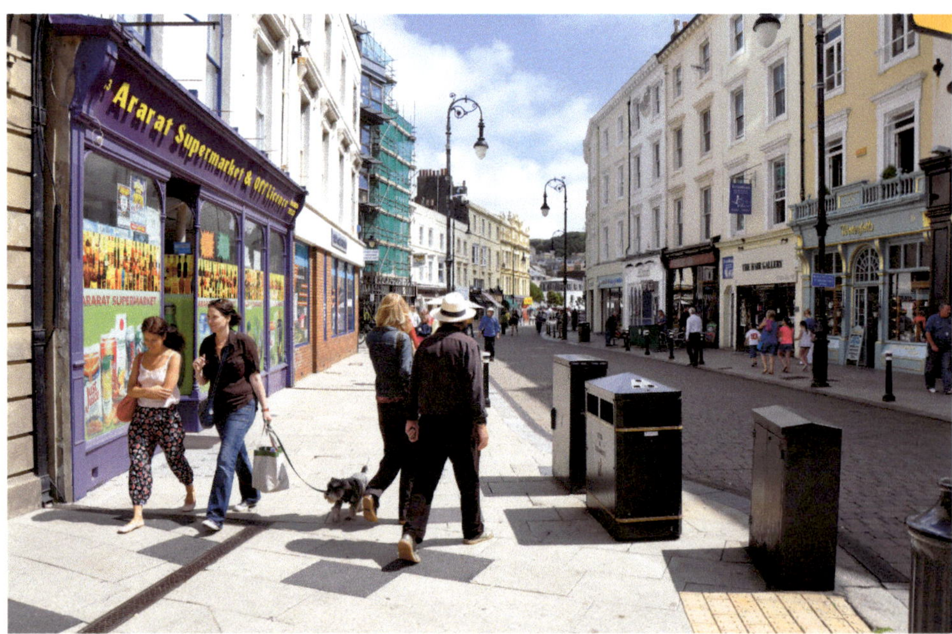

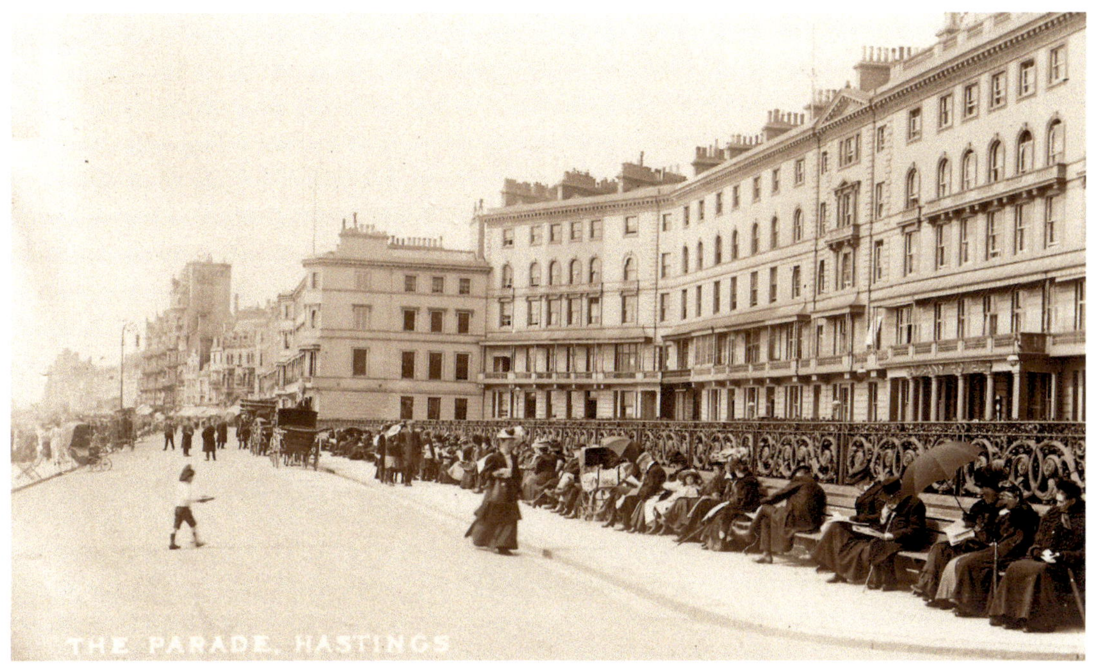

Robertson Terrace

A heavy air raid on 23 May 1943 saw a bomb penetrate the walls of the Queen's Hotel without detonating. It came to land on the nearby Albany Hotel – the large building in the old photo that curves around Robertson Terrace – where it exploded, killing eleven Canadian soldiers inside. The building was eventually rebuilt and is now part of Debenhams and a block of flats. The inset shows the plaque fixed to the site of the Albany Hotel, commemorating the eleven Canadian soldiers.

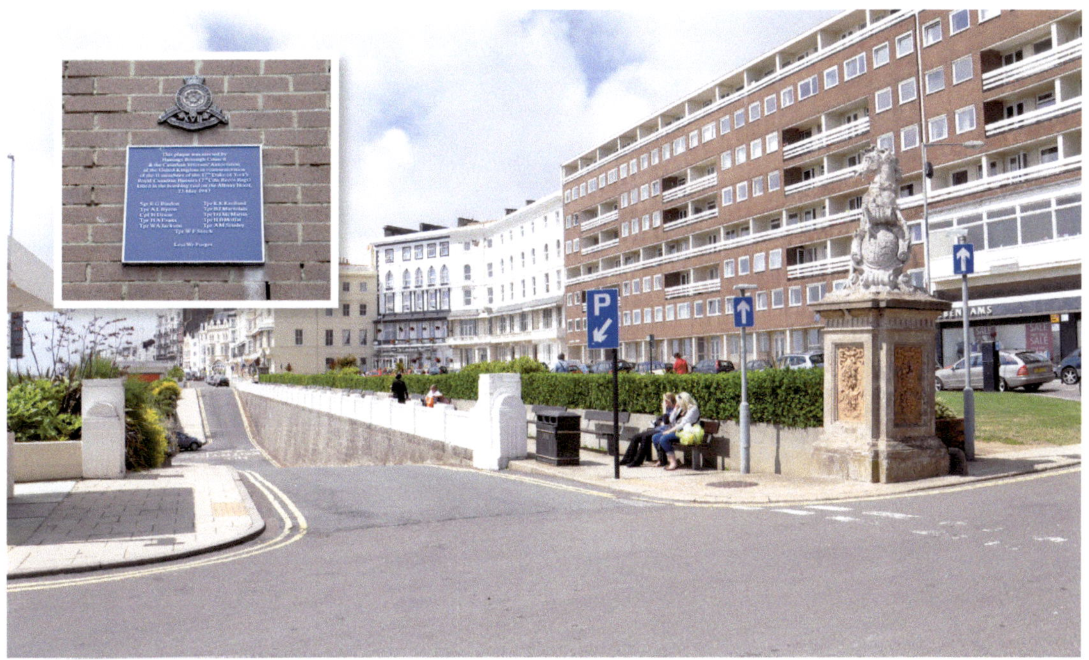

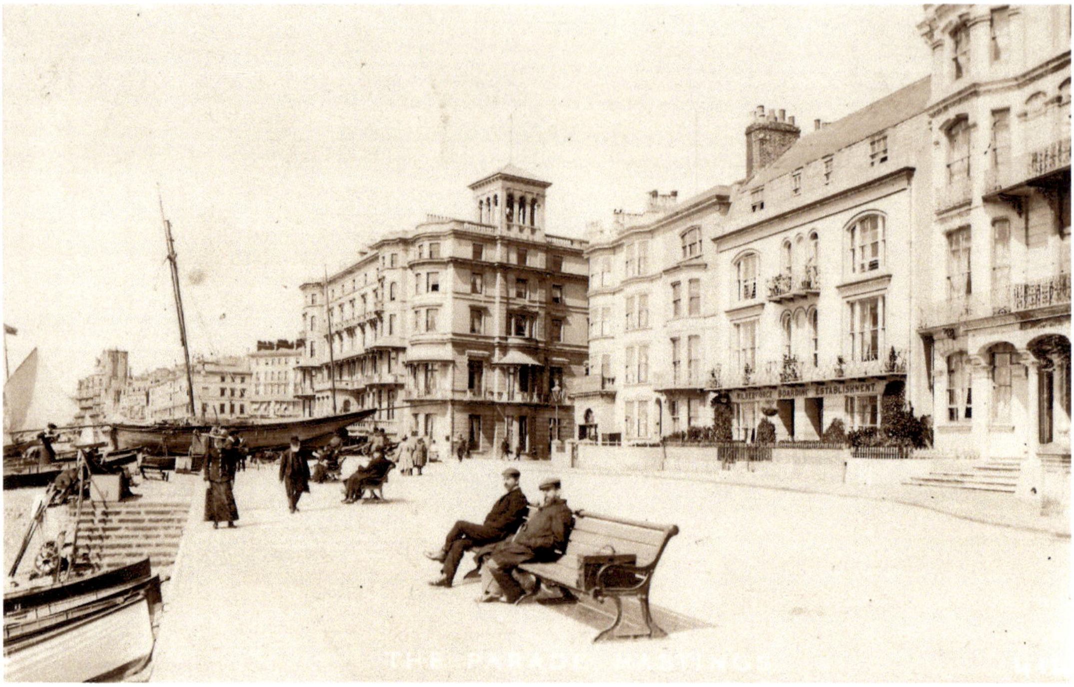

Denmark Place

Dominating the old photograph of Denmark Place is the imposing building of the Queen's Hotel, situated just a few feet from the shingle beach. The hotel was built in 1862 and underwent significant renovation in 1894 when electric lighting was installed. It suffered badly from storm damage during the 1987 hurricane and subsequently shut down. After lying empty for several years the hotel was recently converted into luxury flats.

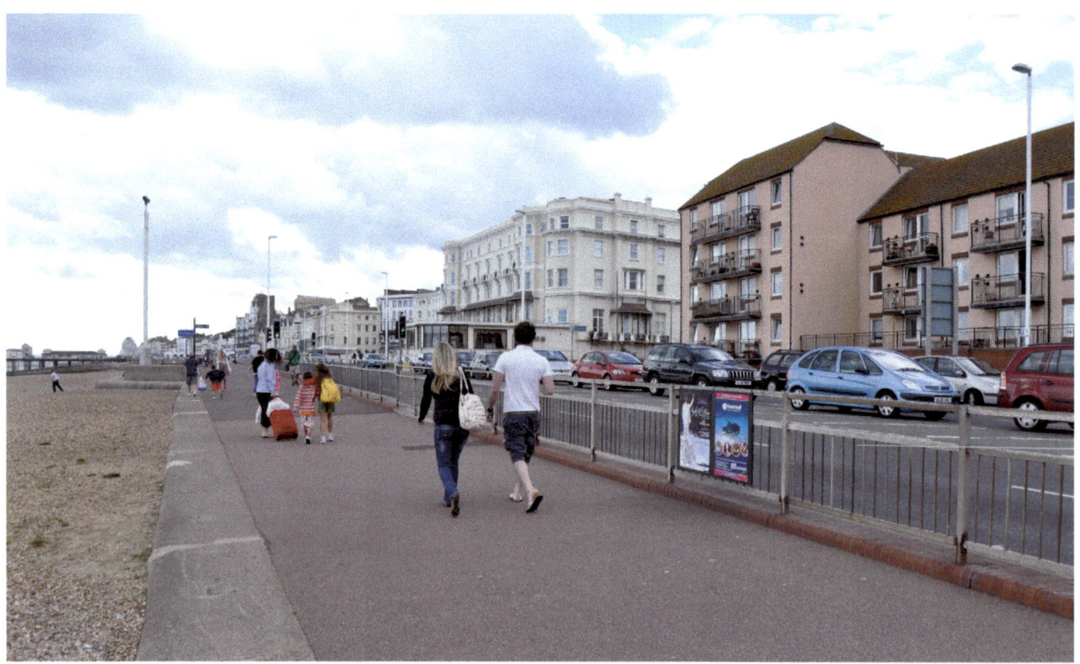

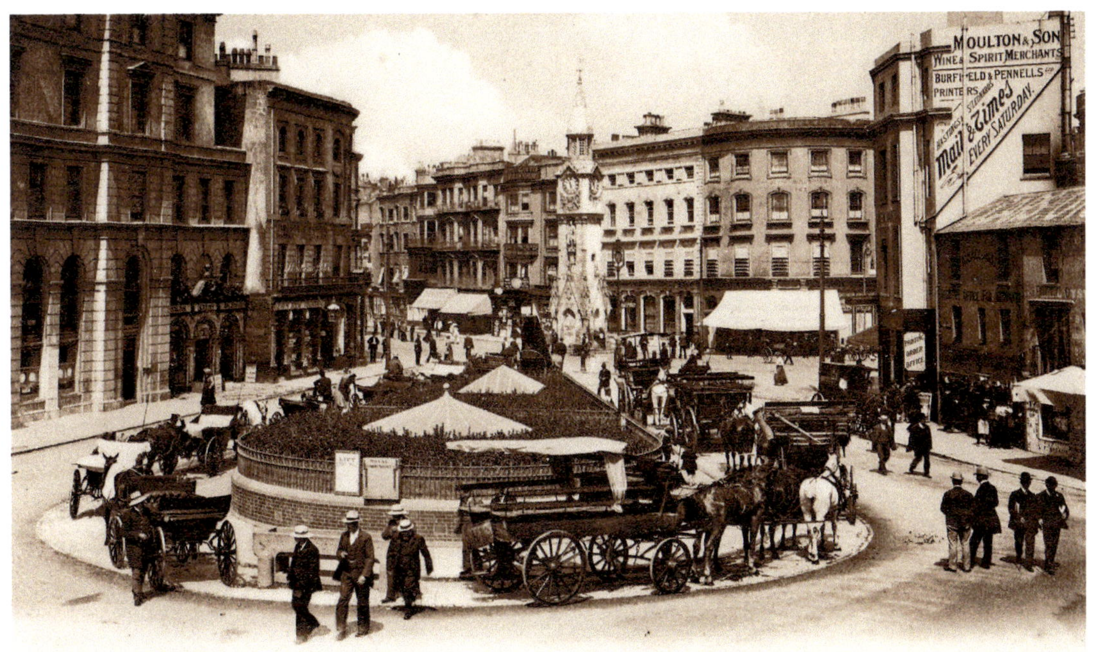

63 HASTINGS. — *Harold Place.* — LL.

The Memorial II

To the right in the image above, the building with *Hastings & St Leonards Mail & Times* advertised on it was where Fred Judge, the renowned local photographer, lived and – from the upper storey of the building – where he would use daylight exposure to develop his large array of Hastings photographs. The image of the Memorial on the right was taken in the summer of 1952 and provides a much more interesting comparison than the tarmac road and public toilets afforded by a 2010 view!

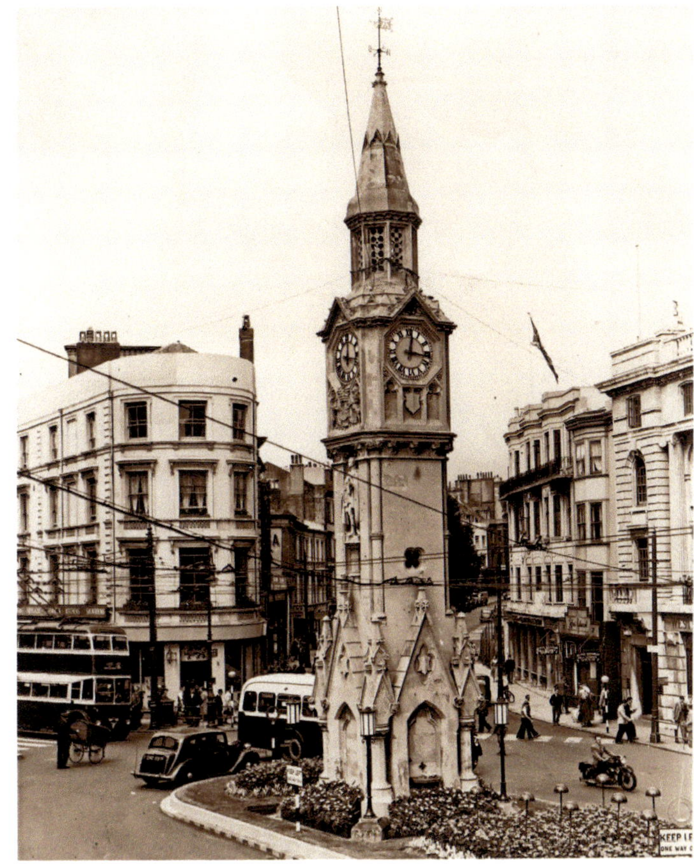

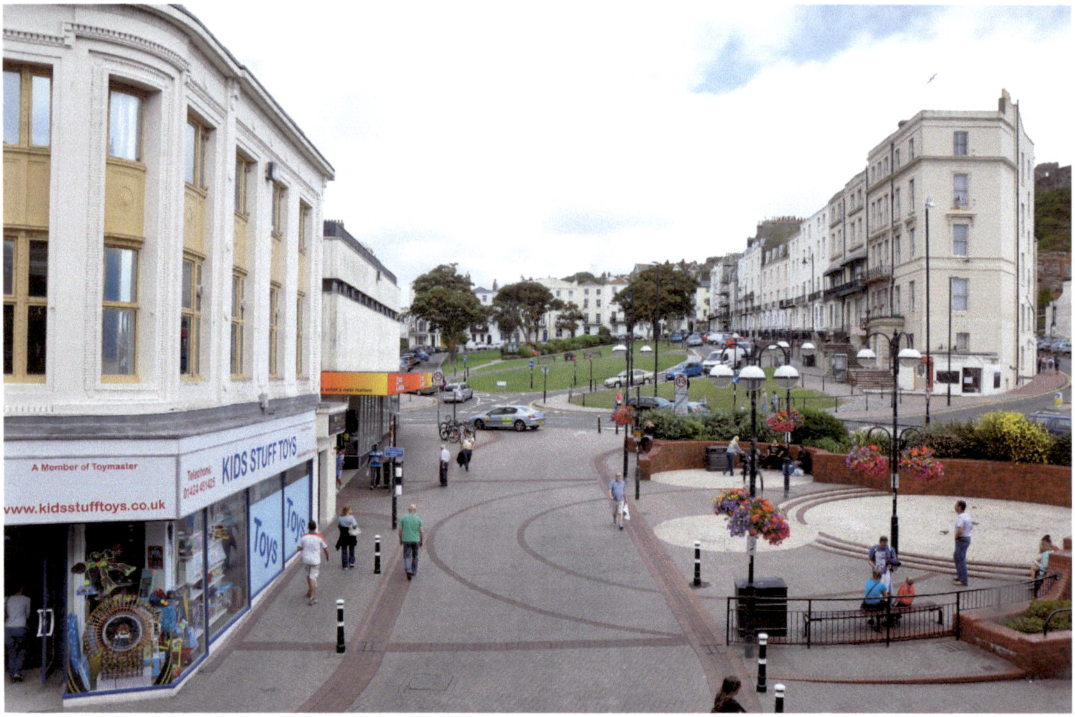

Wellington Square

Hastings' rise to become a fashionable seaside resort began following the Battle of Waterloo. In 1815 the Breeds family purchased the Priory Field from the Milward family and began developing Wellington Square (first called Wellington Place), the Castle Hotel and Russell Street.

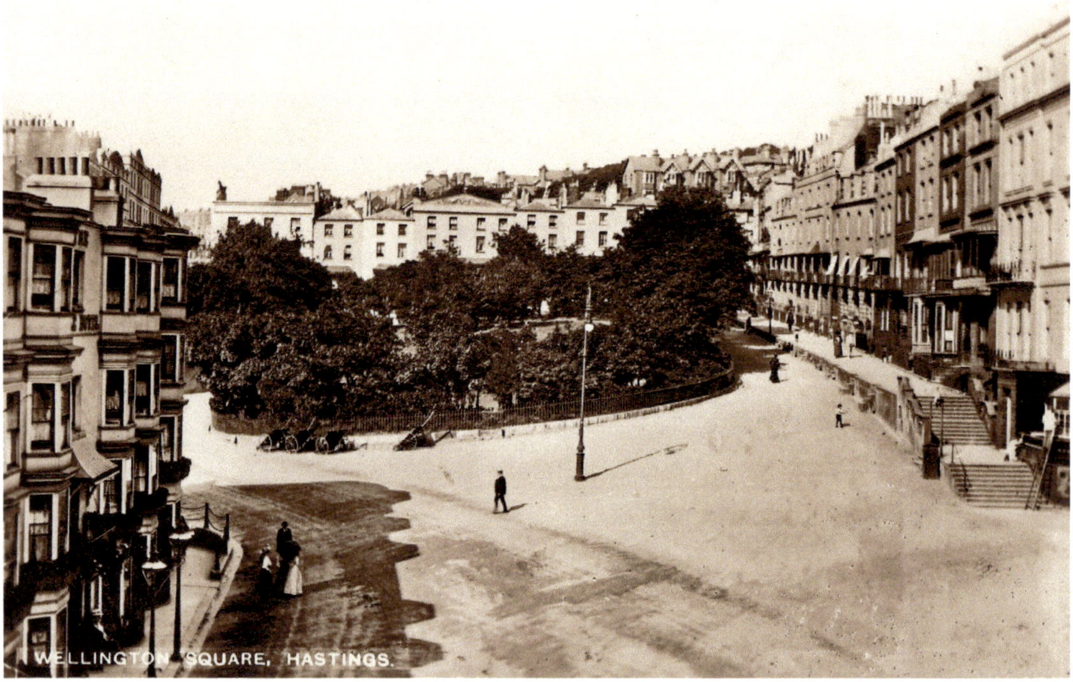

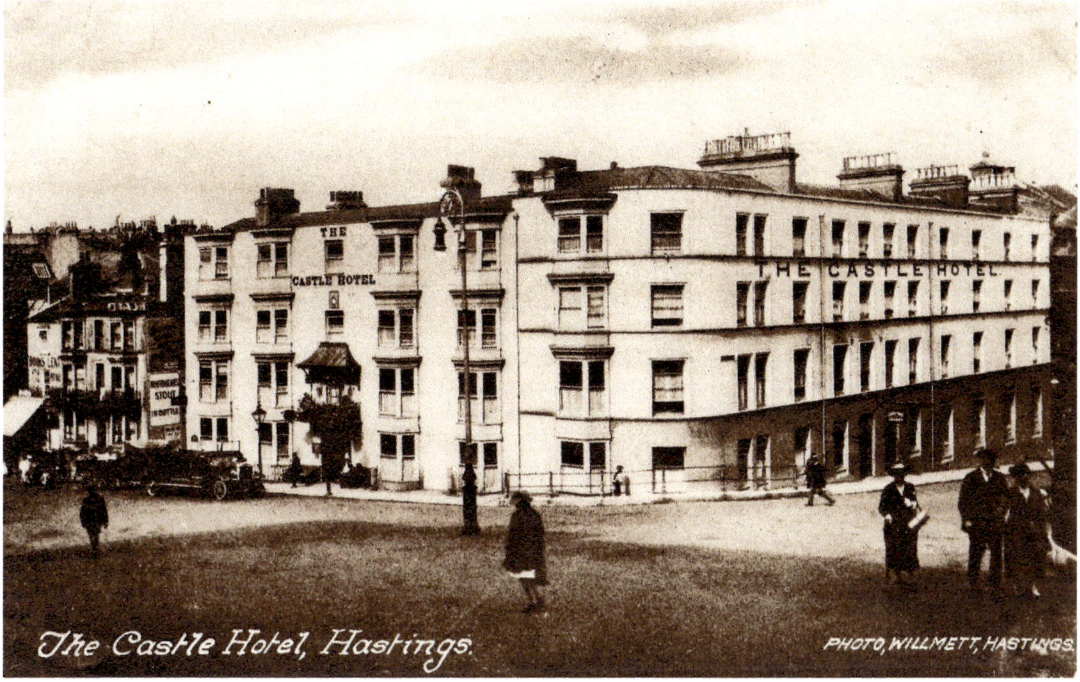

The Castle Hotel, Hastings.

PHOTO, WILLMETT, HASTINGS.

The Castle Hotel

This regency-style hotel, opened in 1818 on the corner of Wellington Square and Albert Road, bore witness to a number of interesting events. In 1908 the hotel was used as a safe house for three suffragettes, including Christabel Pankhurst, after a meeting they were conducting in Wellington Square grew hostile. The suffragettes were in Hastings in the run-up to the local elections, in which the Conservative MP, Arthur du Cros, opposed to women's suffrage, was elected.

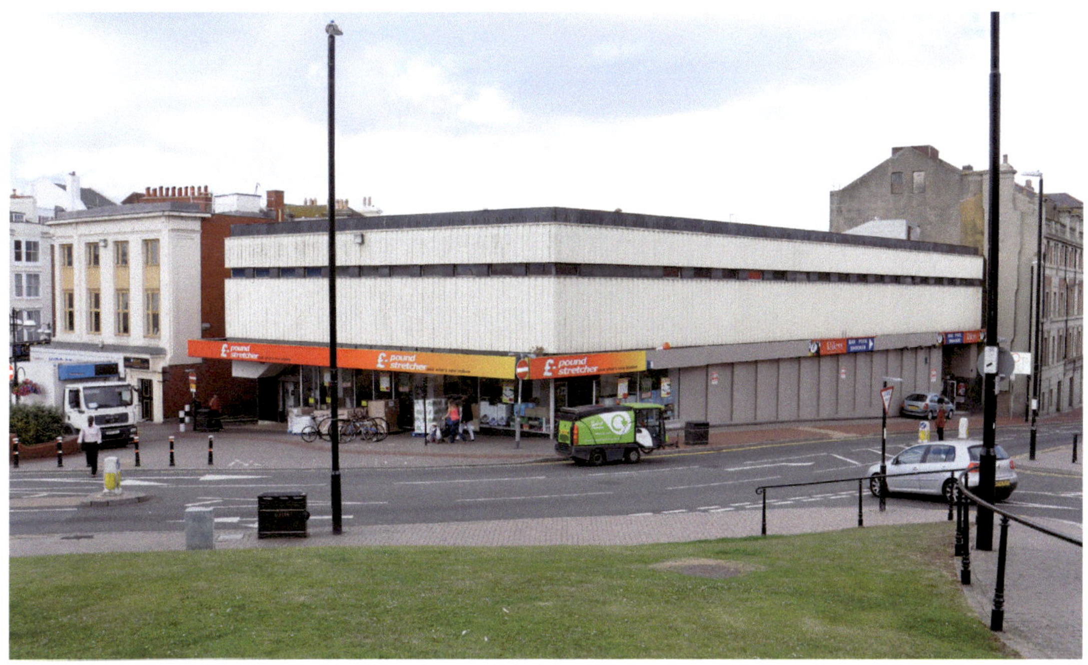

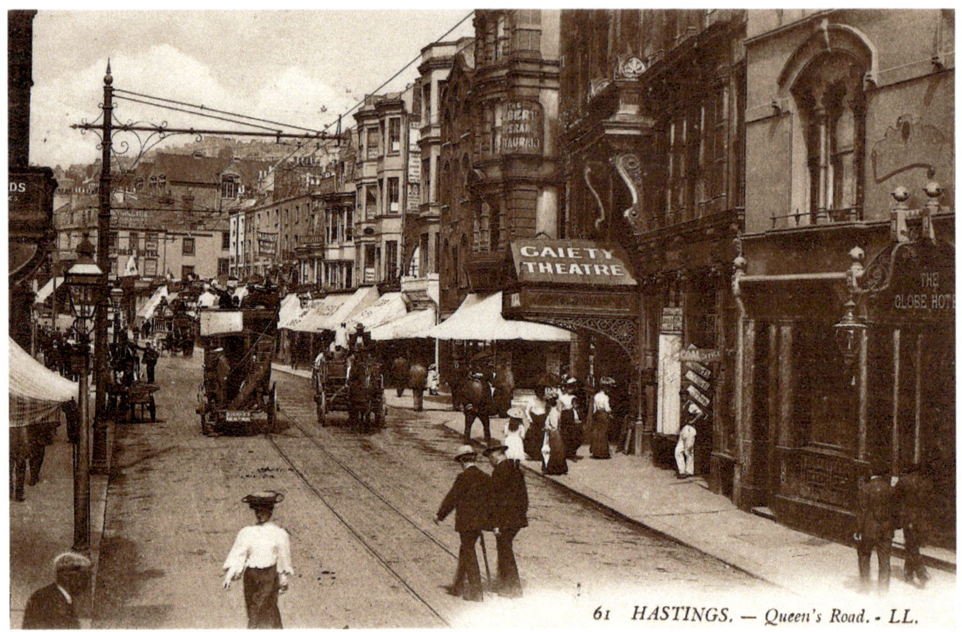

61   HASTINGS. — *Queen's Road.* - LL.

Oscar Wilde at Hastings

Oscar Wilde visited the Gaiety Theatre – shown here on the right of Queen's Road – in 1883, one year after it had opened, to give a talk entitled 'The House Beautiful'. The lecture dealt with the 'practical side of asceticism' and home decoration and drew a large audience. A number of years later, in 1904, the famous stage actress Ellen Terry played Portia here in *The Merchant of Venice*. The Gaiety has changed hands and names several times over the years but still continues to provide entertainment in the form of the town's only major cinema.

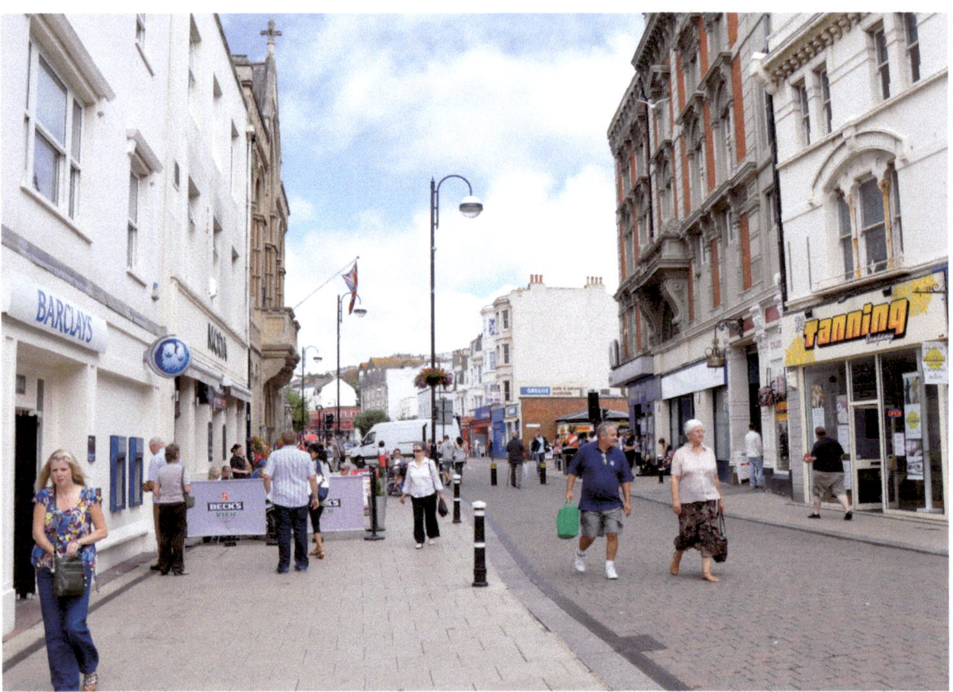

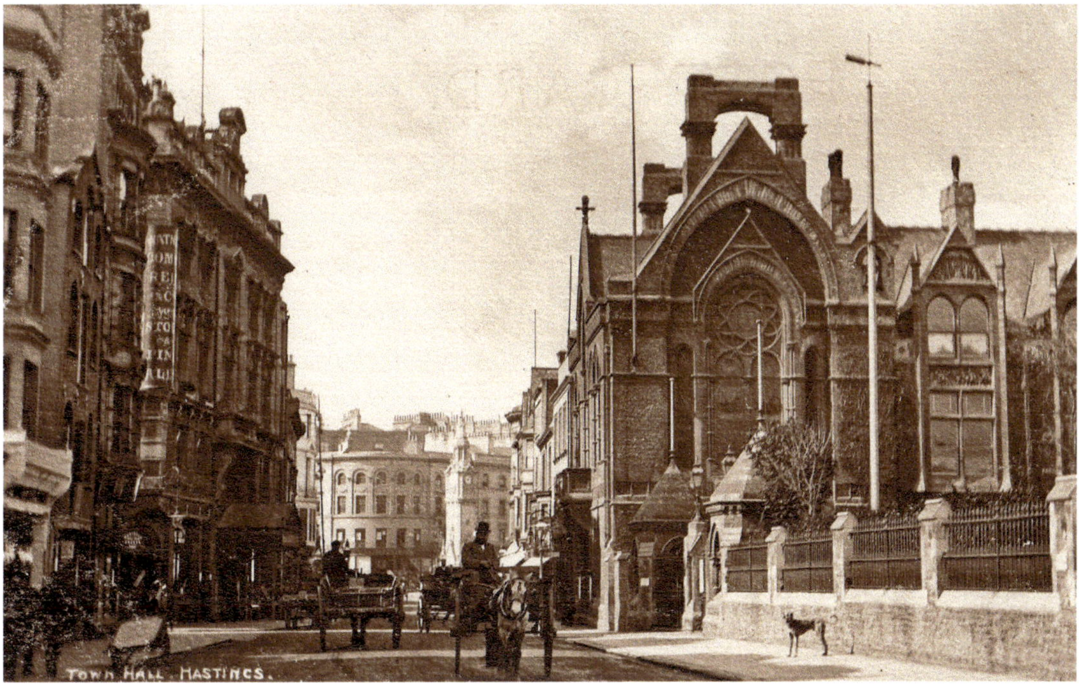

Queen's Road

This view of the Town Hall (on the right) was taken by local photographer Fred Judge around 1904. The imposing Town Hall buildings were opened on 7 September 1881, replacing the much smaller premises in the High Street. The building continues to serve as the Town Hall and many important decisions concerning Hastings' future have been taken here. It has also been the site of many historically important announcements, such as the coronations and deaths of monarchs.

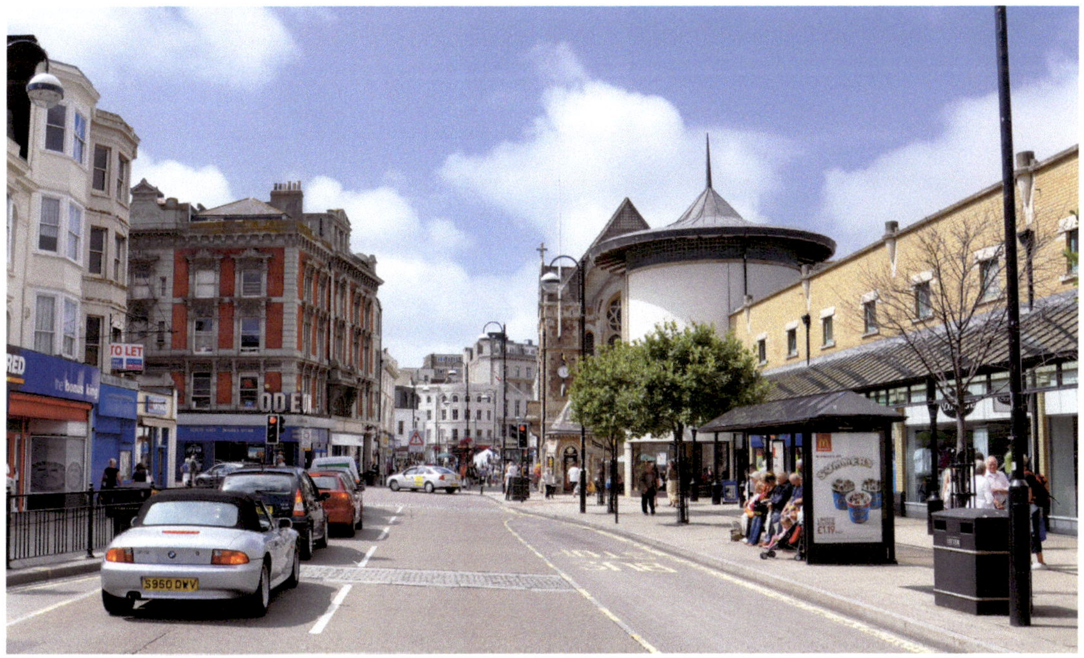

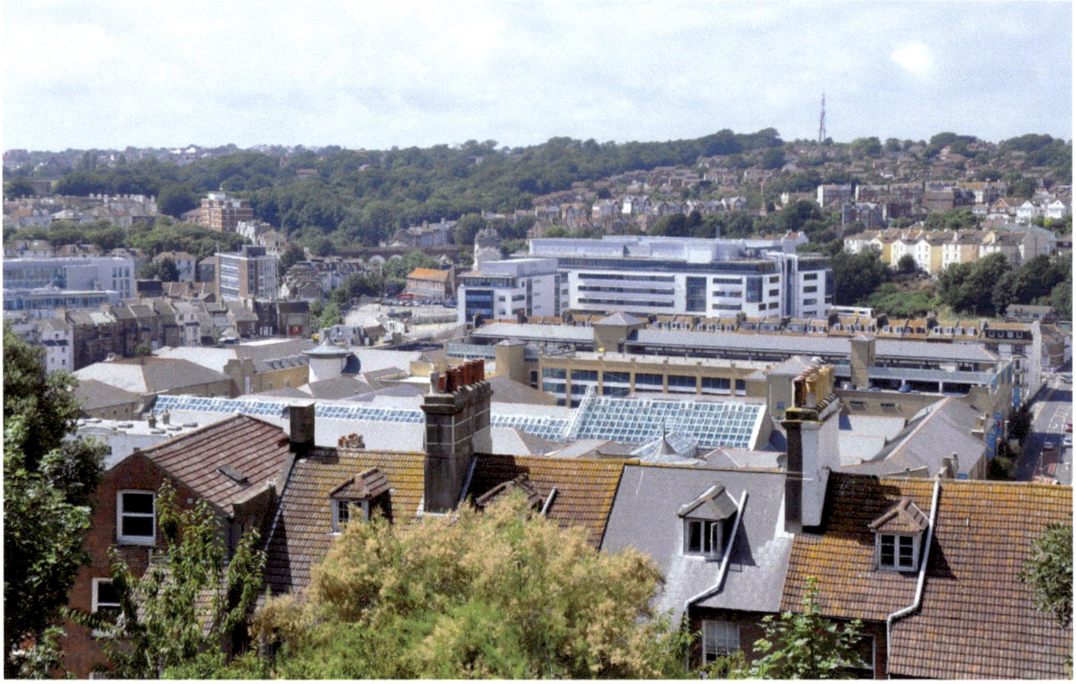

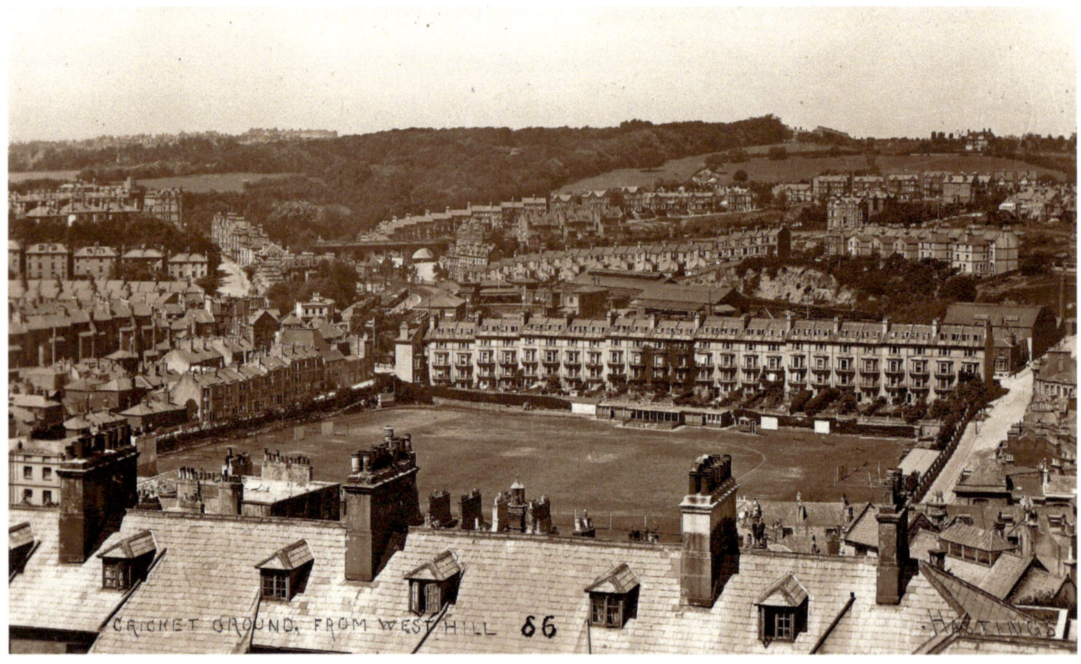

Priory Meadow

The Central Cricket Ground, built on six and a half acres of drained marsh land, was opened on 20 July 1864. Until 1872, when it was purchased outright for £5,000, the land was leased from Countess Waldegrave and the Viscountess Holmesdale. This area served as the main Cricket Ground for the town until the development of the Priory Meadow Shopping Centre, which was opened by Her Majesty the Queen in 1997.

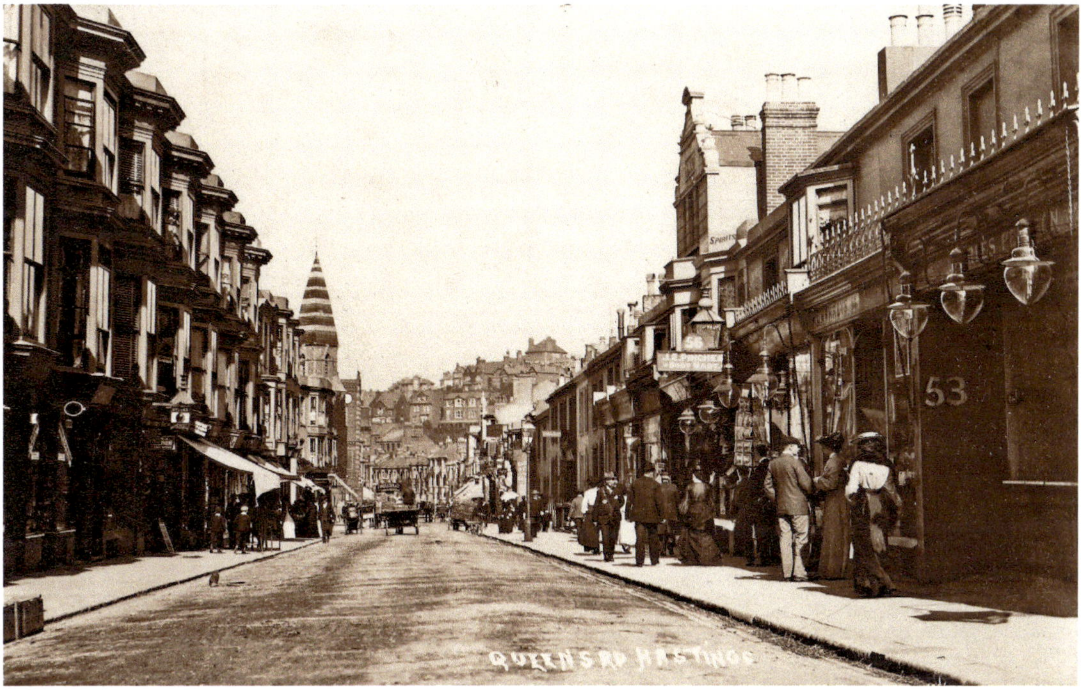

Queen's Road II

On the left of Queen's Road the spire of St Andrew's church can be seen. The church was consecrated in November 1870, serving a new parish which did not have a single building in it ten years previously. Although this was a new parish, there had been a St Andrew's church in Hastings since at least the thirteenth century, situated in Castle Hill Road. This church was demolished in 1970 – Morrison's petrol station now occupies the site. Shortly prior to the demolition of St Andrew's church a section of a mural, painted by the Hastings author Robert Tressell, was saved and is now displayed in Hastings Museum.

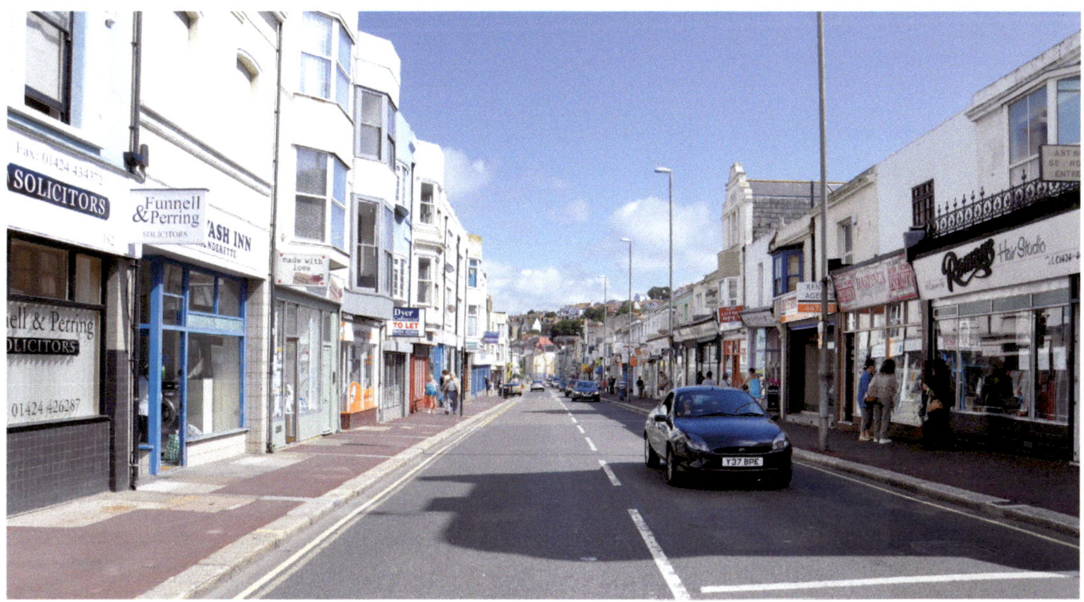

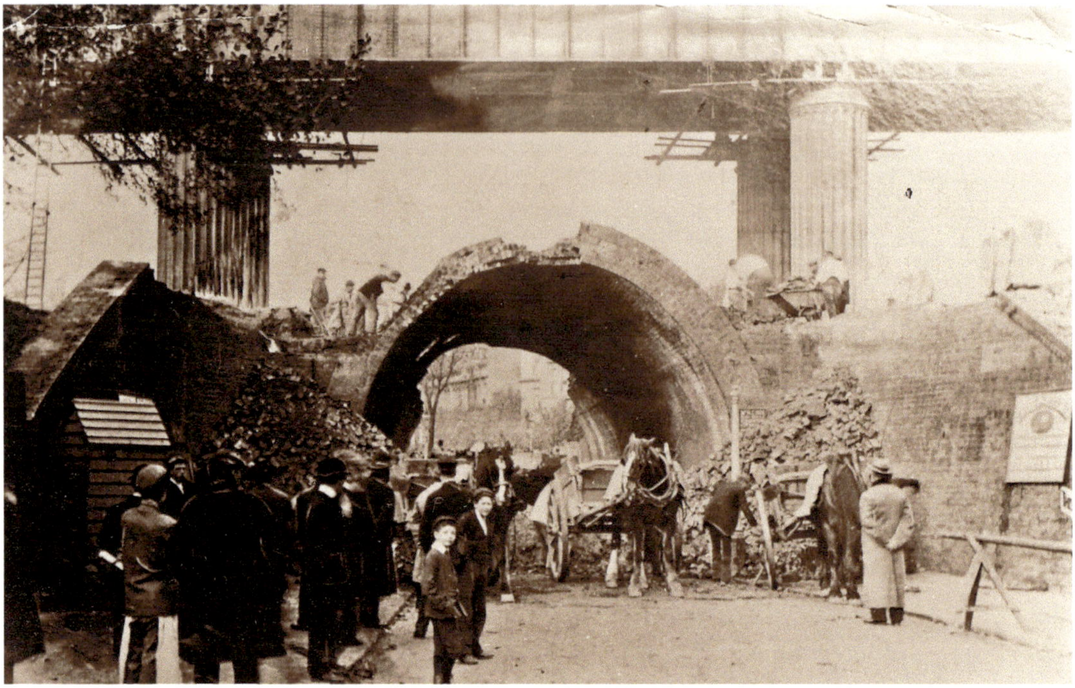

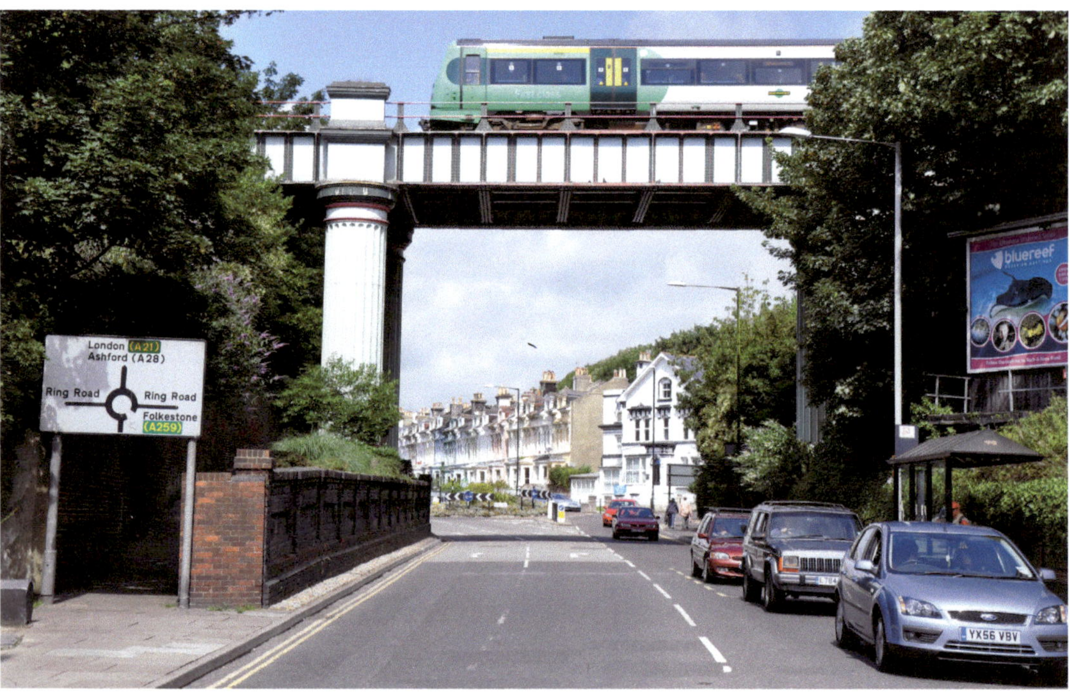

St Andrew's Archway

In November 1898 the dark and narrow St Andrew's Archway under the railway was finally demolished under the watchful eye of the town's mayor, Mr F. Tuppenney, in whose ward the objectionable archway stood. A new iron bridge with fluted columns was built prior to the tunnel's demolition and is still in use today.

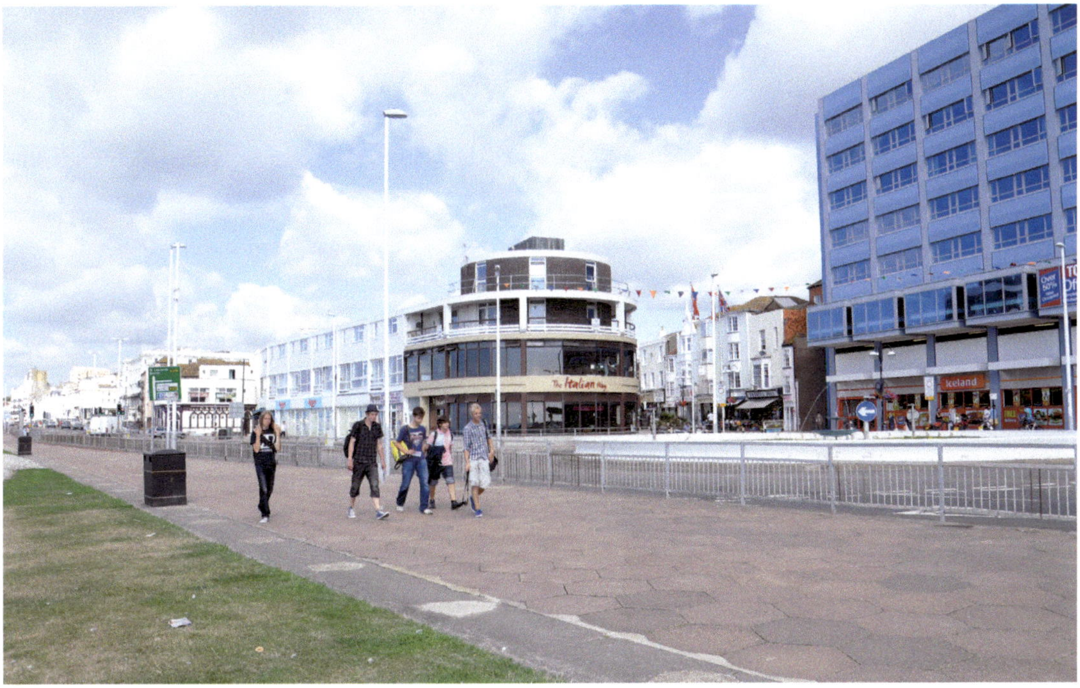

Caroline Place

In the older photograph, a First World War tank can be seen on display in Caroline Place. Several tanks were displayed around the country in order to raise funds. Caroline Place was badly damaged in June 1944 when a doodlebug crash-landed there. Fortunately, nobody was killed.

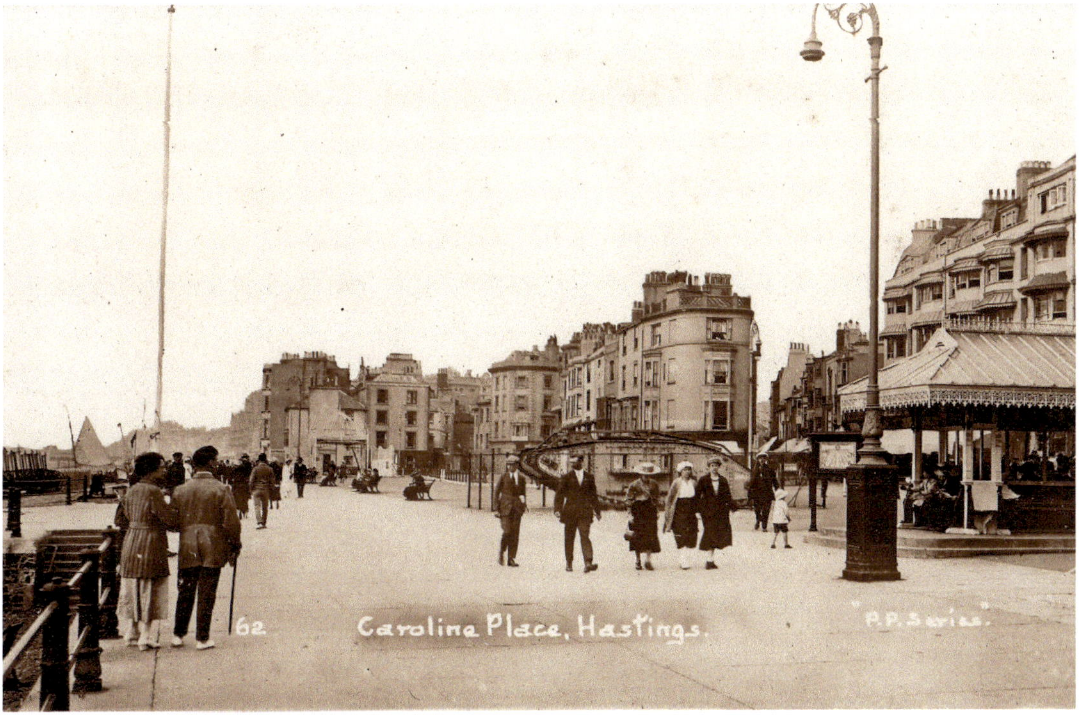

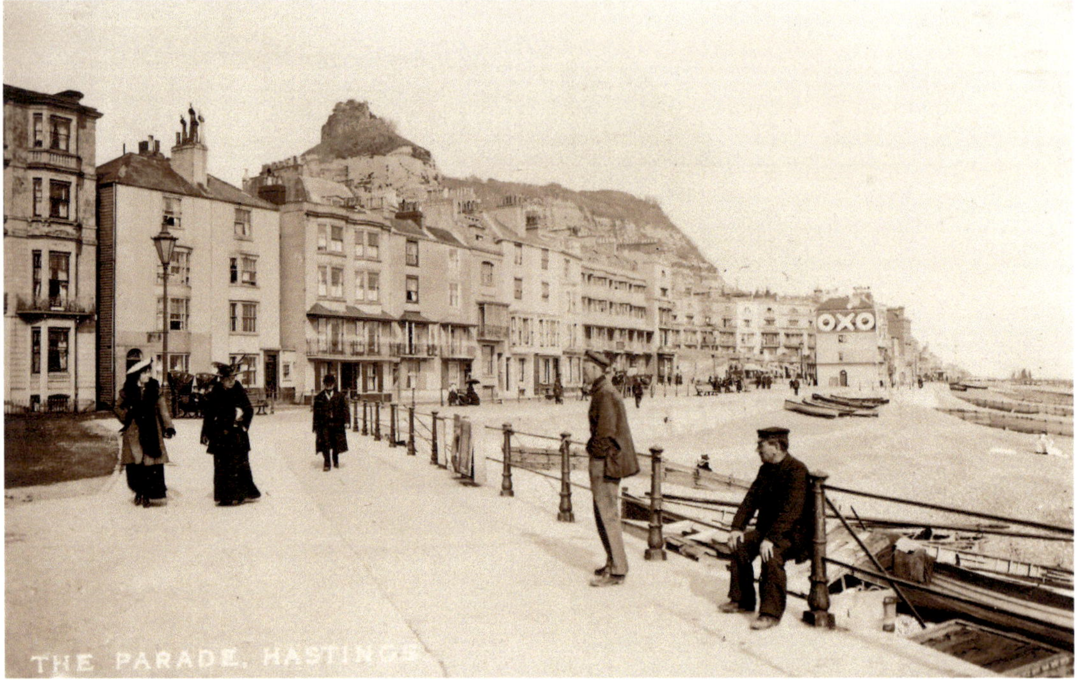

A Change in Sea Defence

But for the castle and a glimpse of Pelham Crescent in the distance, this view is virtually unrecognisable in 2010. Buildings have been replaced and the shoreline moved considerably to protect the seafront from the pernicious waves that have wrought much damage over the years.

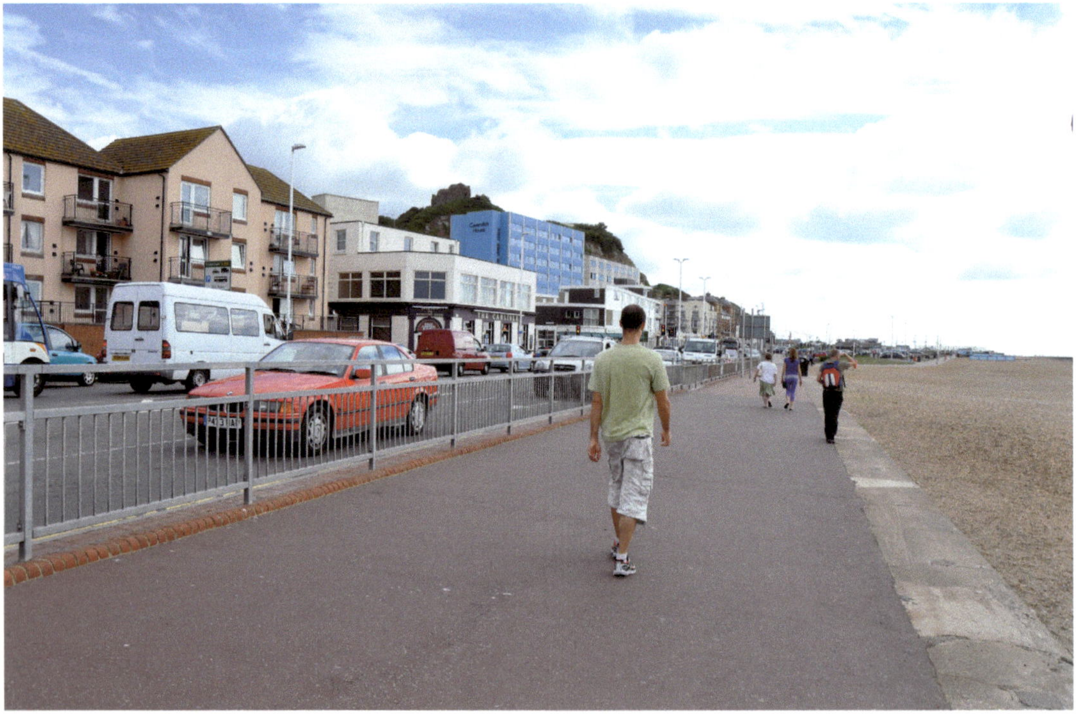

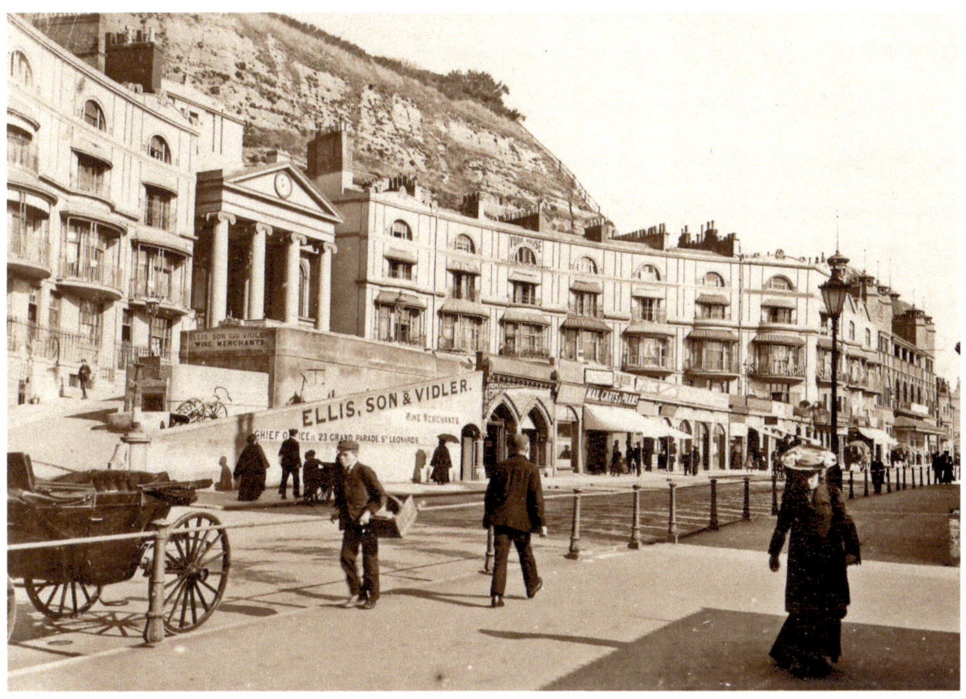

Pelham Crescent

Pelham Crescent and St Mary-in-the-Castle were built between 1824 and 1828 under the direction of the Earl of Chichester, Sir Thomas Pelham. For several months during 1818 the cliffs under the castle were excavated in preparation for the development. Hastings Castle remained in the Pelham family from 1591 until 1951. Although difficult to discern in the modern photograph, the sign advertising the wine merchants, 'Ellis, Son & Vidler', painted on the rise up to Pelham Crescent, is still legible today.

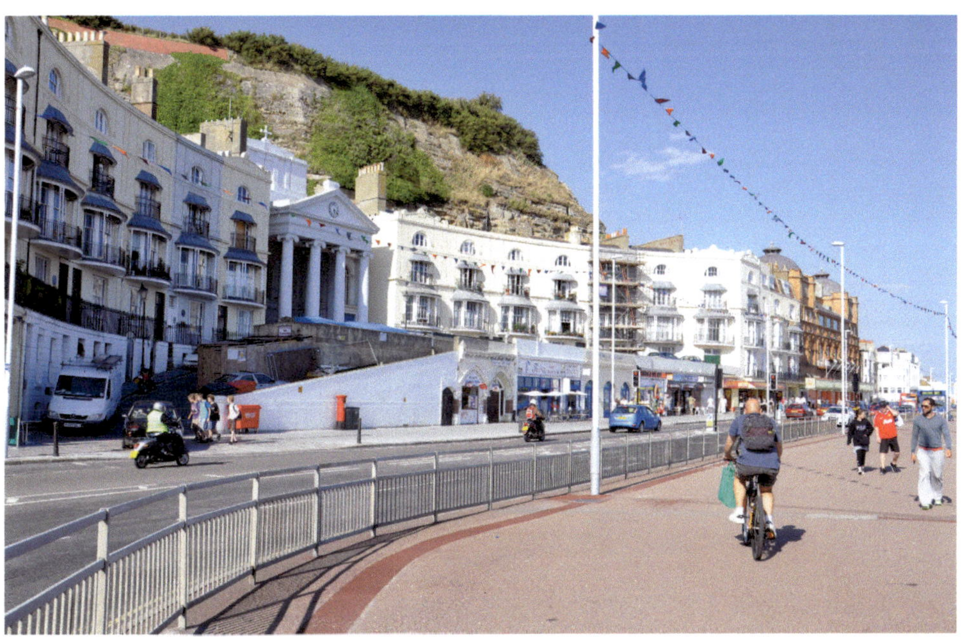

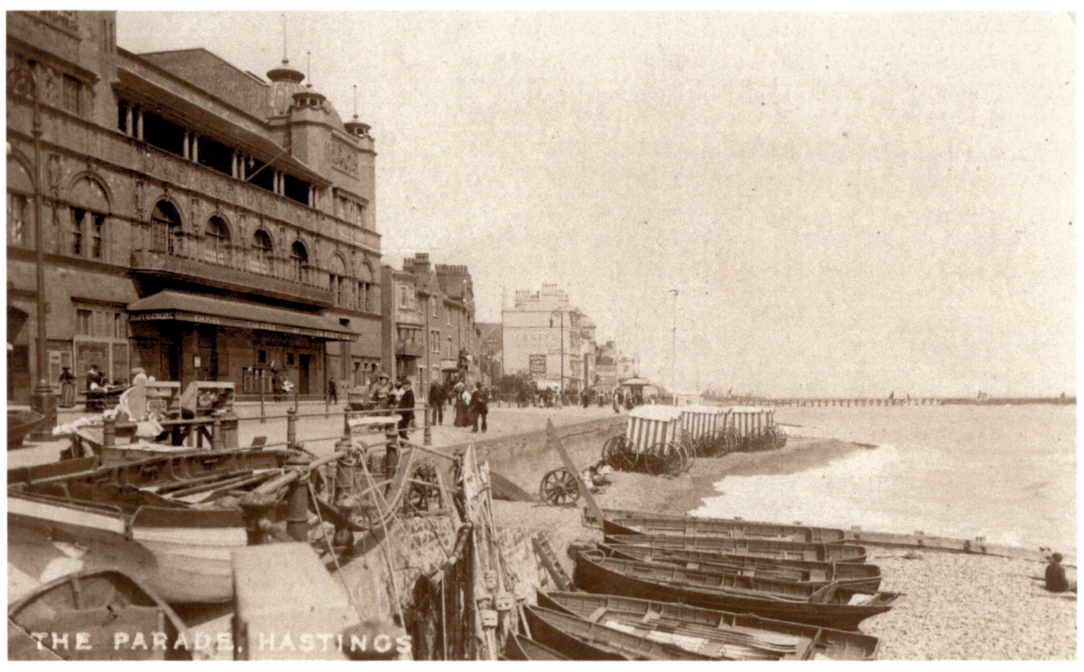

Empire Theatre of Varieties

The building to the left in the photo, on Pelham Place, was the Hippodrome. Opened on 30 March 1899, it was built on the former site of the Royal Marine Hotel and was first named the Empire Theatre, before changing to the Hippodrome and then, in 1910, to the Cinema de Luxe. Among its many performers was, in 1905, the escapologist Houdini, who drew large crowds to the venue.

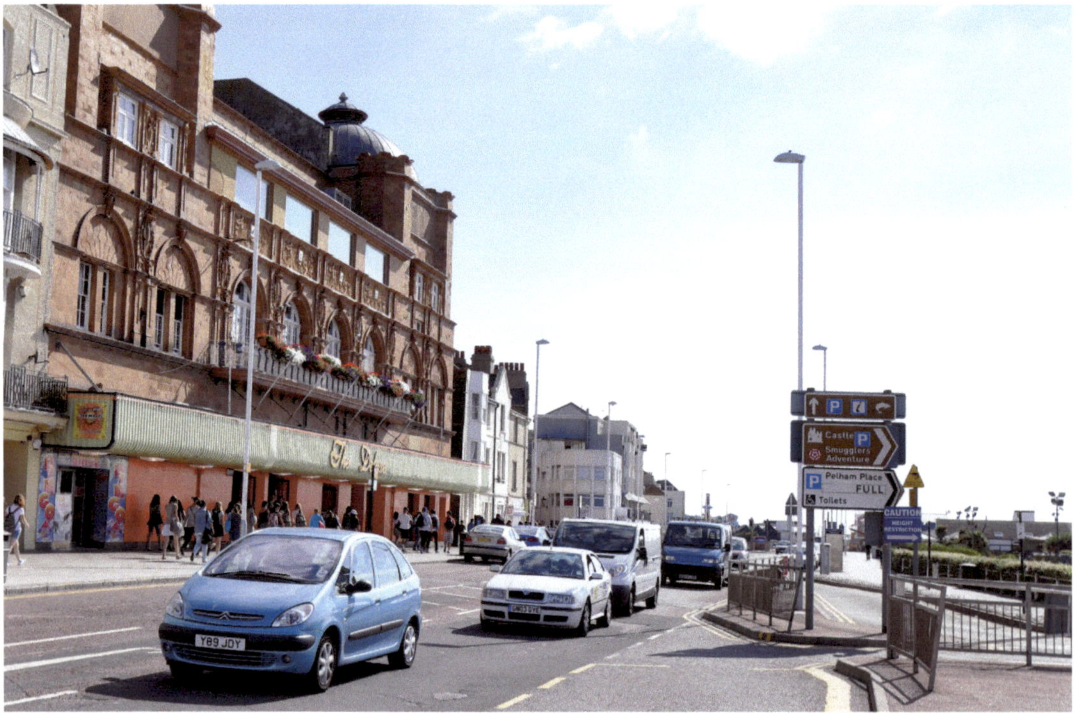

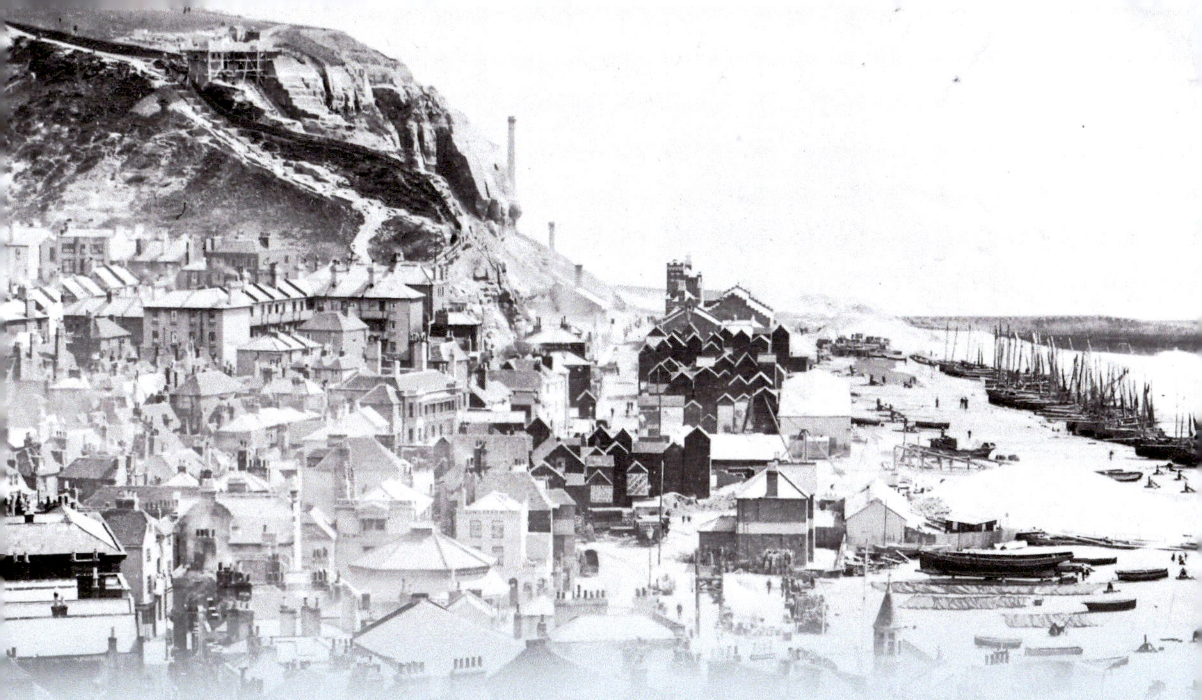

CHAPTER 2

The Old Town

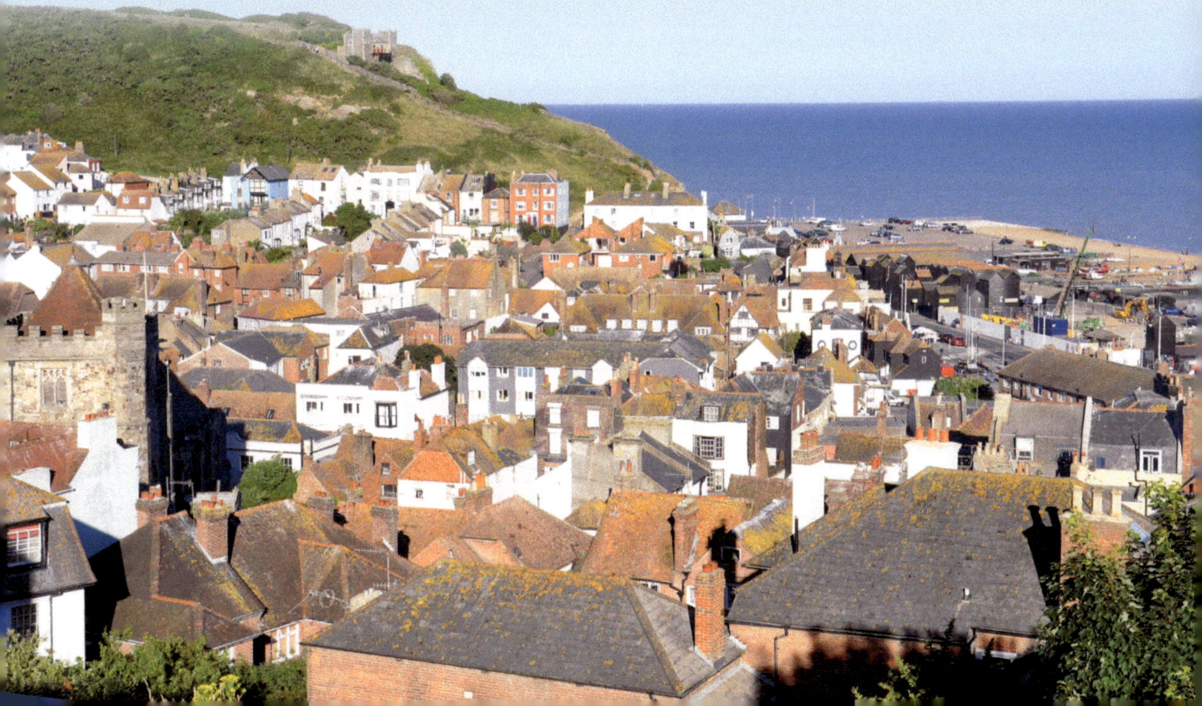

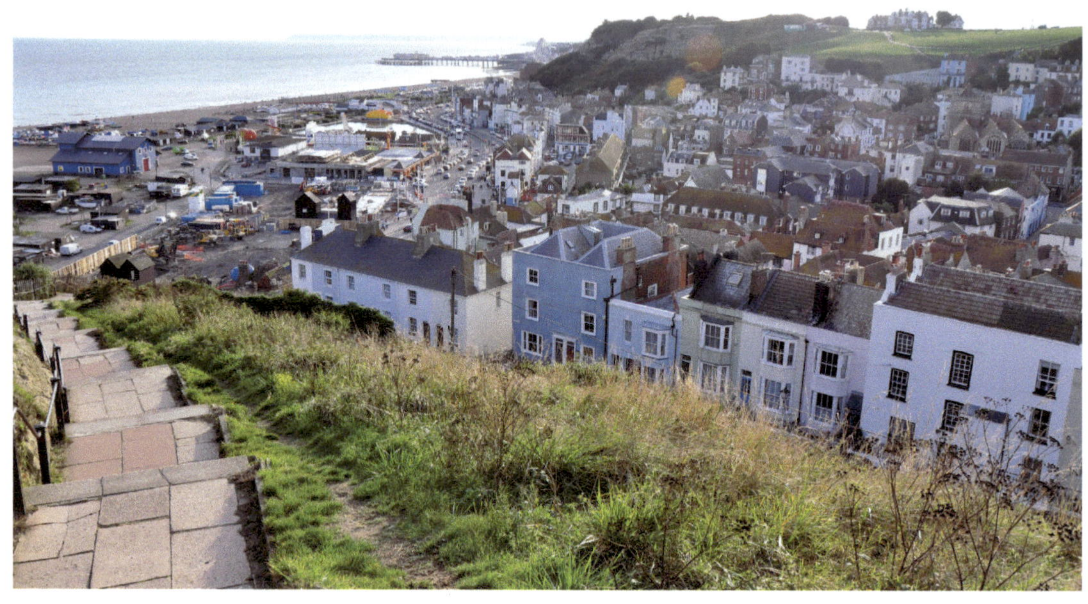

View from the East Hill

This view of the Old Town shows how densely populated the area had become by the turn of the century, the East and West Hills providing natural boundary points. The Bourne stream, of which there is now no visible evidence, once separated the parishes of All Saints and St Clements, providing the town with both a water supply and a natural drain.

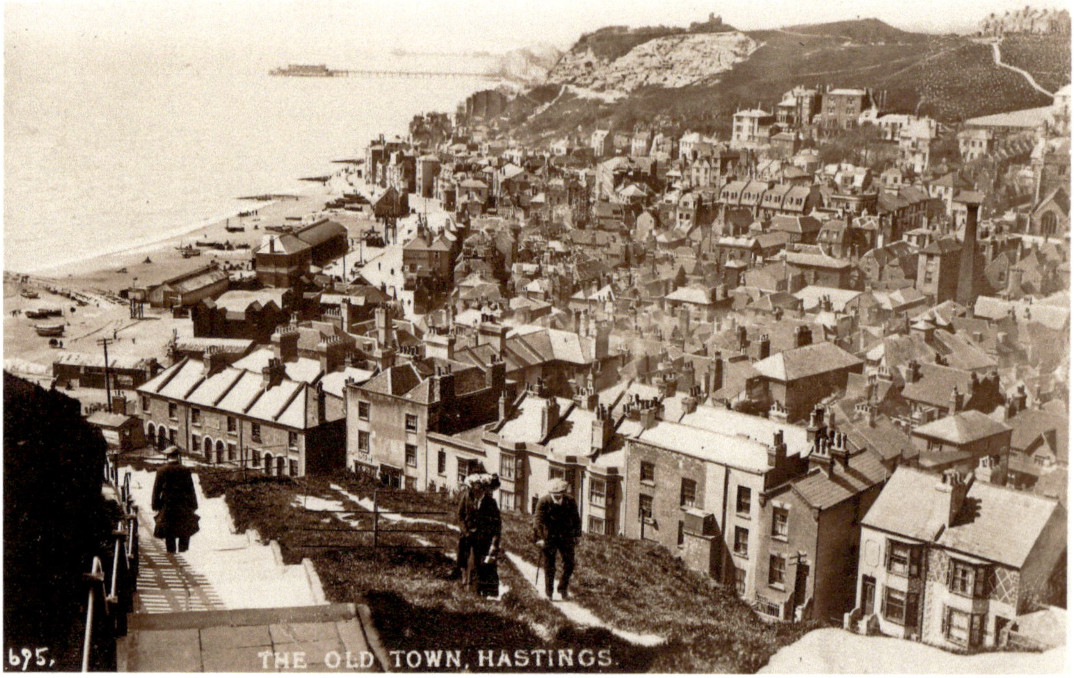

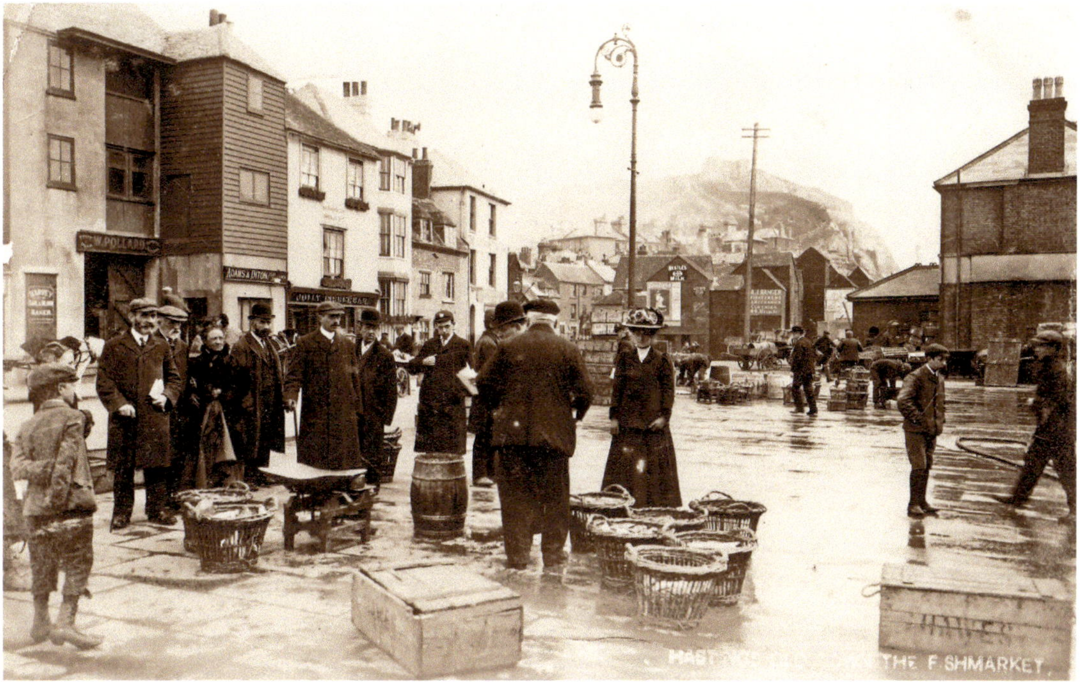

The Fish Market

This evocative image, taken by Frederick Broderick, the prolific photographer of Edwardian Hastings, bears little resemblance to the same area today, where only a few buildings betray its being the same location. In the top photo a group of men and women gather around baskets of fresh fish and a large set of scales.

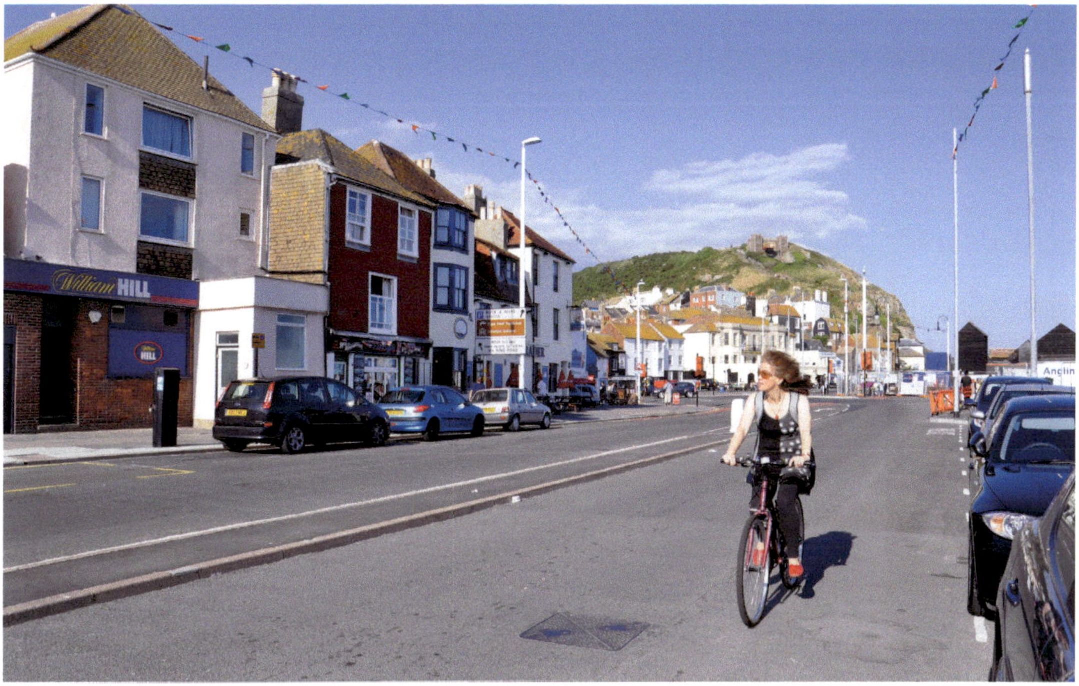

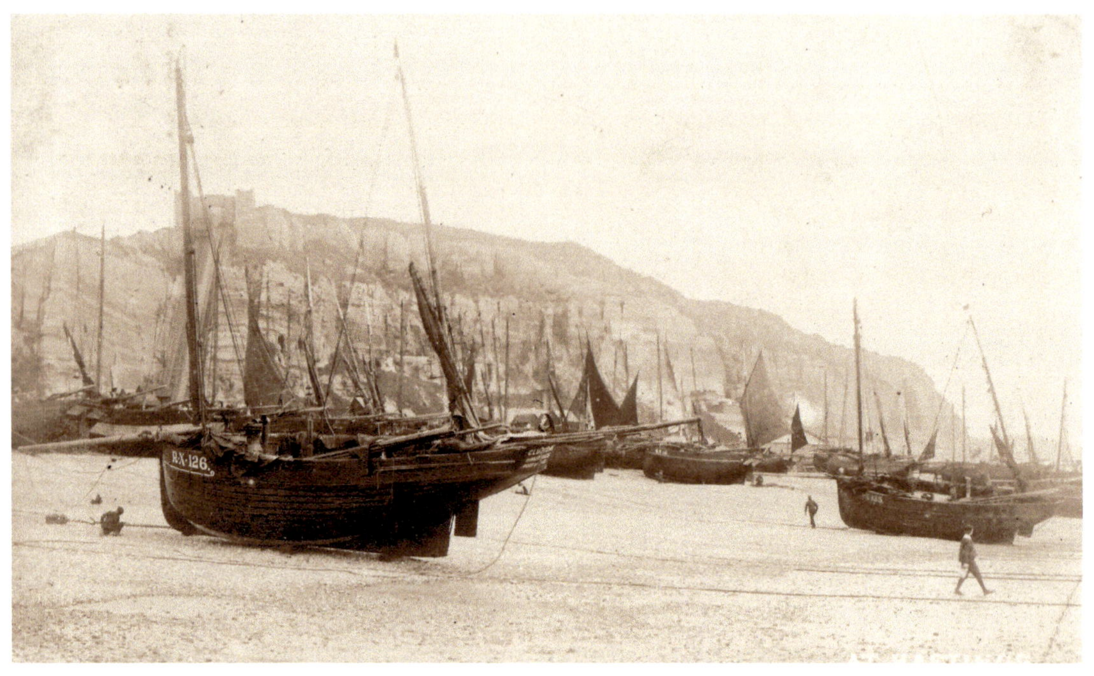

Fishing Boats at Rock-a-Nore

Hastings Old Town boasts the location of the largest beach-based fleet of fishing boats in the country. For a thousand years Hastings has been a centre for maritime activities, with fishing at its heart. Recently, the fishermen have been engaged in a dispute over EU fishing quotas, which the fishermen argue are unfair.

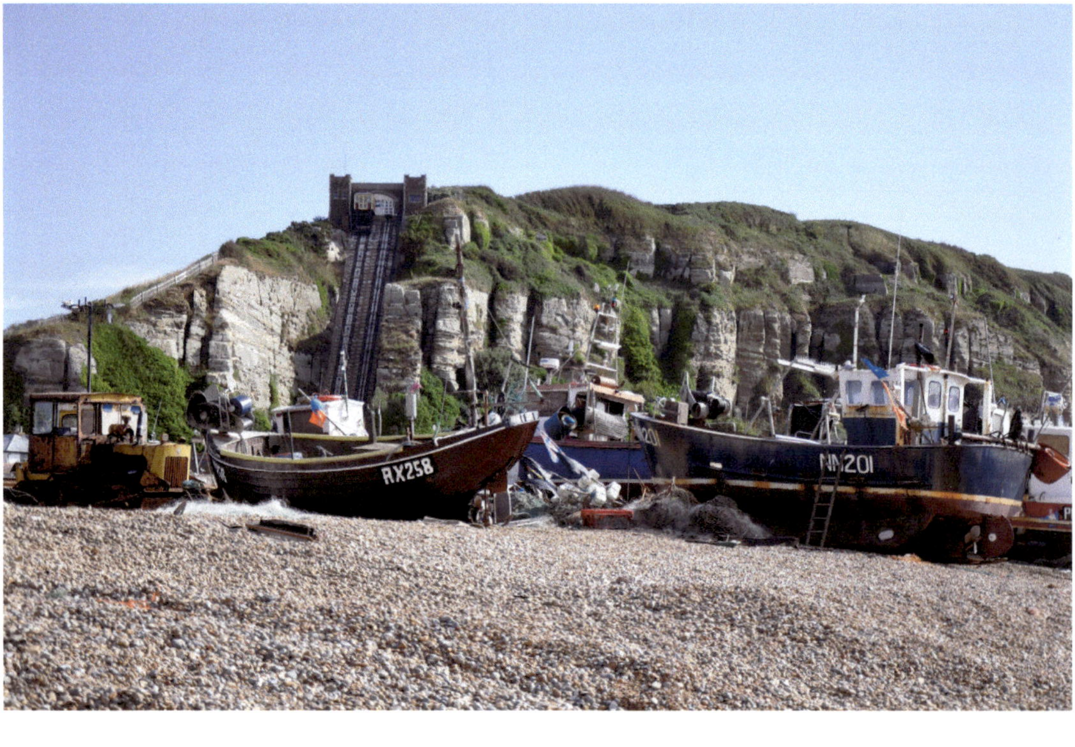

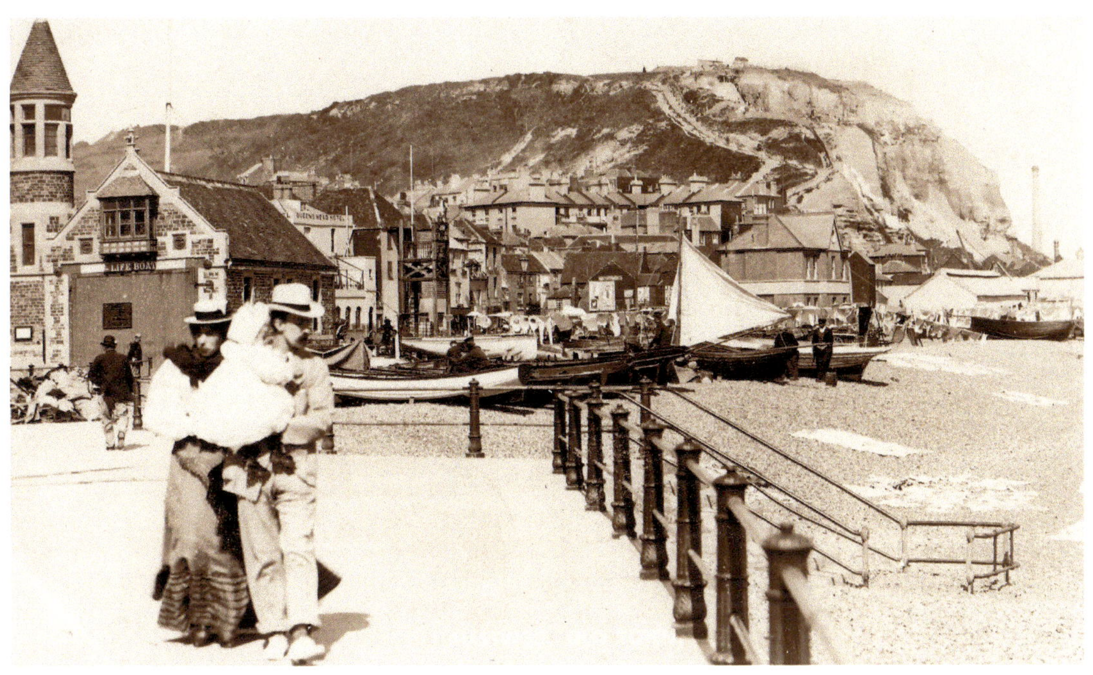

Old and New Lifeboat Houses

These photos show the old and new lifeboat houses. In the distance of the older image is the East Hill lift being constructed, dating this photograph to around 1900. The lifeboat house in the top photograph, on East Parade, was opened on 3 July 1882 and it remained there until the road was widened as part of general improvements to the Old Town in December 1959. The town's very first lifeboat house was situated in Rock-a-Nore and housed the lifeboat *Victoria*.

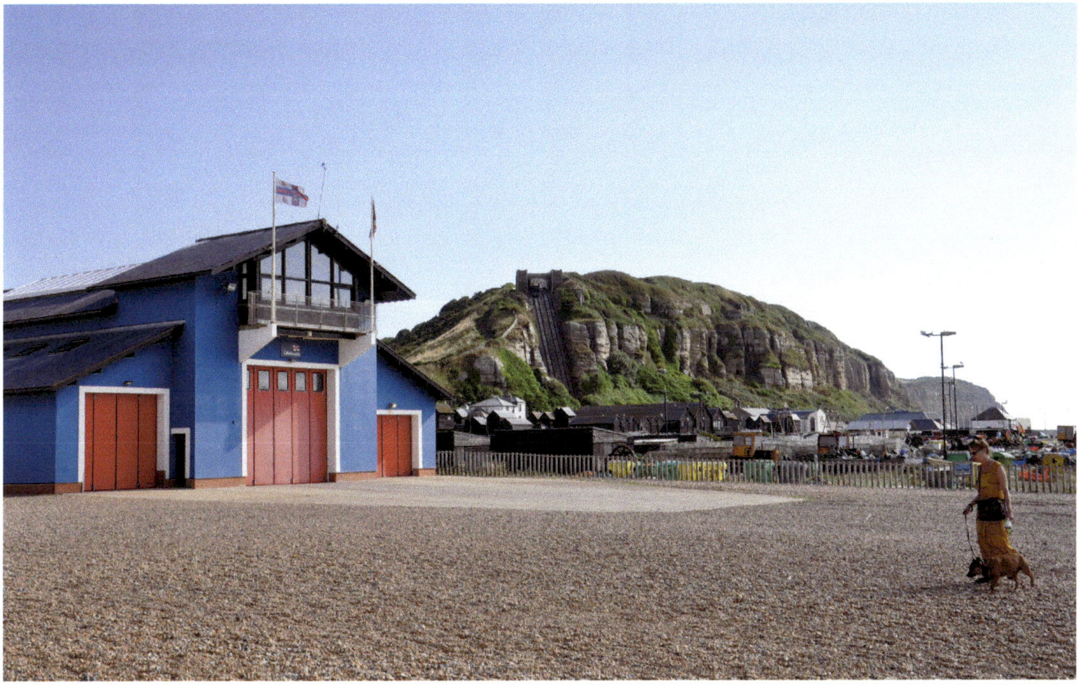

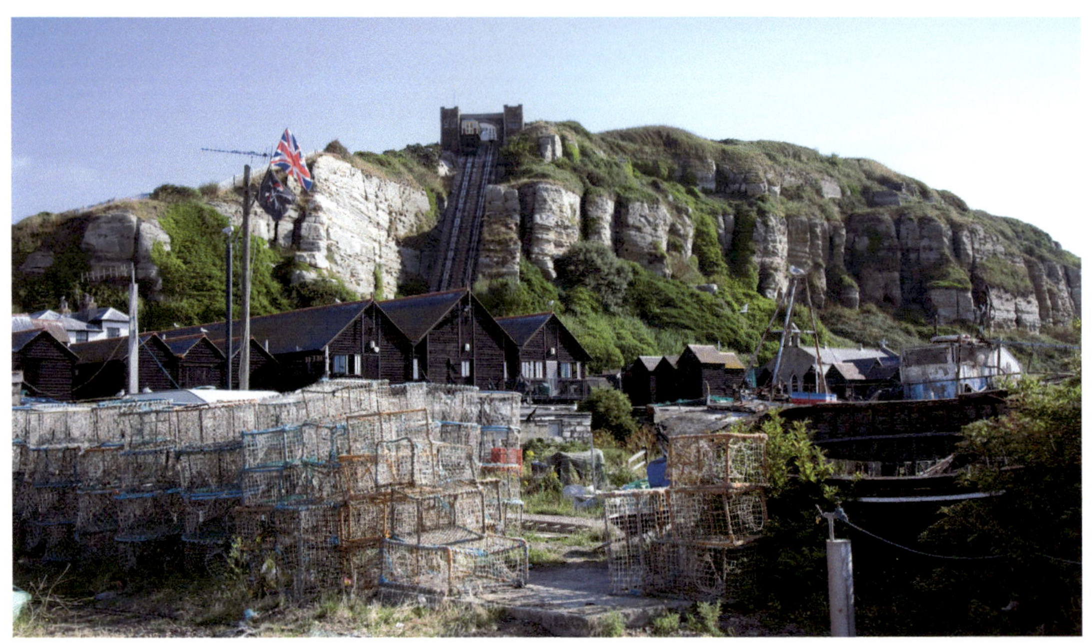

The Old Town and the Famous East Hill Lift

The East Hill lift has the distinction of being the steepest funicular railway in the country. It opened on 10 August 1902 after being beset by complex planning negotiations, difficult construction and an unfortunate derailment (with the carriage containing council officials) near the top. The lift has recently had a £200,000 revamp following a major brake failure which resulted in the two lifts crashing to the bottom. Recent problems have been overcome and the lift continues to serve Hastings as an important tourist attraction.

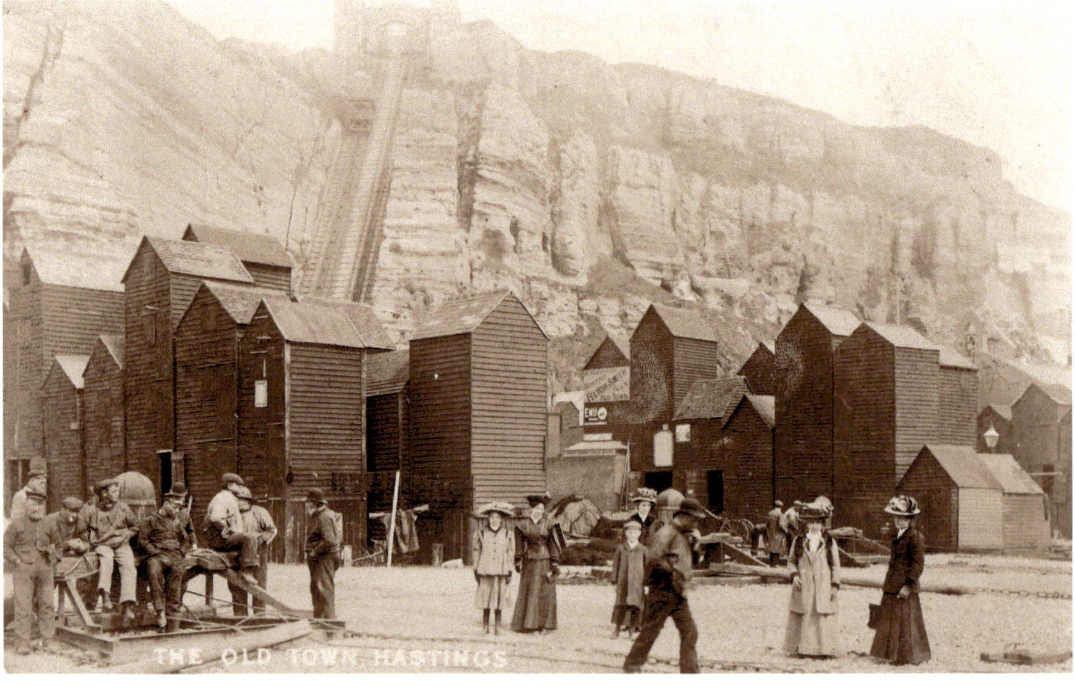

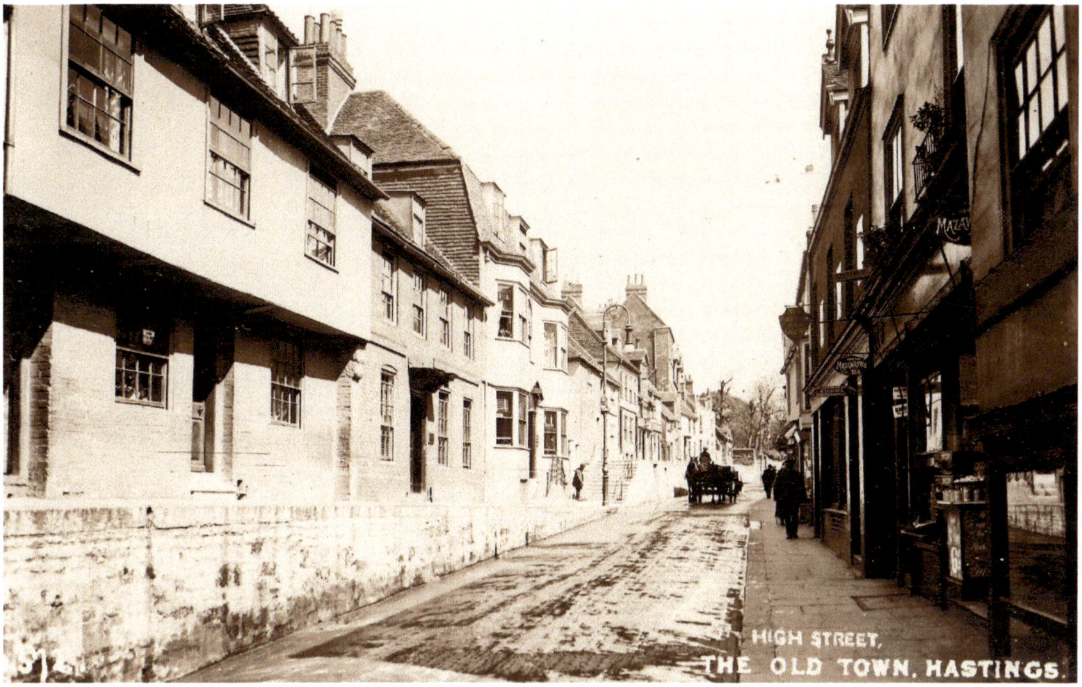

High Street

But for the modern cars and white lines on the road there has been little change in the more than one hundred years separating these two images. The High Street was so designated in 1814; prior to this date it was known as Market Street. In 1700 a town hall was built on the High Street. The structure survived until 1823, when it was replaced by the building that now functions as the Old Town Hall Museum.

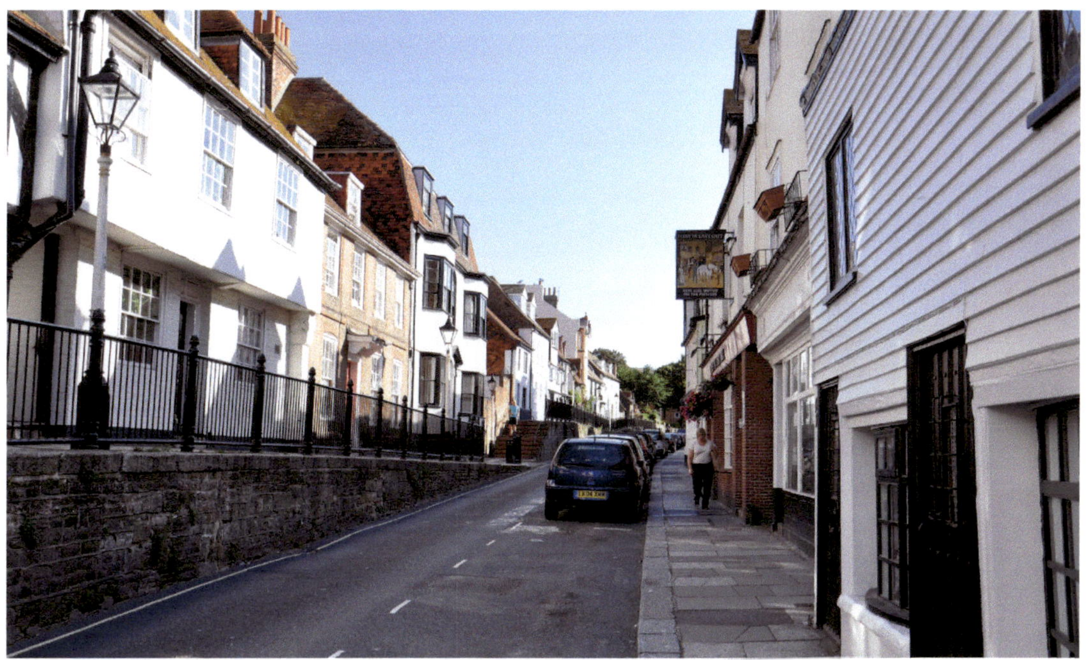

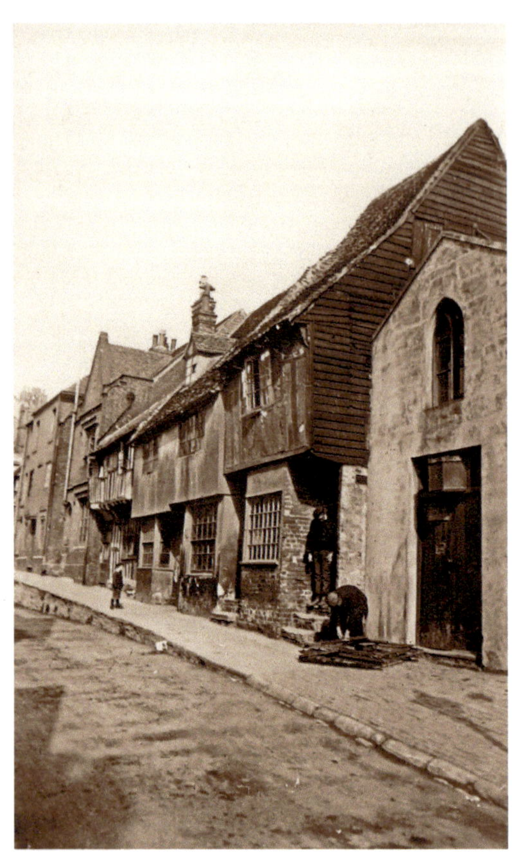

All Saints Street

Time has little altered All Saints Street; some of the houses in this quaint part of the Old Town date back to the fifteenth century. The road takes its name from the parish church and was once nicknamed Fish or Fisher Street owing to the large number of fishermen who resided there. It was generally the poorest of the Old Town parishes. In 1835 Sarah Milward, whose father had been rector at All Saints church, paid for the first elementary school to be started at 57 All Saints Street. In 1914 the school moved to Harold Road and became All Saints School before moving again to Githa Road in 1959.

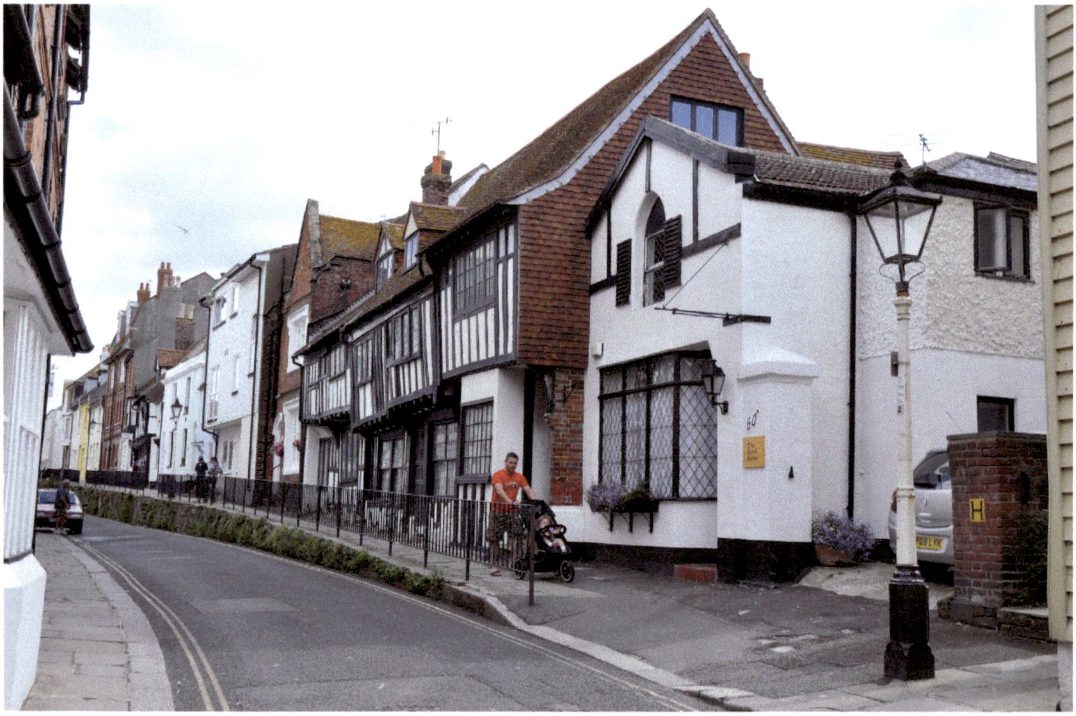

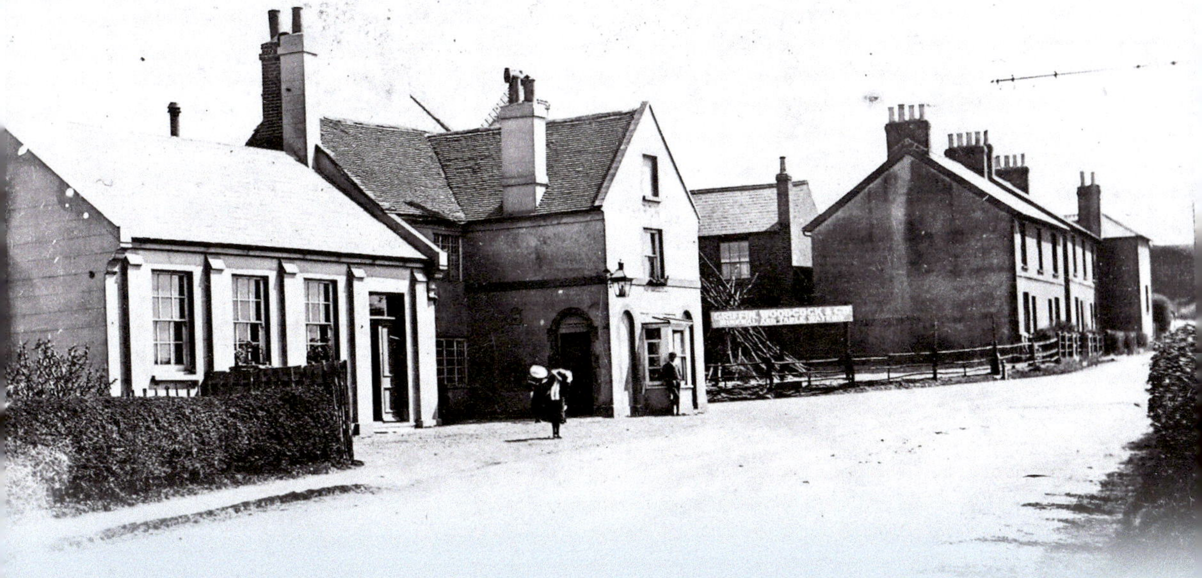

CHAPTER 3

General Views

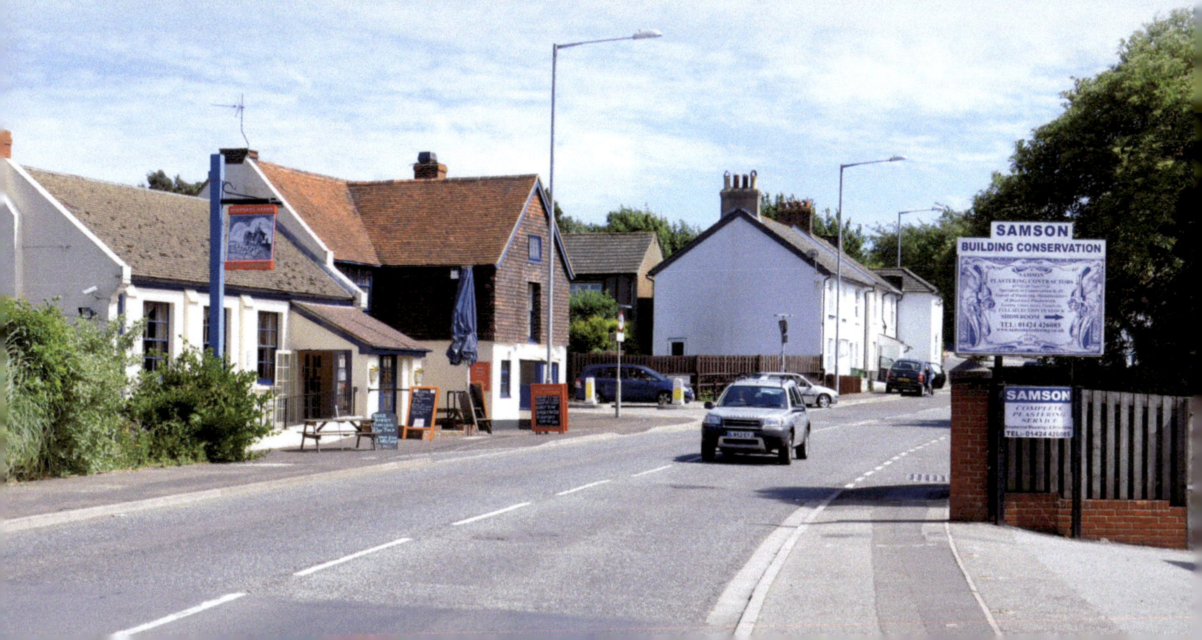

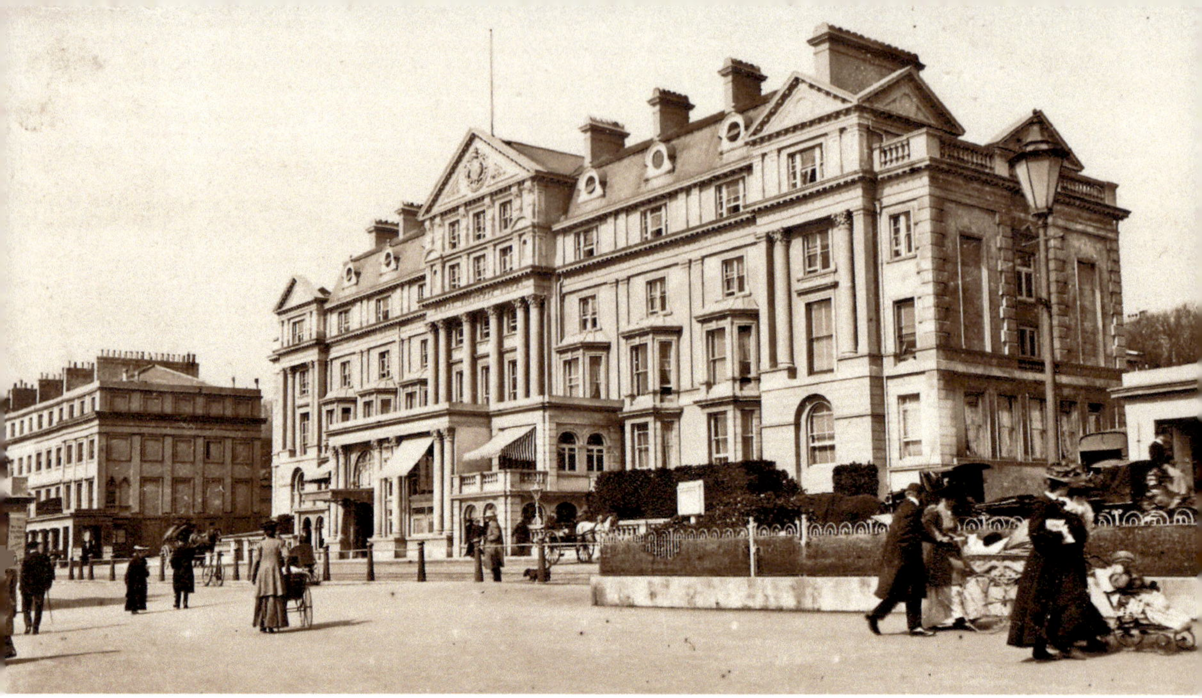

The Royal Victoria Hotel

The Victoria Hotel (later the Royal Victoria Hotel) was originally named the St Leonards Hotel and was the centrepiece of James Burton's new town of St Leonards, which was built on farm land once belonging to the Eversfield estate. The hotel was built in 1828 and opened the following year on 26 October 1829. Prince Albert, Edward VII and George V are among the hotel's famous visitors.

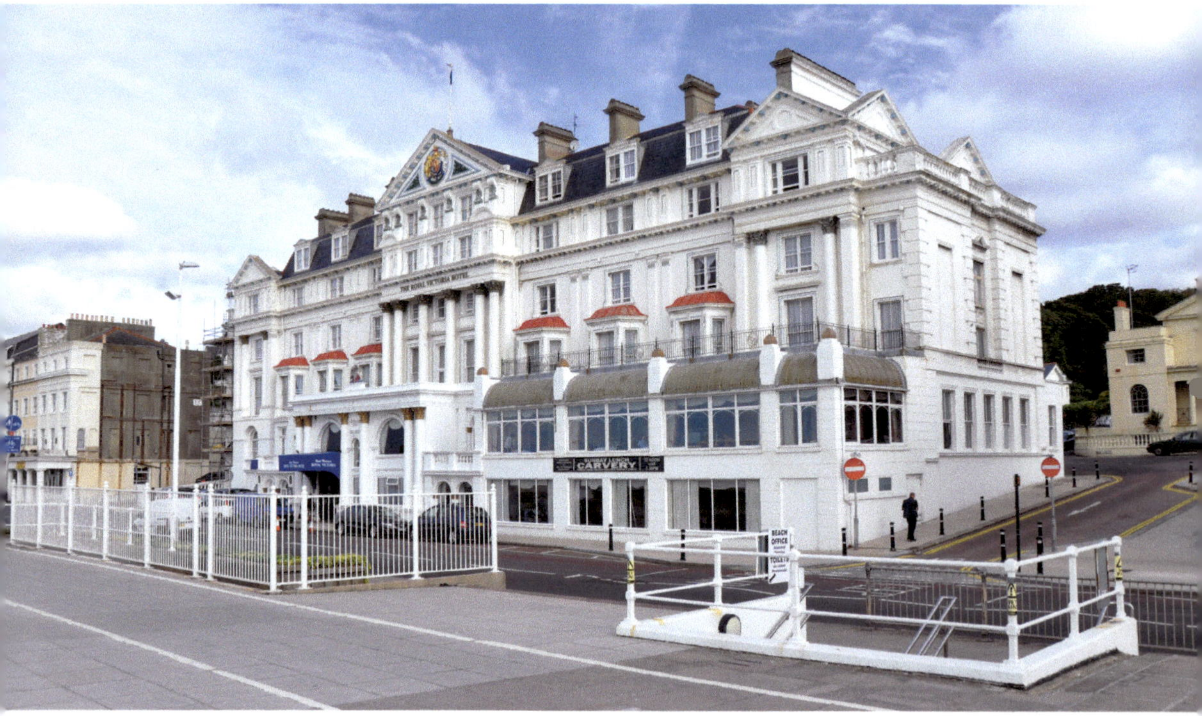

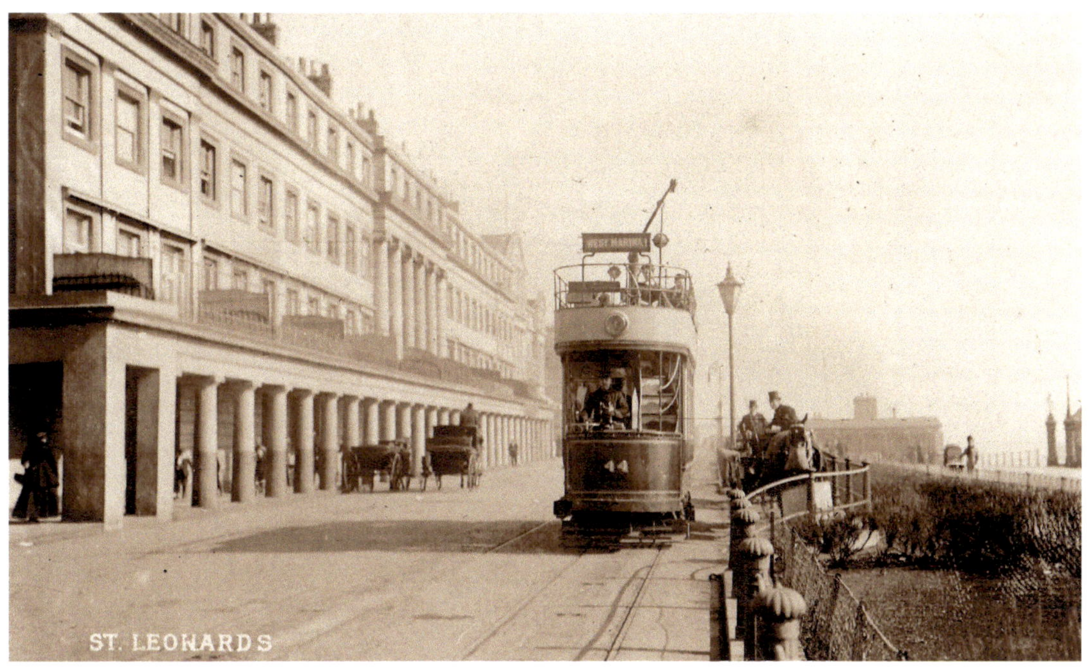

The Marina

The modern photo shows the west end of Marine Court, a hulking great 170-feet-tall block of flats, which was, at the time it was opened in 1938, the highest dwelling place in Britain. The Art Deco-style building was modelled on the ocean liner *Queen Mary* and from the front it clearly resembles a large boat, a fact that caused much controversy at the time of its creation. Marine Court was listed Grade II by English Heritage in 1999.

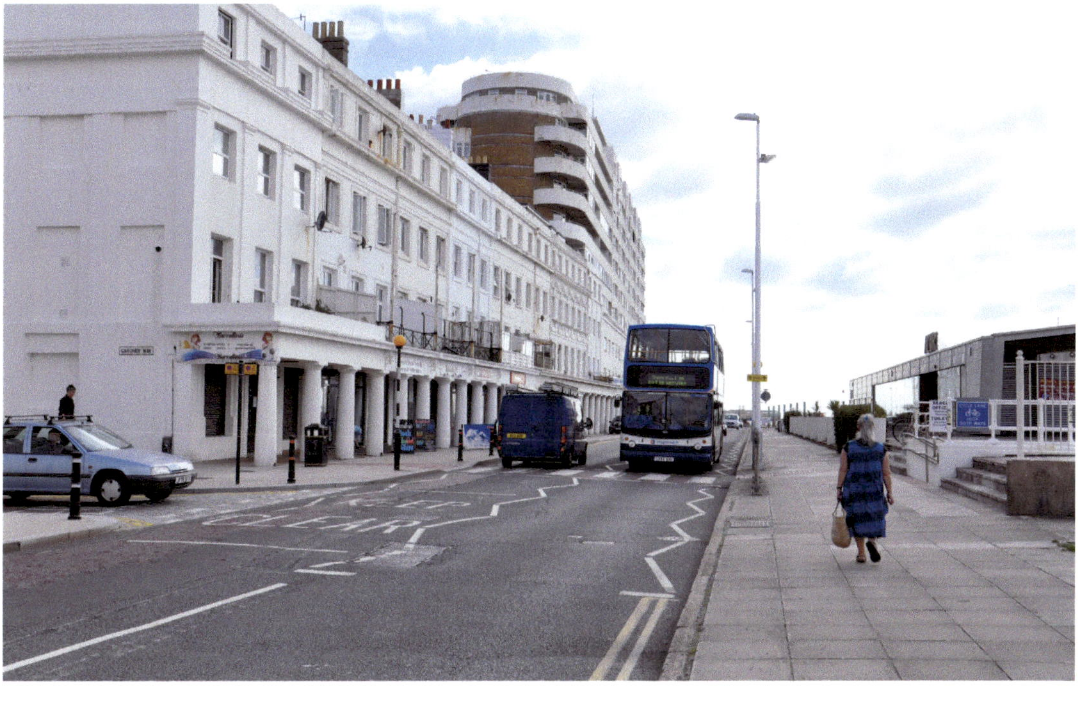

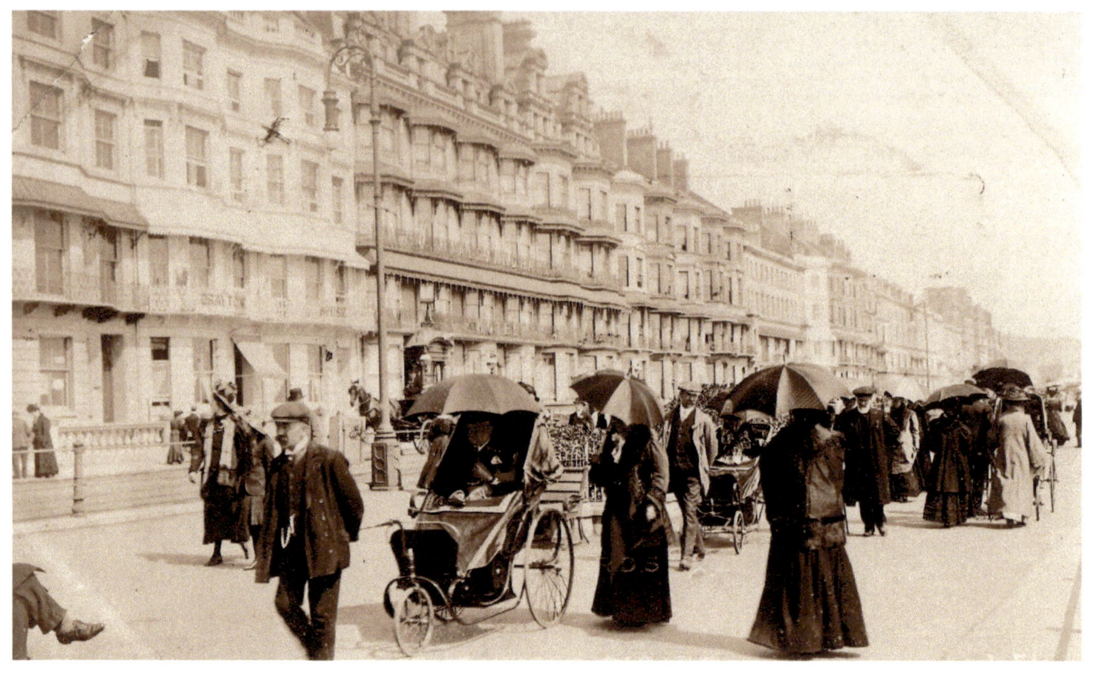

St Leonards Parade

'The marvellously low death rate of the borough, and especially the almost entire absence of zymotic diseases, is an eloquent practical vindication of the hygienic character of the town, which now stands unrivalled in the very front rank among English watering places as a winter and summer retreat for invalids.' These words, taken from the 1897 *Views and Reviews*, are manifest in this photograph of St Leonards seafront. The bath chair shown in the photo was typically used by the elderly and disabled.

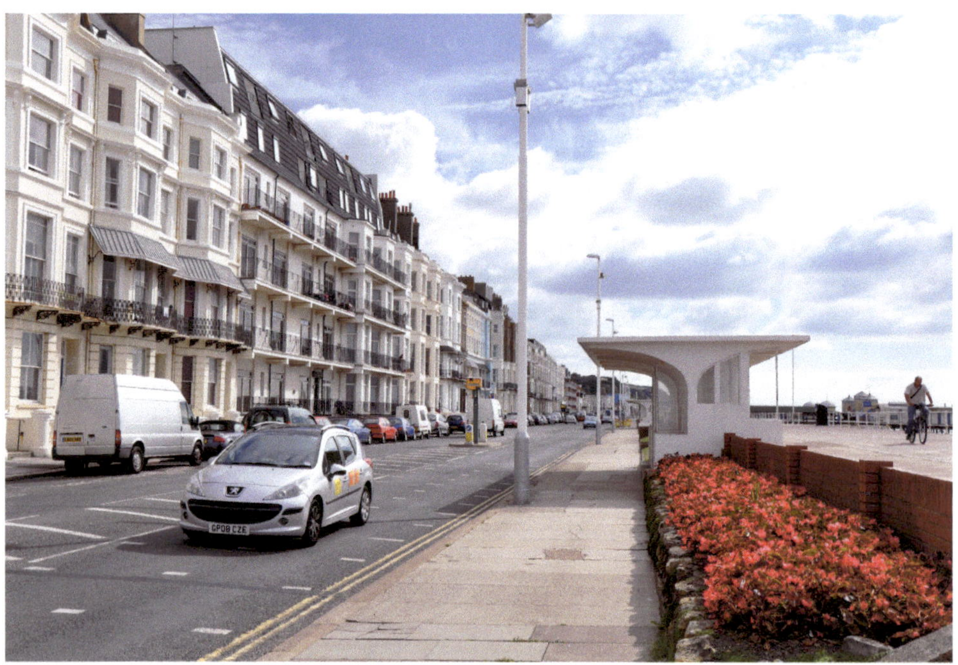

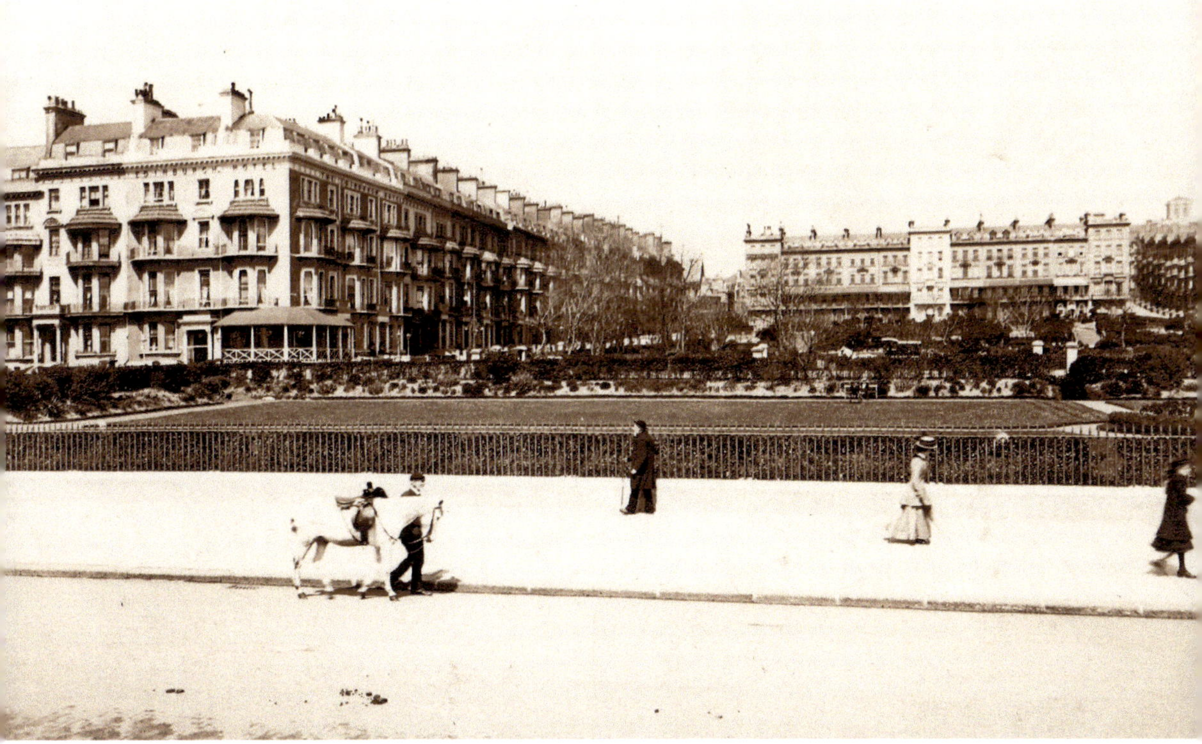

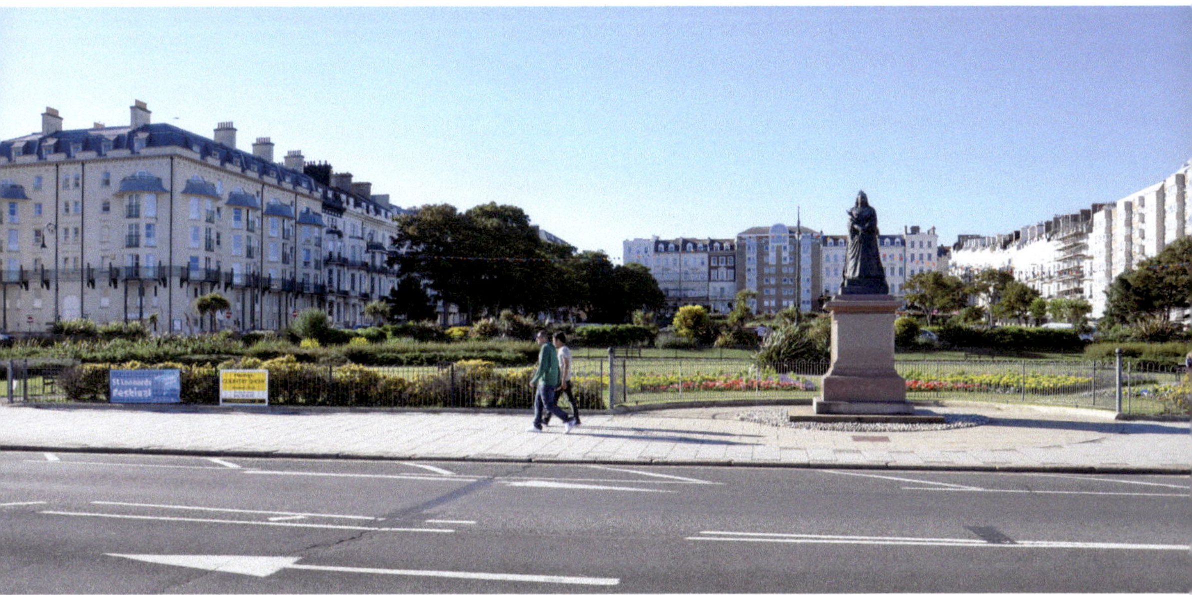

Warrior Square

At the turn of the twentieth century Warrior Square was, due to its well-manicured gardens and lawns, considered to be an excellent place in which to hold political or military gatherings. It was only fitting then that a new statue to honour the reign of Queen Victoria be situated on the edge of the square. The bronze statue, unveiled on 31 December 1902, was sculpted by Francis John Williamson and was based on Victoria at the time of her Golden Jubilee in 1887.

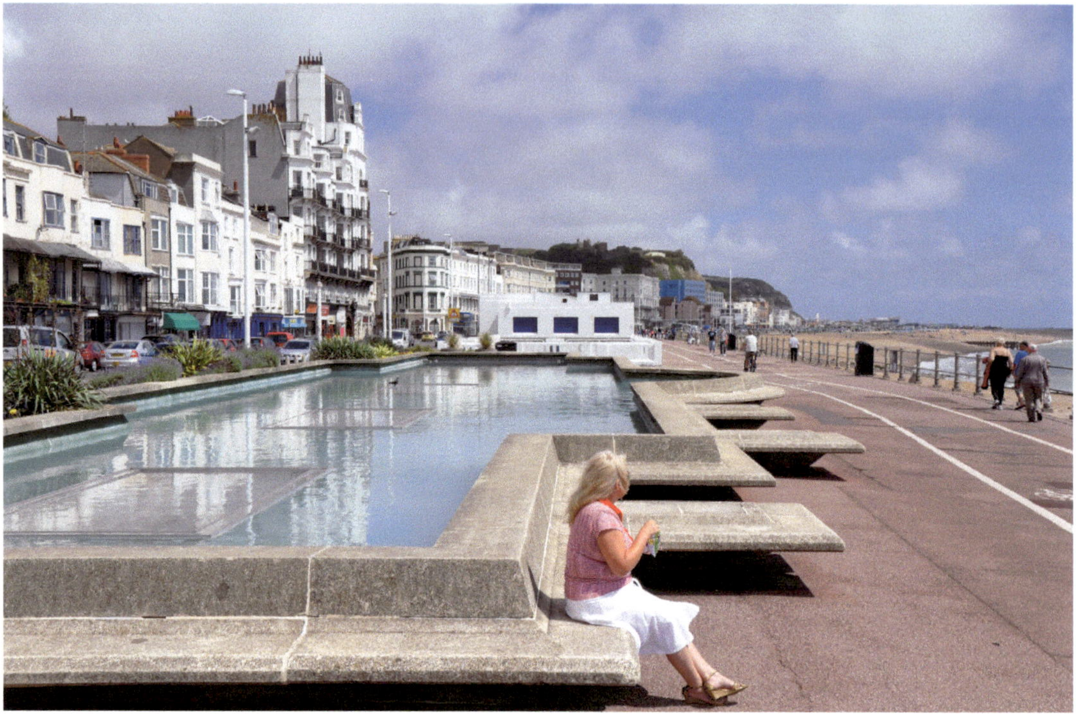

The Parade, Hastings

This very busy scene along Hastings seafront (below) clearly demonstrates just how popular the seaside town was during its heyday at the turn of the century. This photograph was very likely taken during the high season when visitor numbers were at their peak. Conversely, the modern version shows very few visitors or locals enjoying a stroll along the promenade.

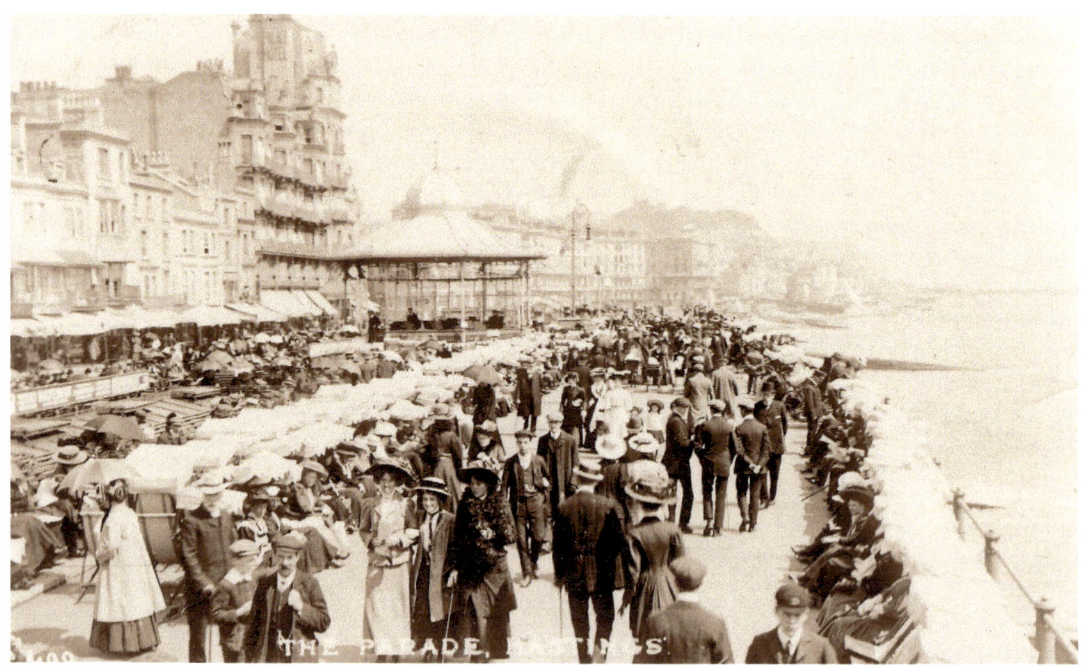

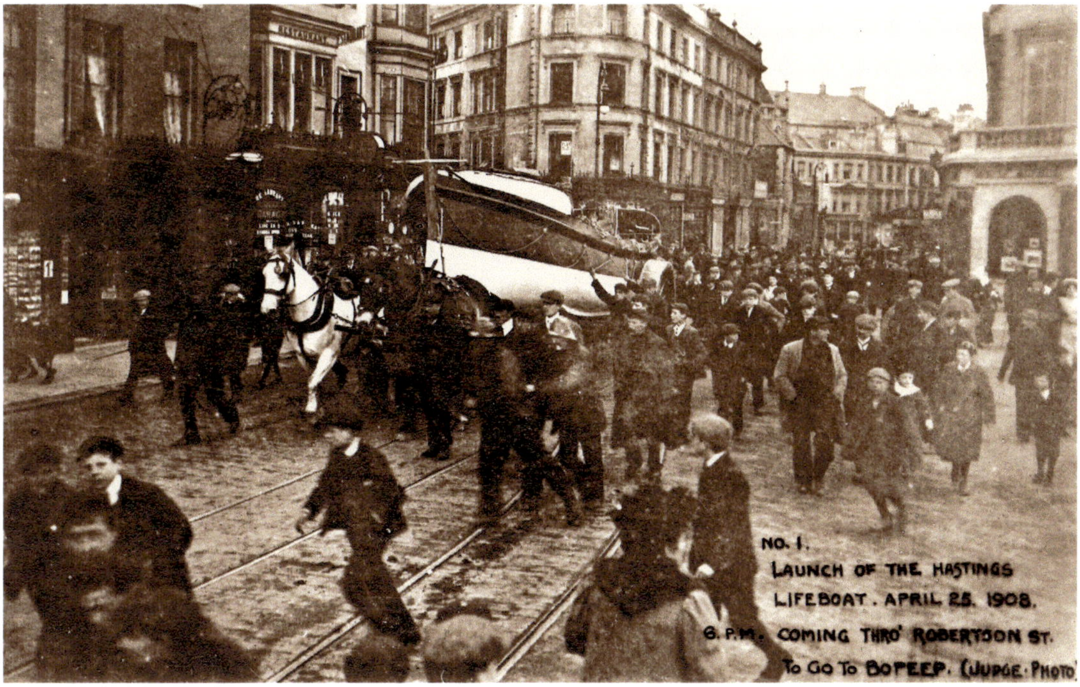

Dramatic Sea Rescue

This scene from 25 April 1908 depicts the Hastings lifeboat *Charles Arkcoll II* being drawn along from Robertson Street for a launch at Bo-Peep to attend the distressed London sailing barge *Amy*. According to Steve Peak in his book *Fishermen of Hastings*, the barge was struggling with rough seas off the coast of Beachy Head, at which point she turned back towards St Leonards. The lifeboat crew rescued the skipper and two crew, then towed the *Amy* to shelter close to Dungeness.

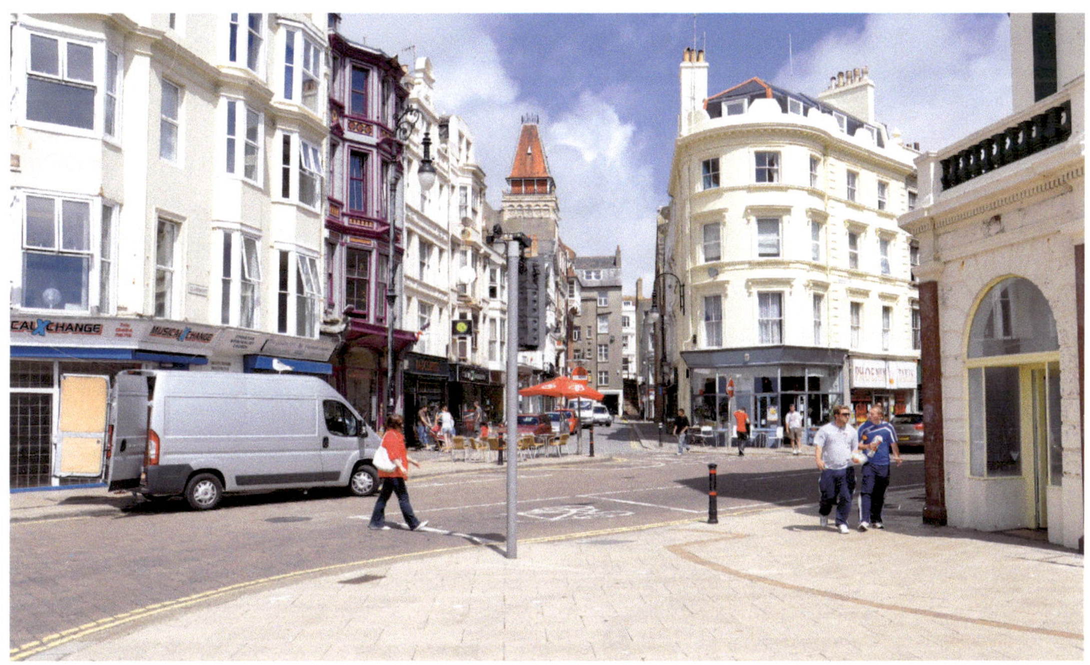

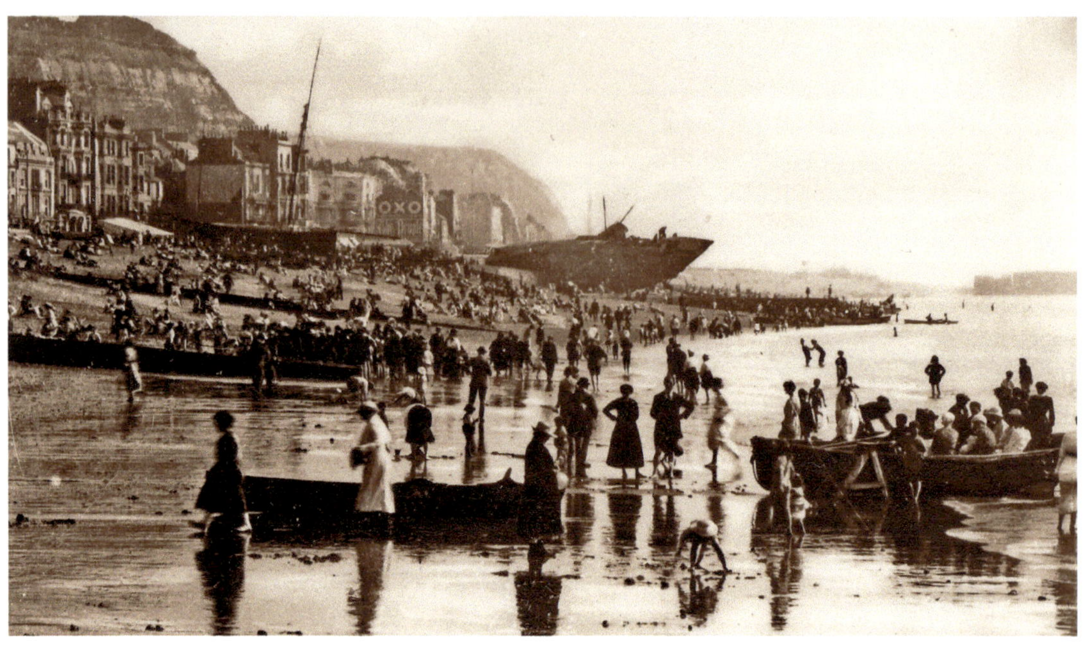

A Sinister Monster

An unusual visitor to Hastings' shoreline washed up onto the beach on 15 April 1919: a German U-boat, which became stranded near Harold Place. U118 was one of two U-Boats being towed from Harwich by the French destroyer *Francis Garnier* when heavy seas separated the vessels. The local paper described the scene thus: 'As the morning advanced and the tide came in the craft was buffeted tremendously. The boat appeared a helpless yet sinister monster as it rolled in the surf only a few yards from the promenade at Harold Place.' Permission was sought from the Admiralty and hundreds of visitors were given permission to board the vessel. Sadly, the two coastguards who had been given the responsibility of showing visitors around U118 both died within nine months, their causes of death being inhalation of noxious substances while on the U-boat.

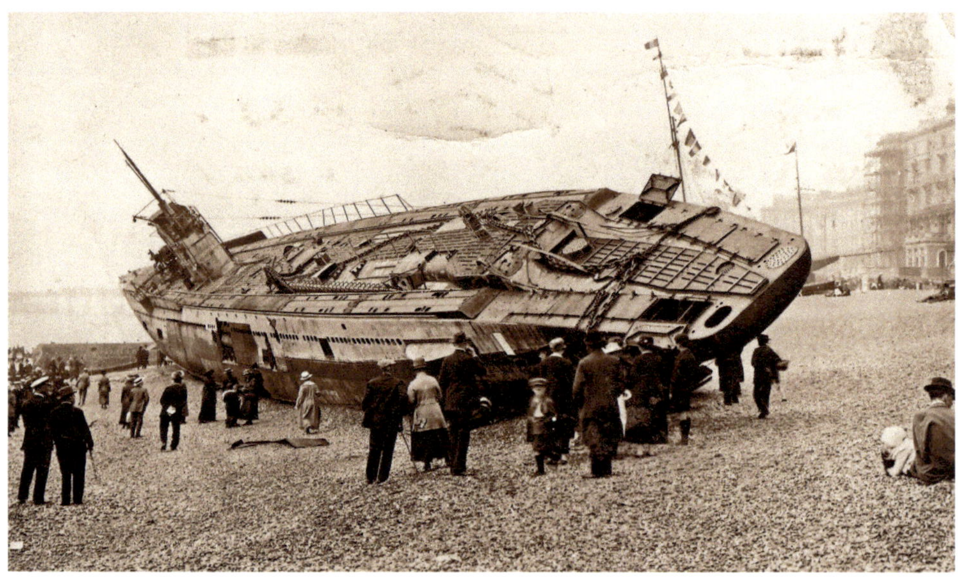

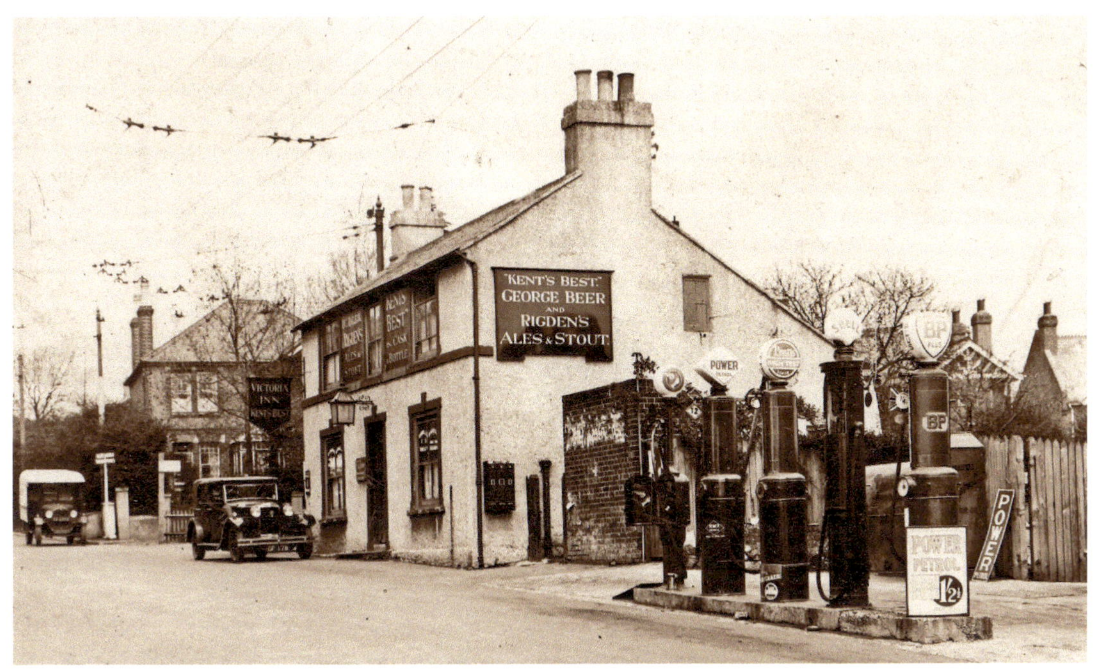

Battle Road

The site of the Victoria Inn on Battle Road, for fifty years in the hands of Charles Albert Bristow until his death in 1970, was the turning point for the trolleybuses from 1928. Prior to this the tram service ran up Battle Road, but not as far as the Victoria Inn. Among the list of accidents in David Padgham's *Hastings Tramways Centenary* was, on 22 April 1921, the death of three-year-old Roland Hoad, who was killed by a tram on Battle Road; the coroner deemed that it was not the fault of the tram driver.

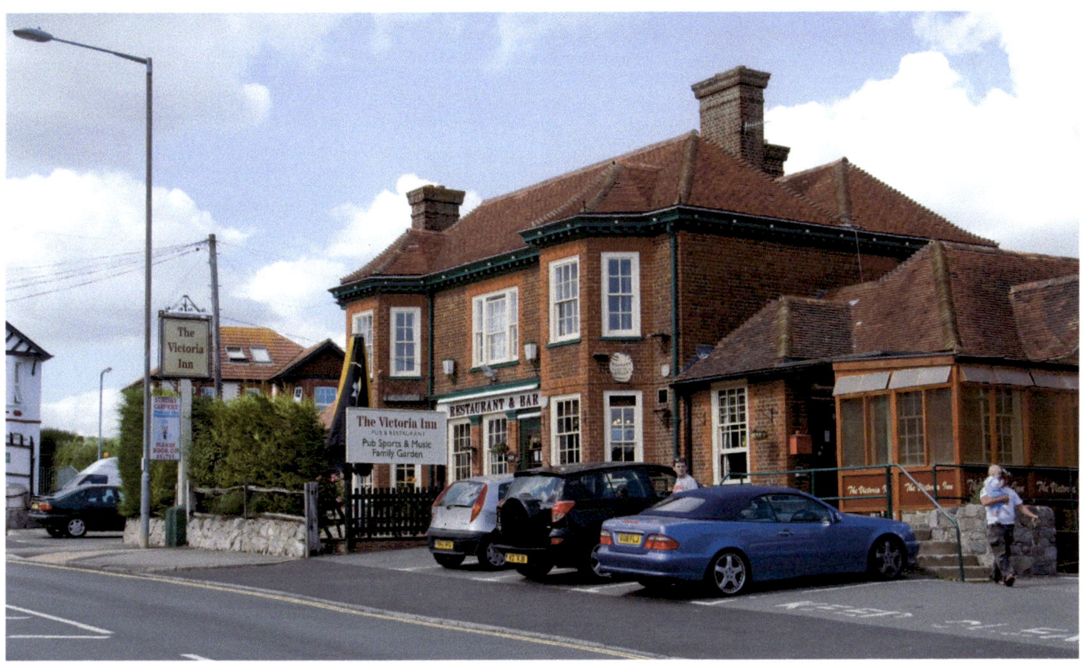

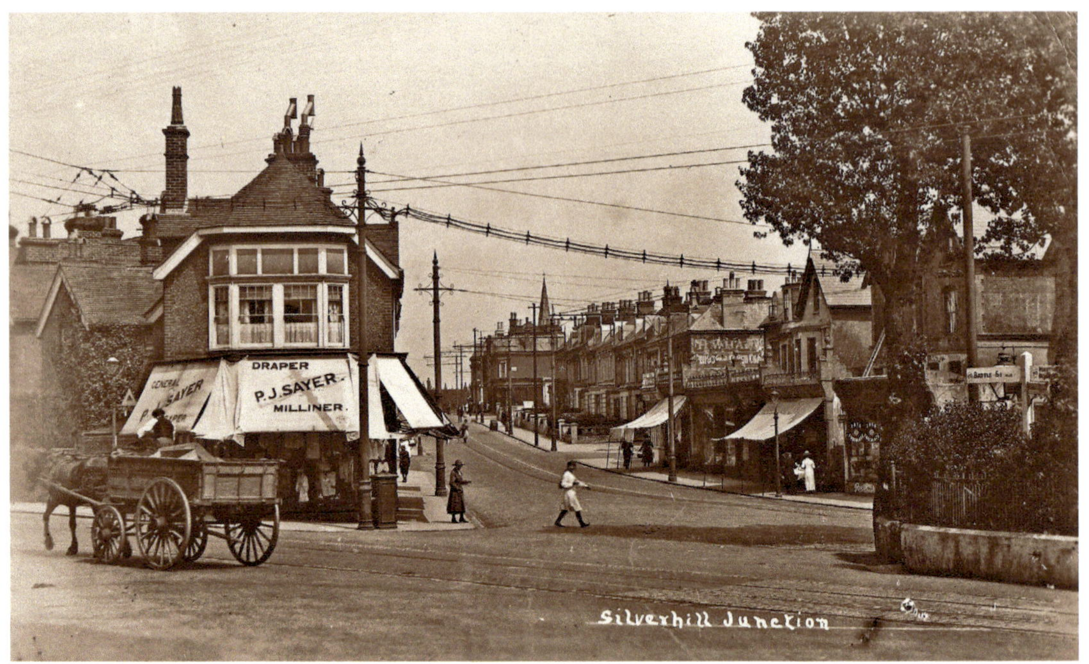

Silverhill Junction

This old photo of Silverhill Junction is dated to around 1910 and shows how Silverhill continued to develop commercially after this date. The buildings on the right-hand side of Sedlescombe Road North are functioning here as houses; today they serve as independent shops to the residents of Silverhill in the form of a post office, florist, undertaker, chemist and greengrocer.

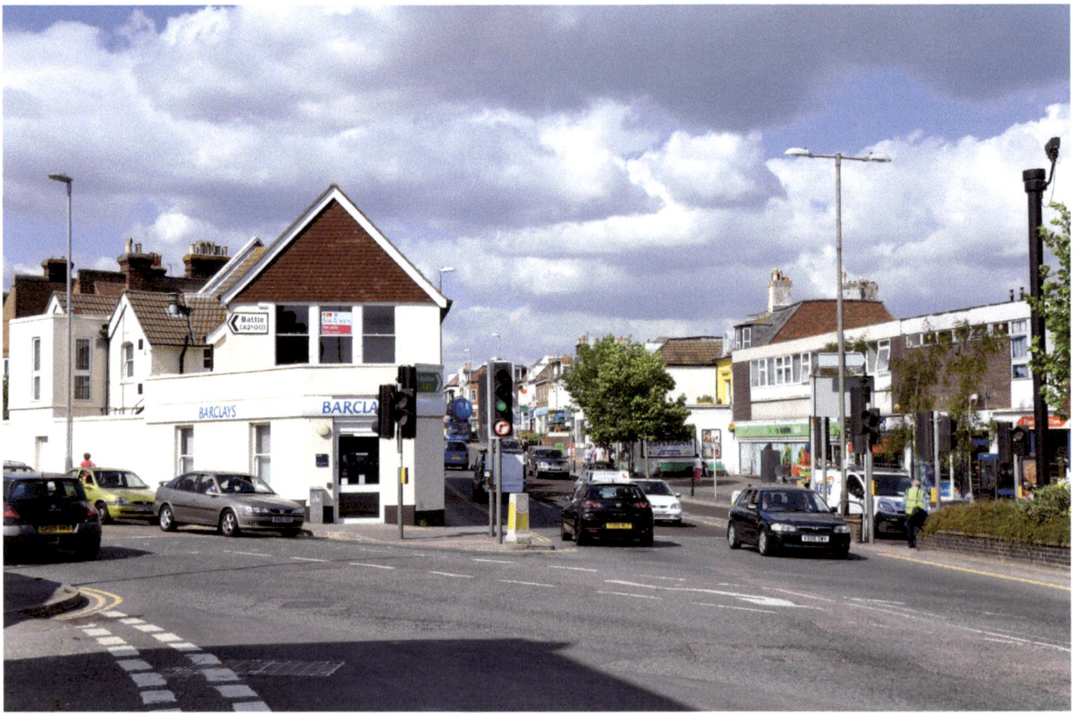

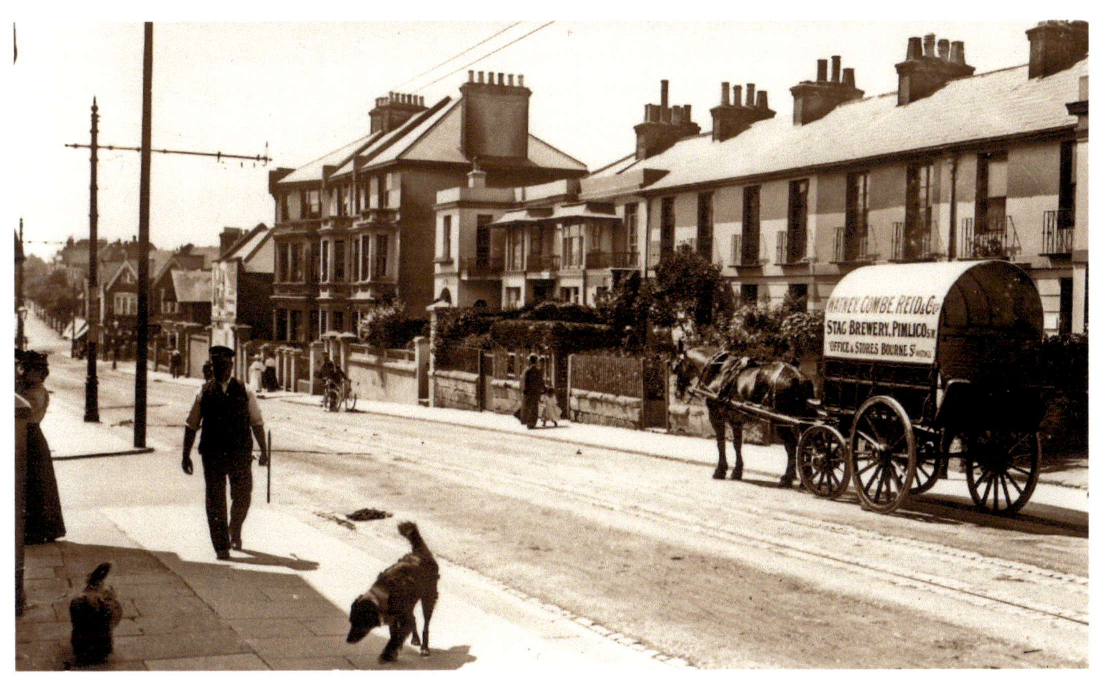

Sedlescombe Road North

This quiet scene of Sedlescombe Road North – in which a horse pulls a cart with 'Watney, Combe, Reid & Co., Stag Brewery, Pimlico' emblazoned on the side – is dated by the presence of the overhead tram wires to around 1905. Only the larger properties at the end of this run of houses have gone, having been replaced by a BP petrol station.

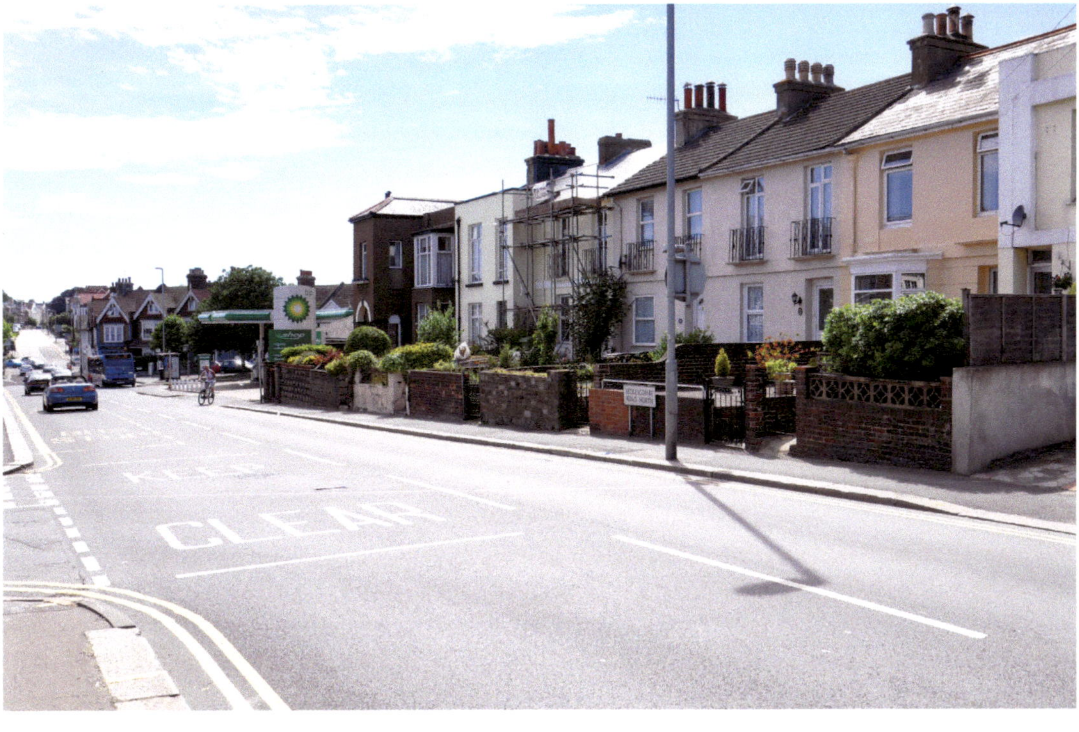

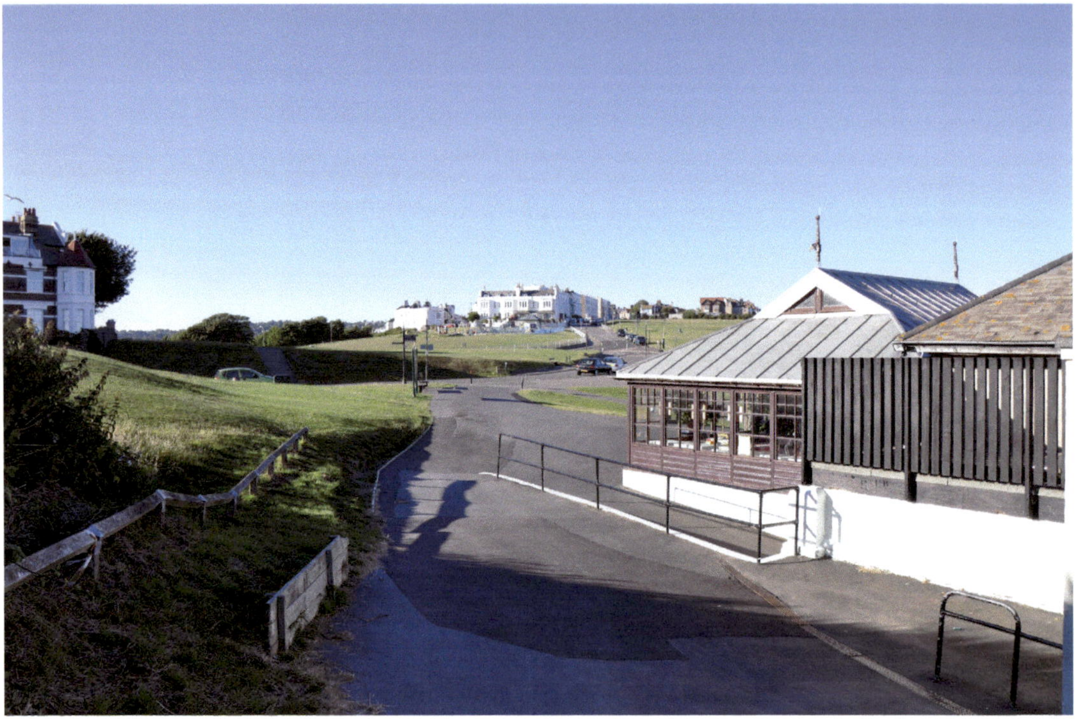

The West Hill

The 1860s and 1870s saw large parcels of land on the West Hill being sold from the Stonefield and Sayer-Milward estates. Perhaps due to the prolific rise and speed of the housing developments, Hastings Council purchased twenty-four acres of land on the East and West Hills in 1888 at a cost of £24,000, preserving them for future generations to enjoy. The West Hill lift was declared open three years later on 25 March 1891.

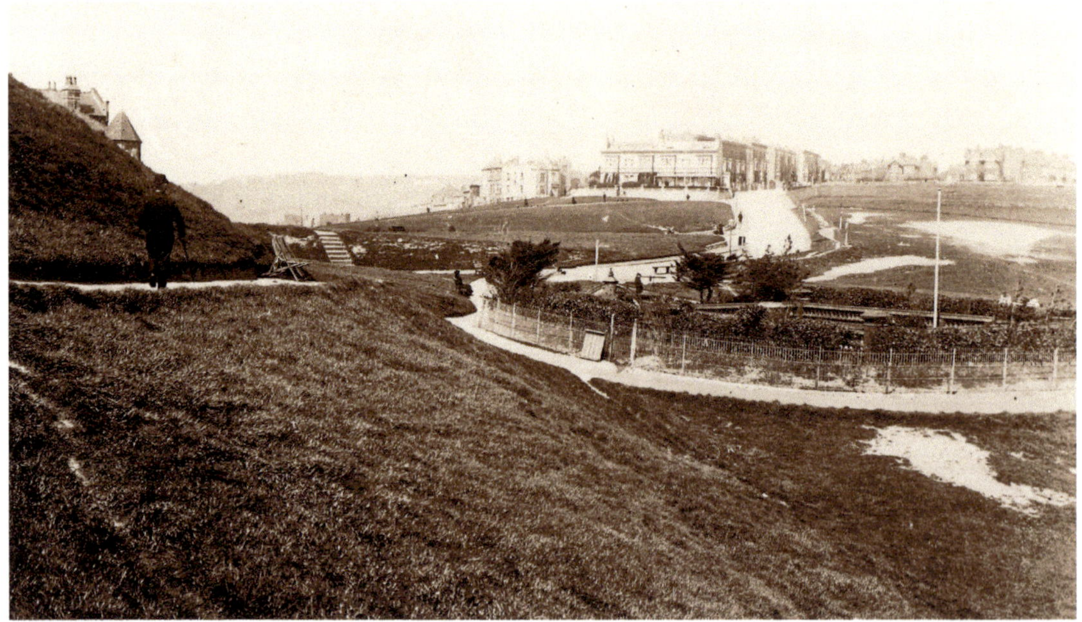

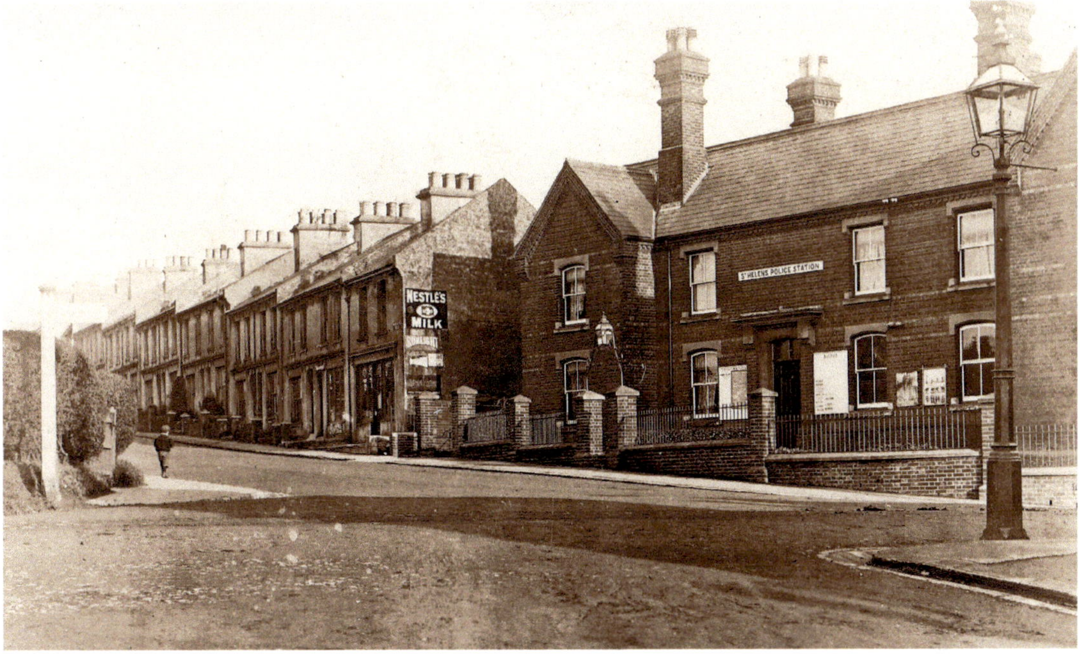

St Helen's Police Station

Without the benefit of the modern picture, it would be very difficult to place this old photograph, taken on the junction of Winchelsea Road and The Ridge. The large building on the right was St Helen's Police Station; the land on which it was built was purchased for £480 in 1882 from Thomas Dennett. It was one of seven police stations in the town at this time.

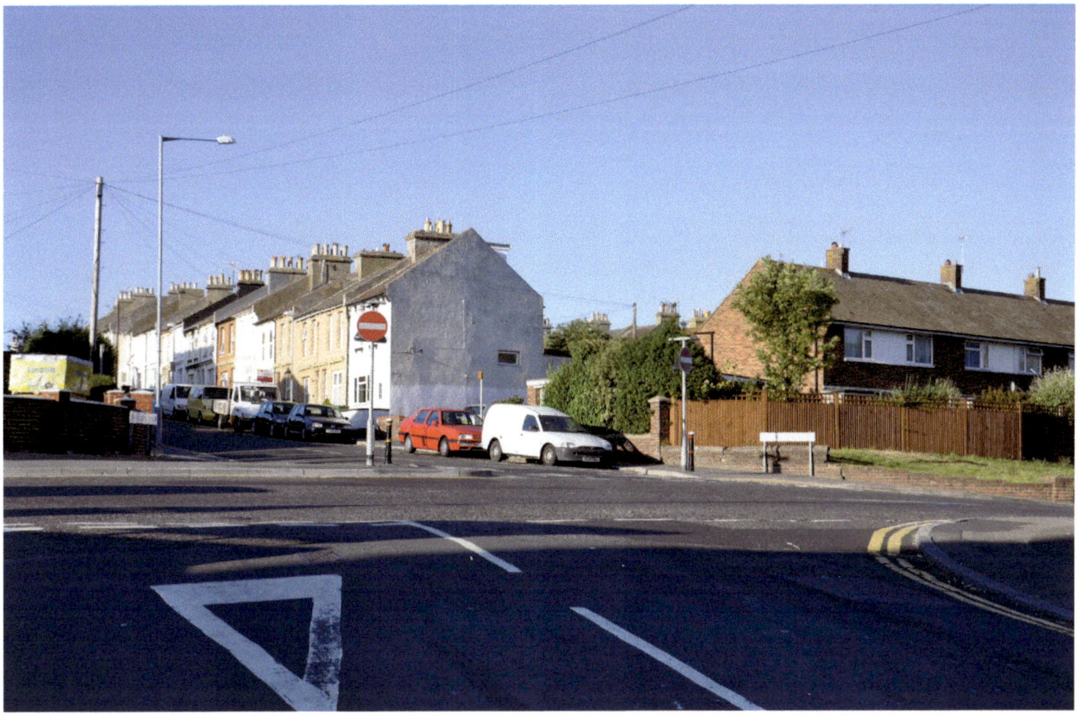

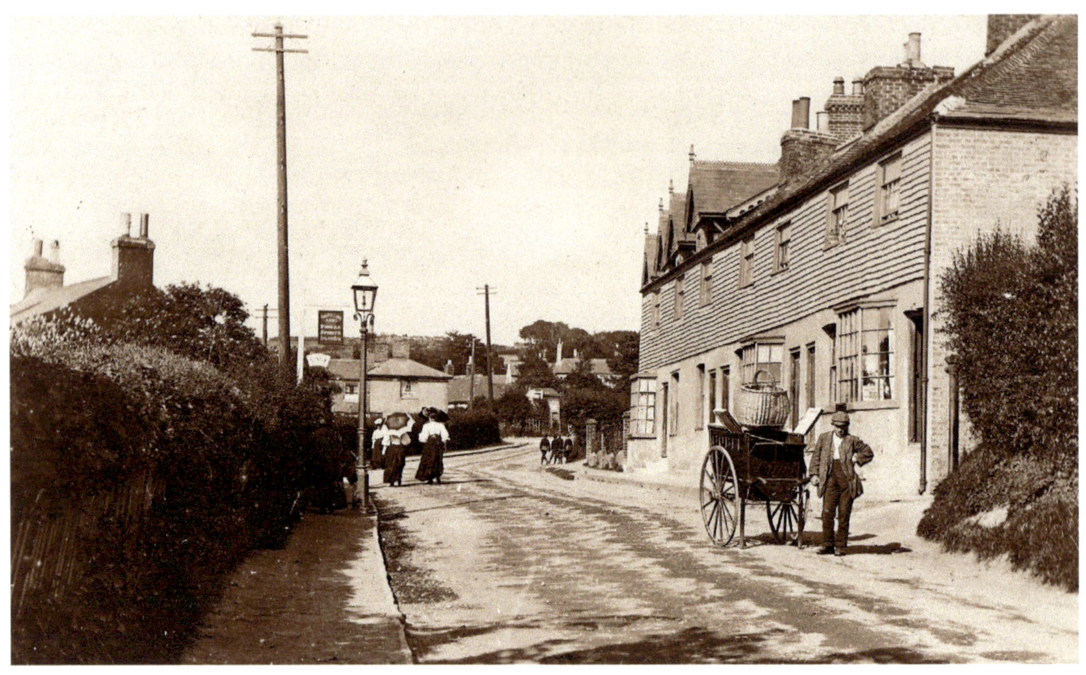

Fairlight Road

A great deal has changed in the years between these two photos of Fairlight Road in Ore, yet the similarities are still clearly visible. The row of cottages on the right have had a complete façade redevelopment and the house on the left in the photo has since been weather-boarded. In the middle-left of the old photograph is the hanging sign for the Oddfellows Arms, which is still situated on Old London Road, though now further south.

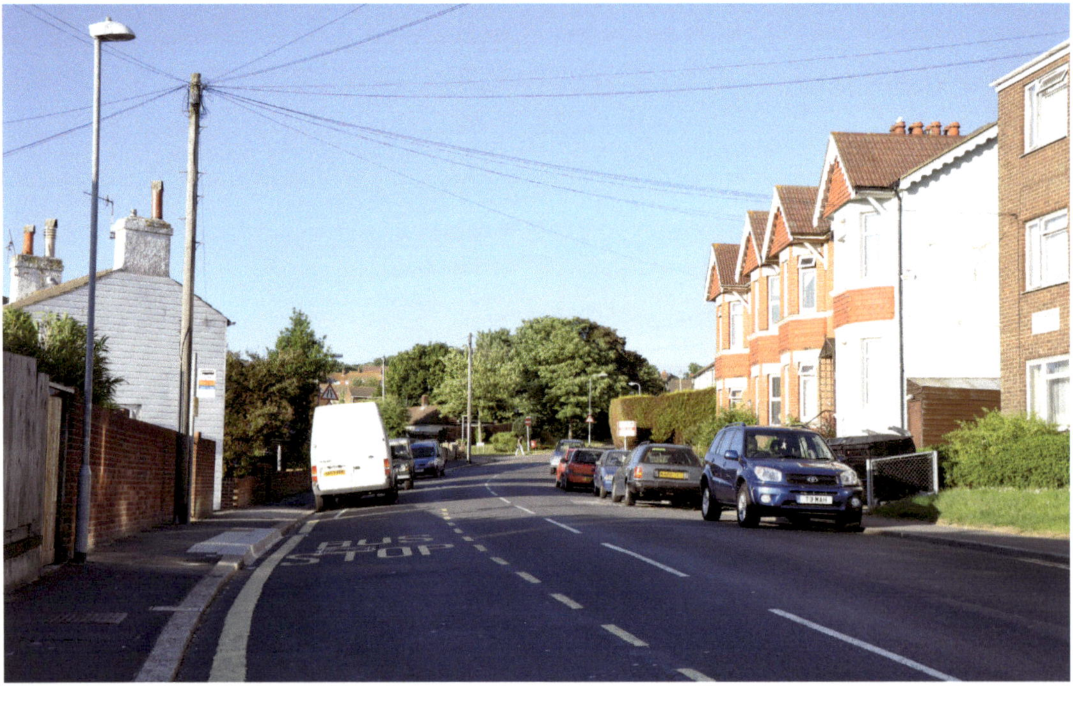

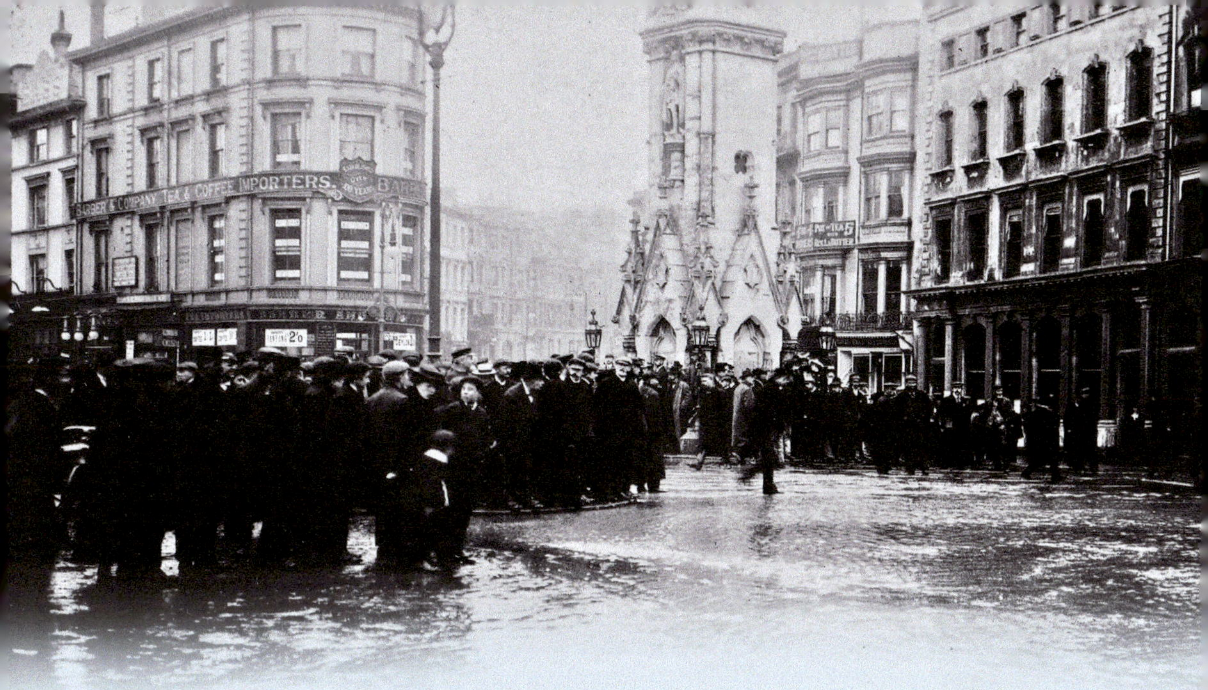

CHAPTER 4

Fire & Flood

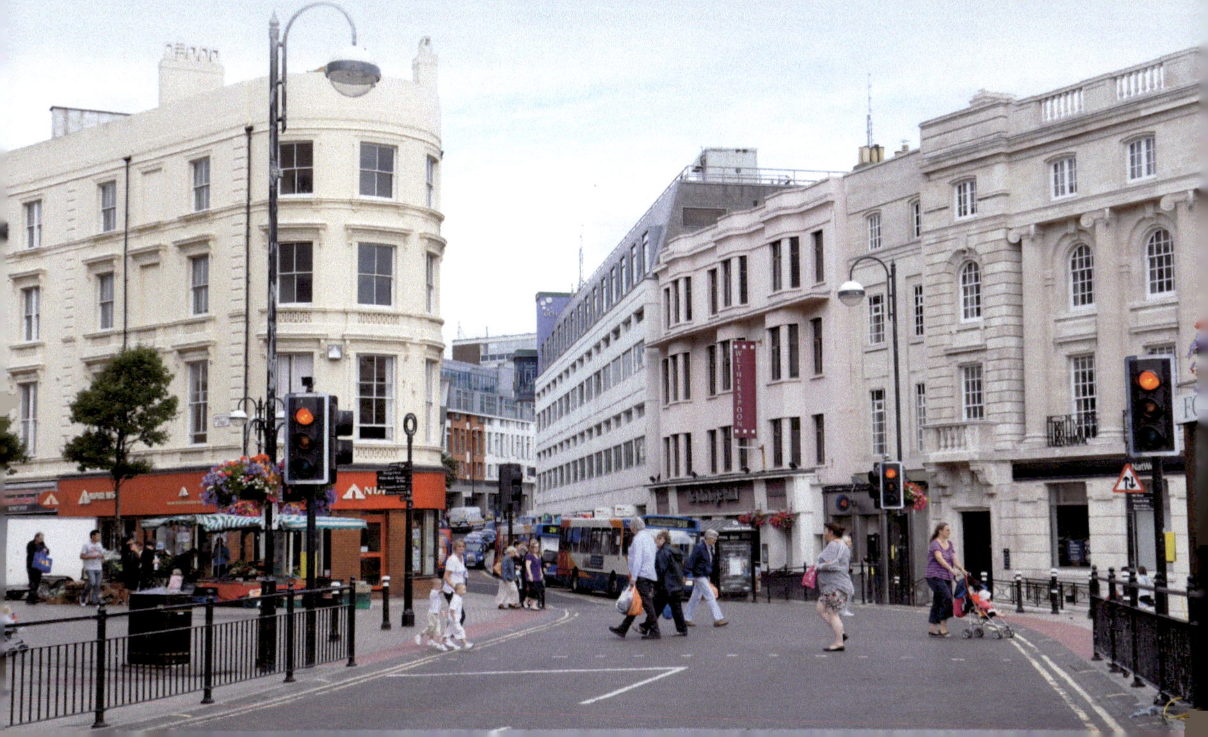

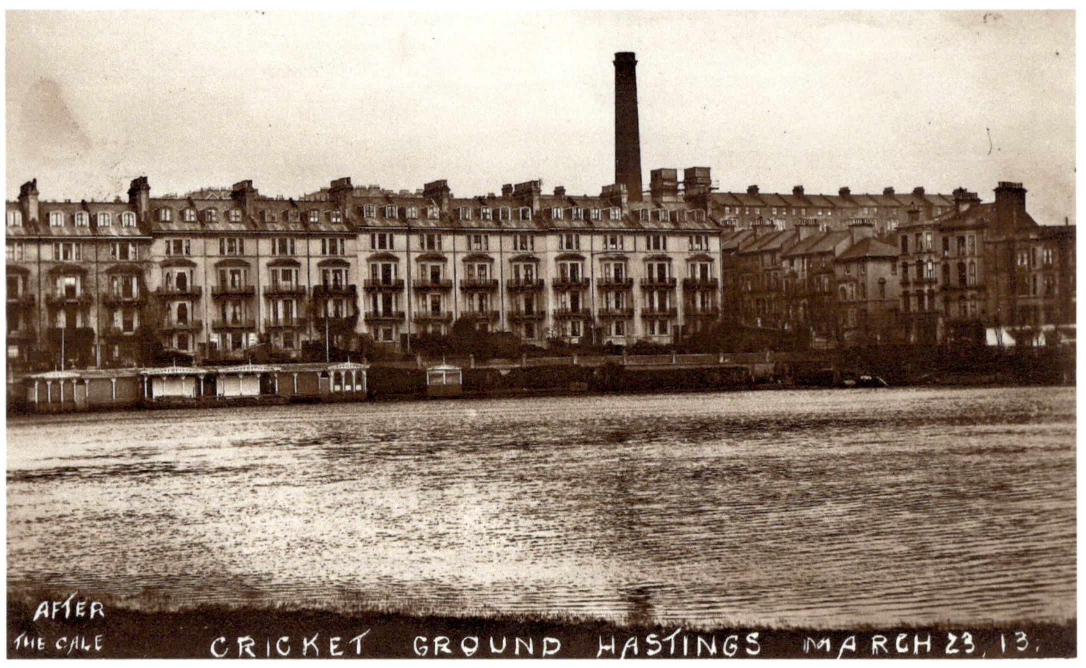

Great Gale at Hastings

The worst flooding and high winds that Hastings had seen for thirty years lashed the town on 22 March 1913. High seas breached the seafront near the Queen's Hotel, flooding down Harold Place to the Memorial. The volume of water was such that the waves reached halfway up Havelock Road. The local paper described the scenes in the town centre: 'The Central Cricket Ground was entirely under water, and gleamed like a huge lake under the lamps and the moonlight.'

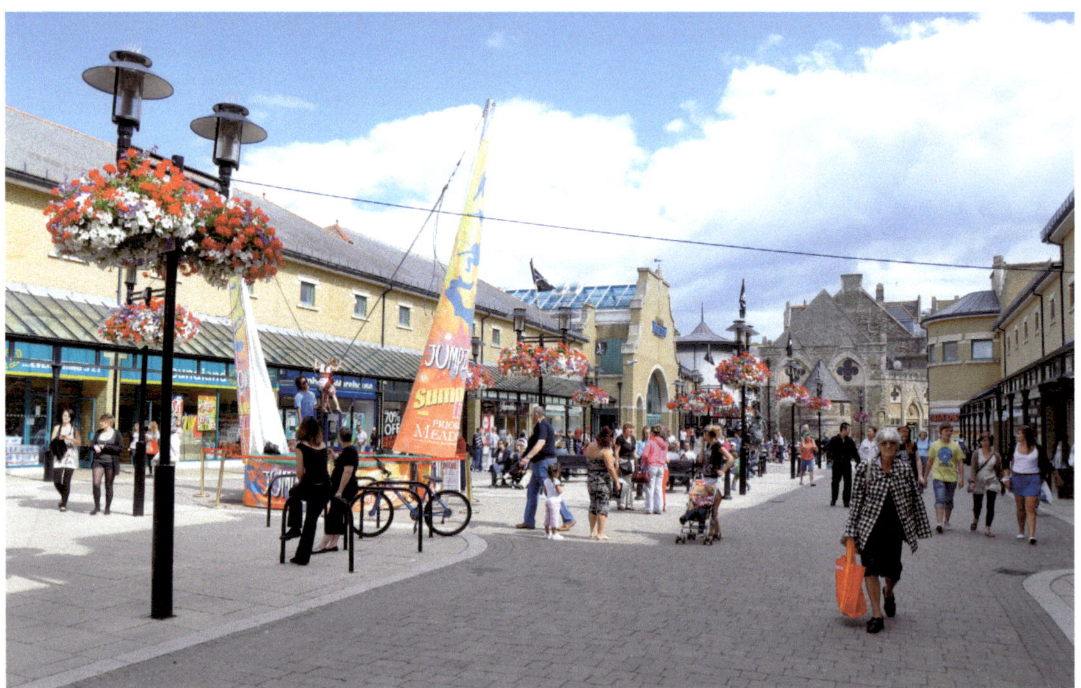

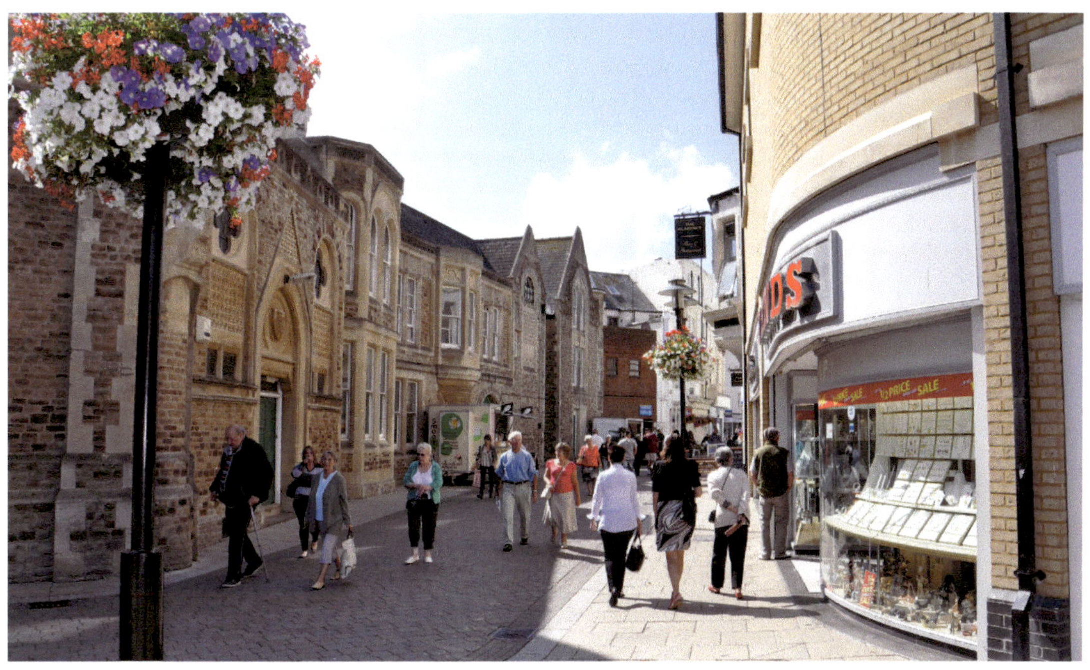

Station Road Under Water

The flooding of 22 March 1913 plunged Station Road under water and it was necessary for two fire engines from Middle Street and Shepherd Street to pump water from the premises along this thoroughfare. This area of the town centre has always been liable to flooding; the most notable recent occurrence was on 20 February 2006 when a tide of sewage flowed down Station Road, despite the creation in 2000 of a £43 million storm tunnel to prevent such flooding.

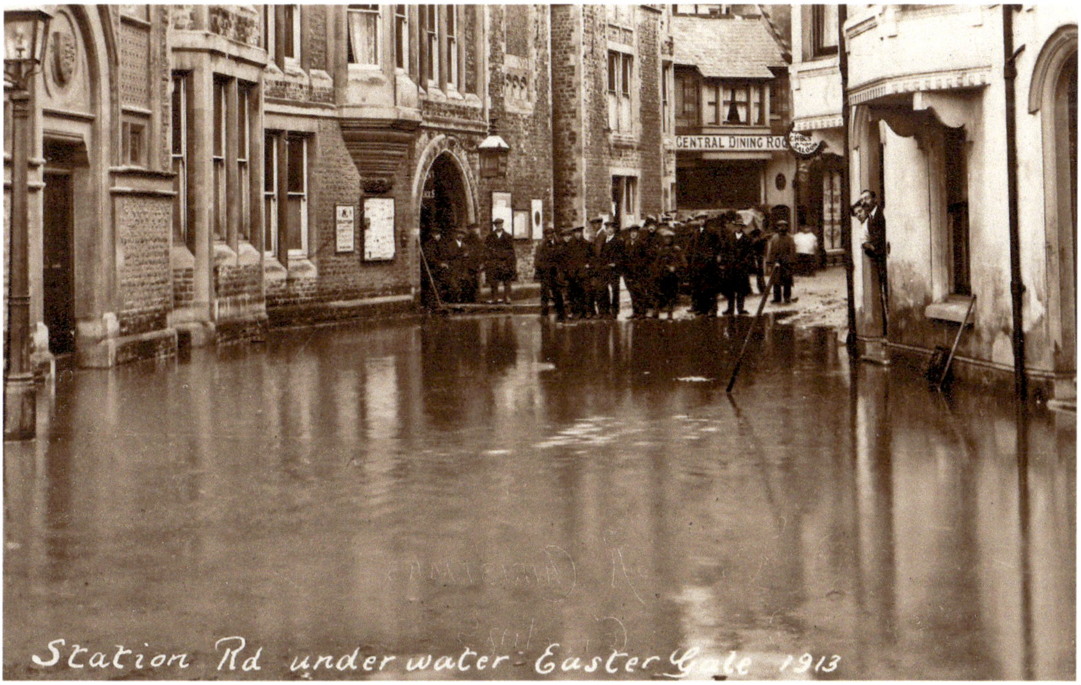

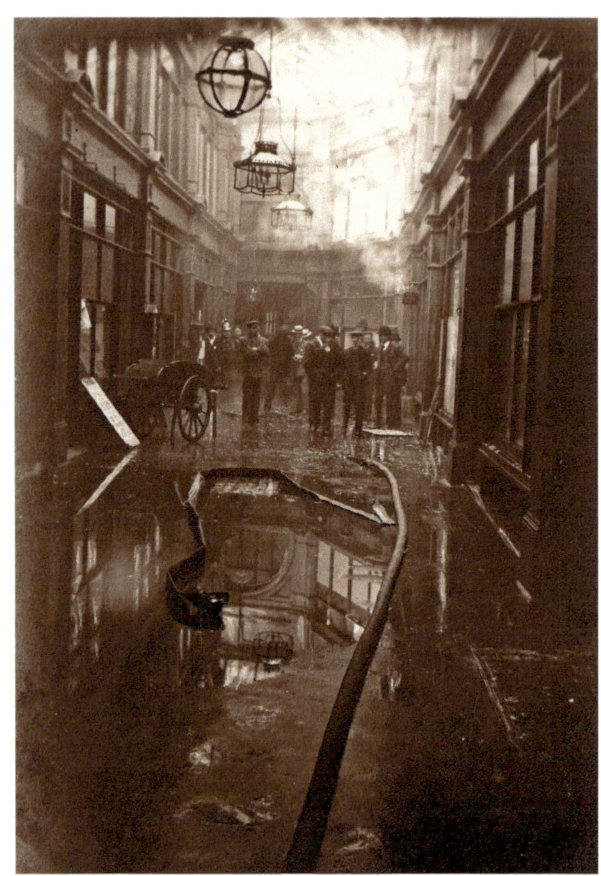

Queen's Avenue Fire

A fire broke out in Queen's Avenue (now called Queen's Arcade) on 25 September 1904. The row of sixteen shops opened in October 1882, providing a covered run of shops linking York Buildings and Queen's Road. It was in 1924 in a workshop situated above the current butcher's shop that John Logie Baird demonstrated the world's first ever television, a hugely significant claim for this charming arcade. Another more severe fire ripped through the arcade on 15 February 1990, causing damage to the tune of £1 million.

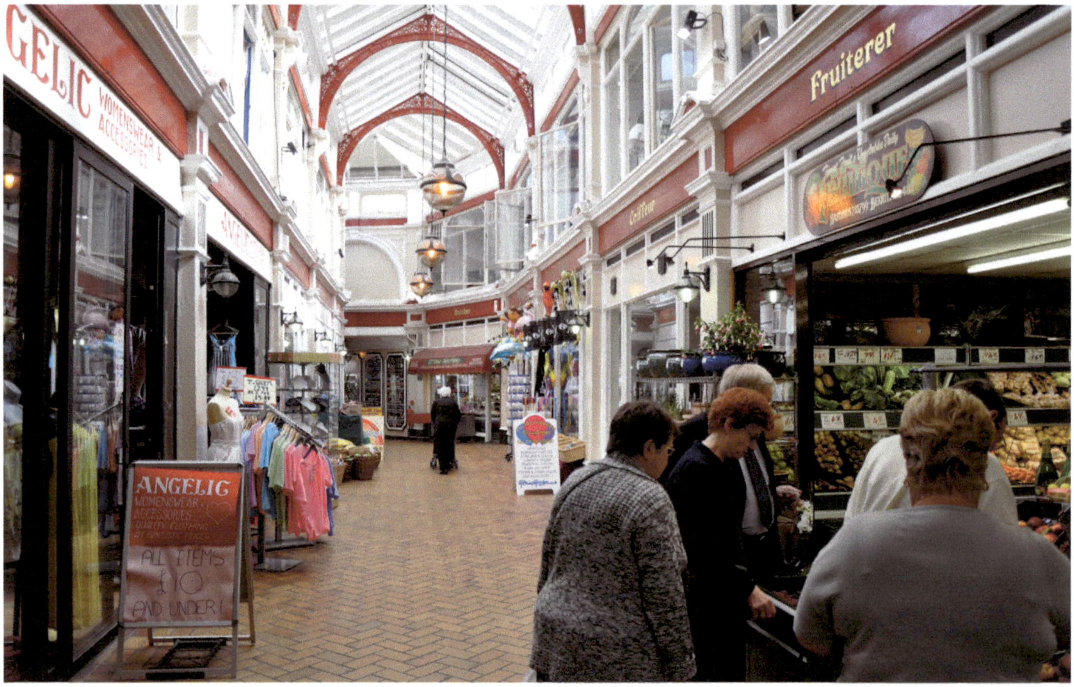

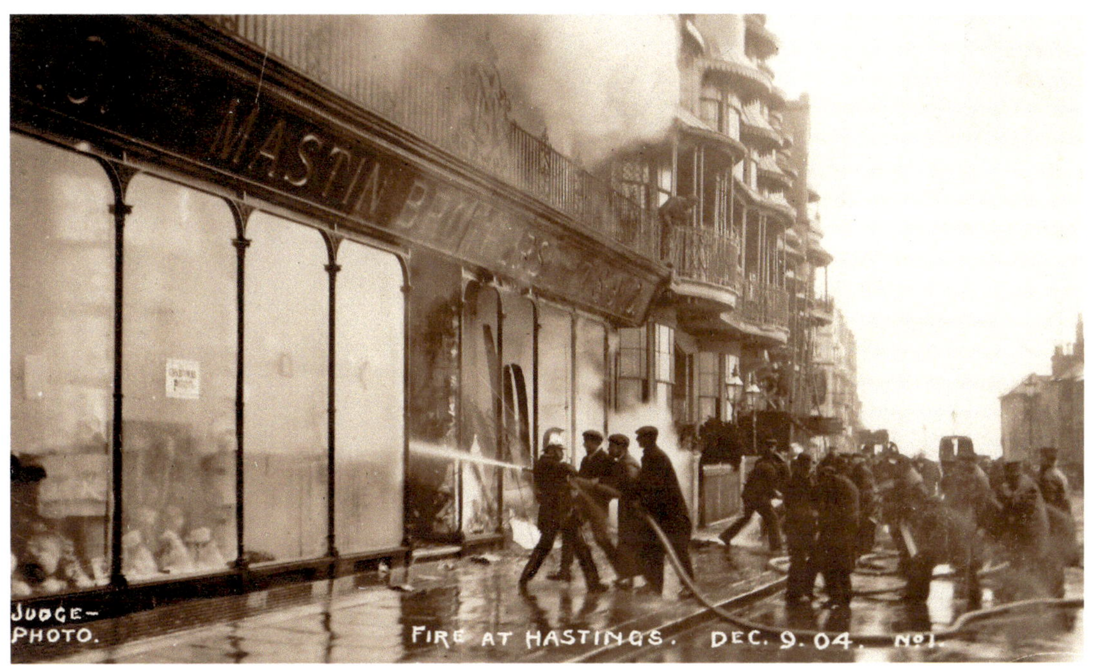

Fire at Mastin Brothers' Store

A huge fire tore through the Mastin Brothers' store at 7–10 Breeds Place on 9 December 1904. Several employees needed to be rescued by firemen. Despite the efforts of the fire brigade, several sections of the department store were lost. The cause of the fire was believed to have been a fall of soot in a blocked chimney, and, as the *Hastings & St Leonards Observer* described it, 'Nothing will beat lace curtains in blazing.'

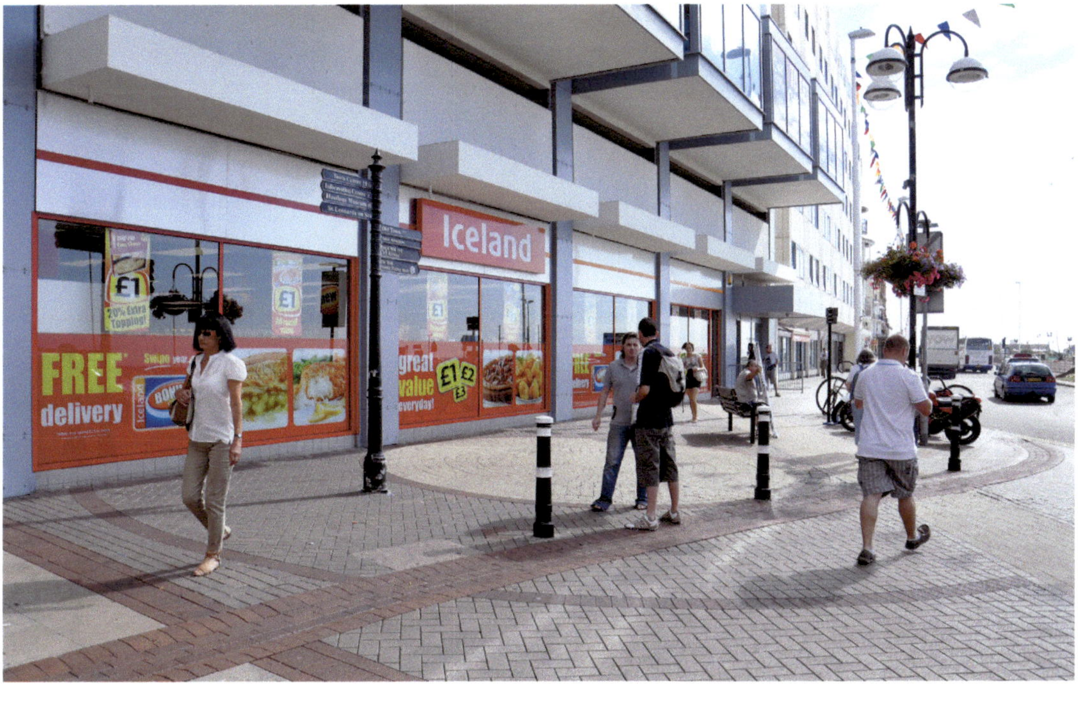

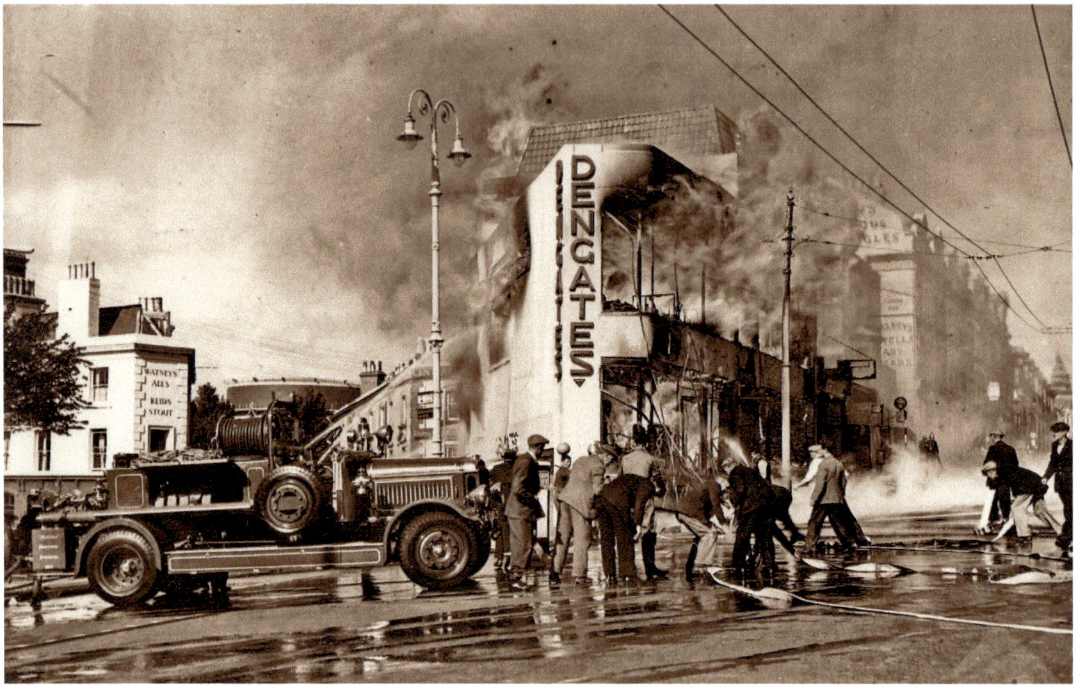

Largest Fire in Hastings

The largest fire that Hastings had ever seen occurred on 31 October 1938 at the Dengates furniture shop at 203–204 Queen's Road. The shop had only been built eighteen months previously and the blaze caused damage worth an estimated £11,000. The upper storeys of Halfords, situated directly across the street, even caught fire. Coincidentally, it was the final ever shift of the Volunteer Fire Brigade, as the following day the new professional Fire Brigade took over.

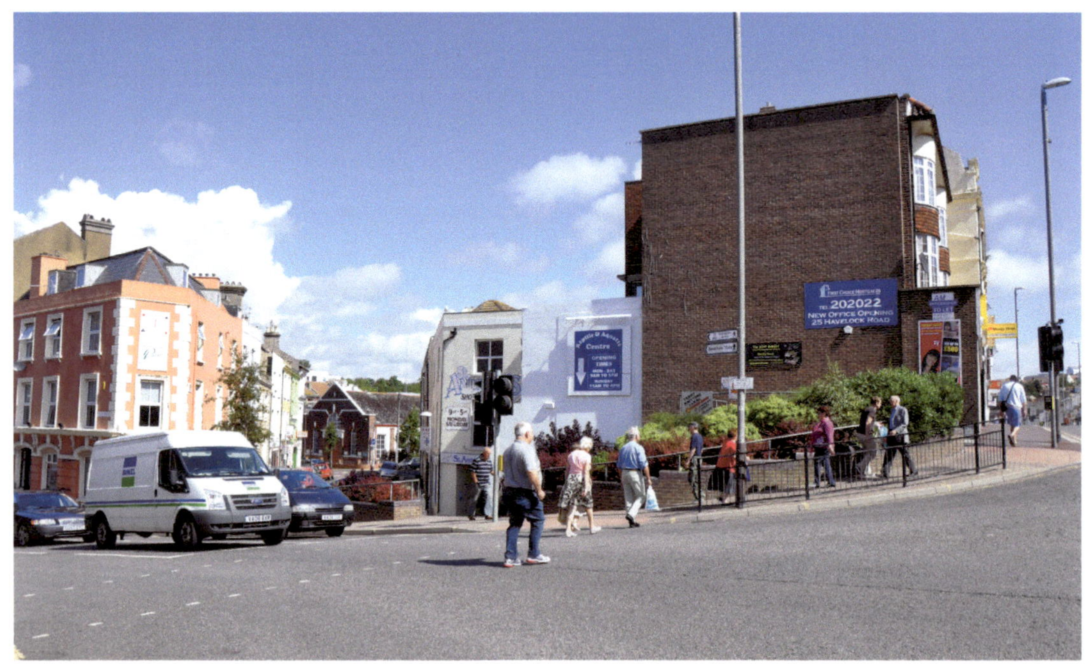

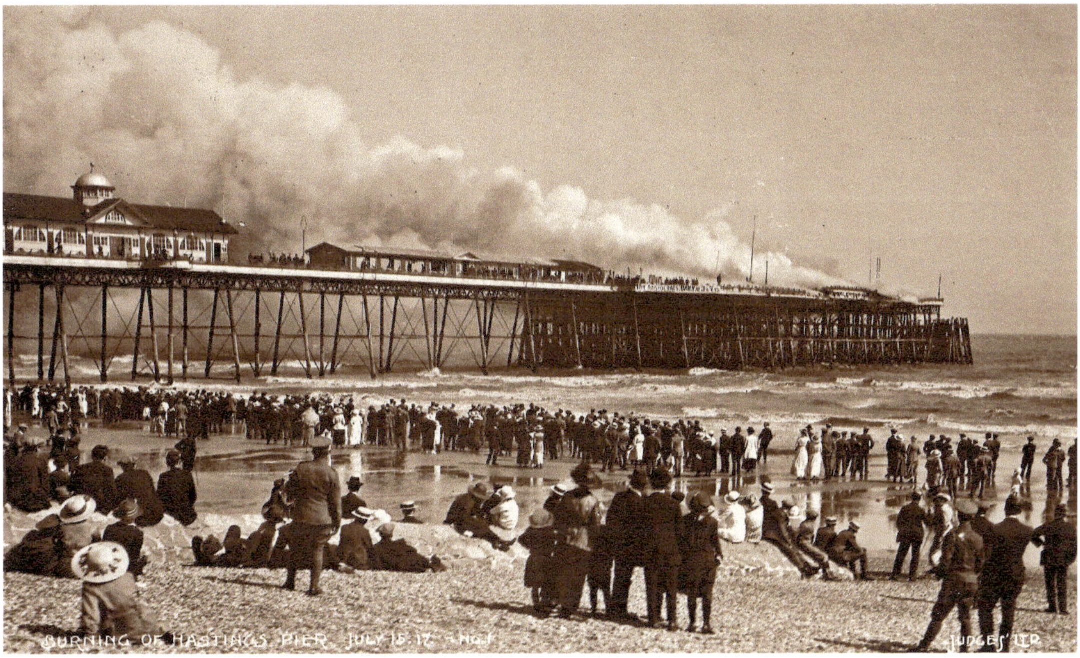

A Wonderful Sunday Afternoon Spectacle

Such was the headline of the local paper after a serious fire ravaged Hastings Pier on 15 July 1917. The fire started at 2.00 p.m. and was thought to have been caused by a dropped cigarette. Over the years a combination of severe storms and lack of care caused irrevocable damage and in 2006 the 'peerless pier' closed to the public. Disaster once again struck the ill-fated pier early on 5 October 2010 when around 95 per cent was destroyed in yet another huge blaze.

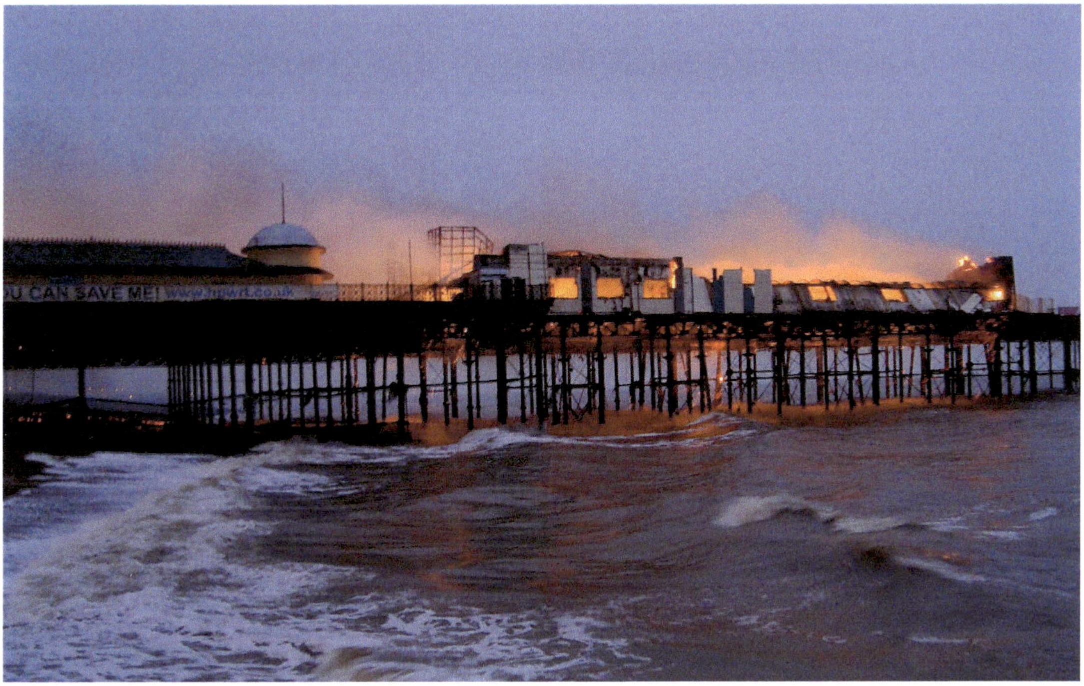

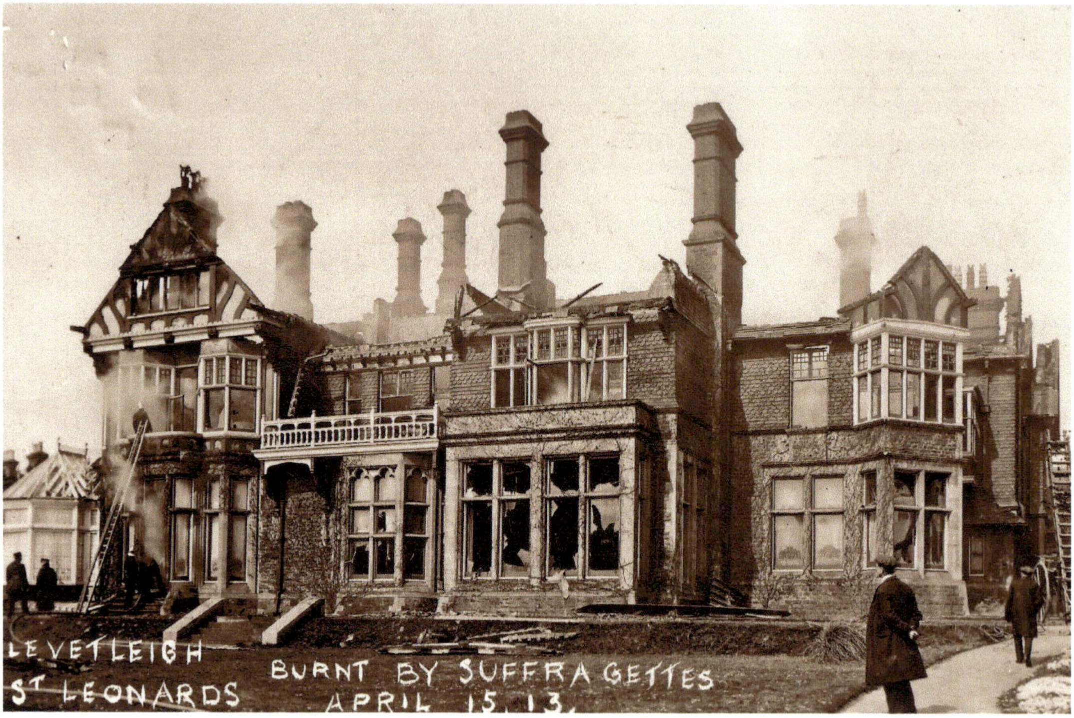

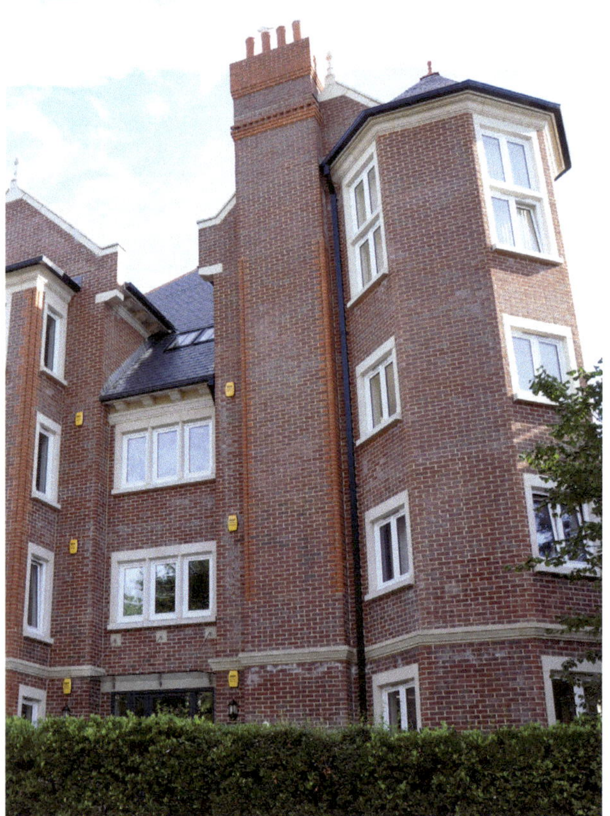

Burnt by Suffragettes

Levetleigh, the former home of the Conservative MP for Hastings and Rye, Arthur du Cros, was severely damaged by fire in the early hours of 15 April 1913. Owing to a quantity of suffragette literature found on the grounds of the property, the fire was blamed on the suffragettes. Ironically, the house had left the possession of du Cros on 25 March and the house had already been stripped of furniture and belongings. Du Cros was interviewed by police the following day, when he made clear his lack of surprise at the fire, as he had been forewarned that an attack by suffragettes was likely. He reiterated his position: he had always been a convinced opponent of women's suffrage and should continue to be. The damaged property was later converted into two bungalows, which were demolished in 2007 to make way for Du Cros House, which now occupies the site of Levetleigh.

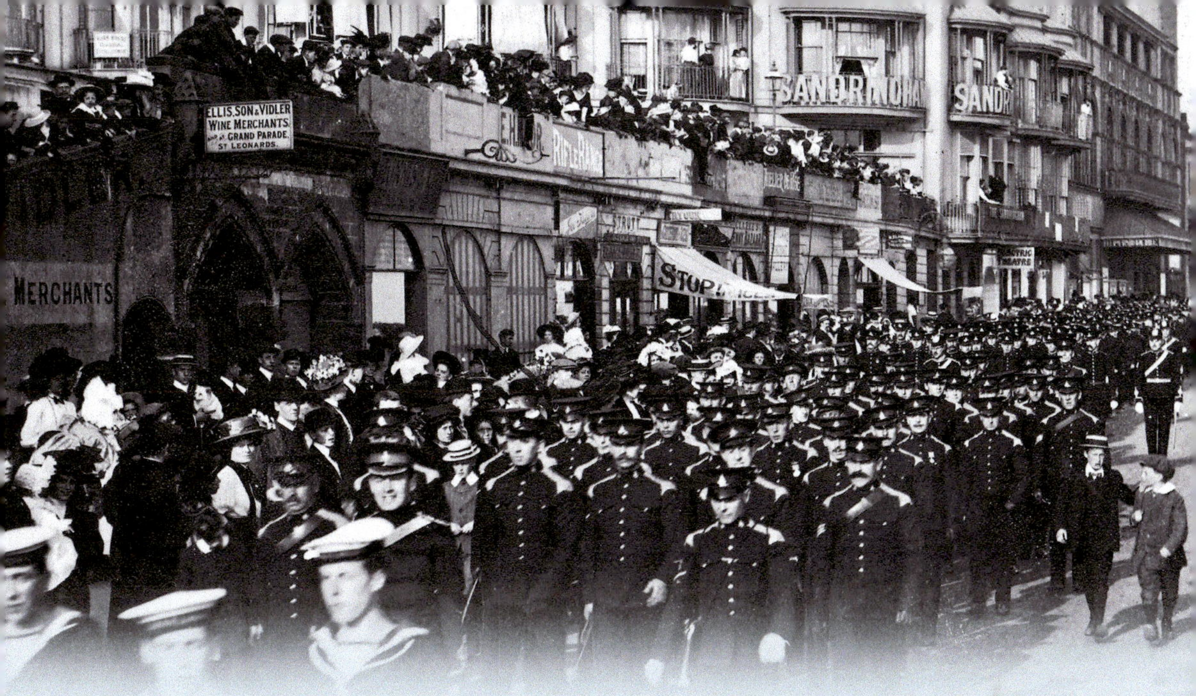

CHAPTER 5

Politics & Pageantry

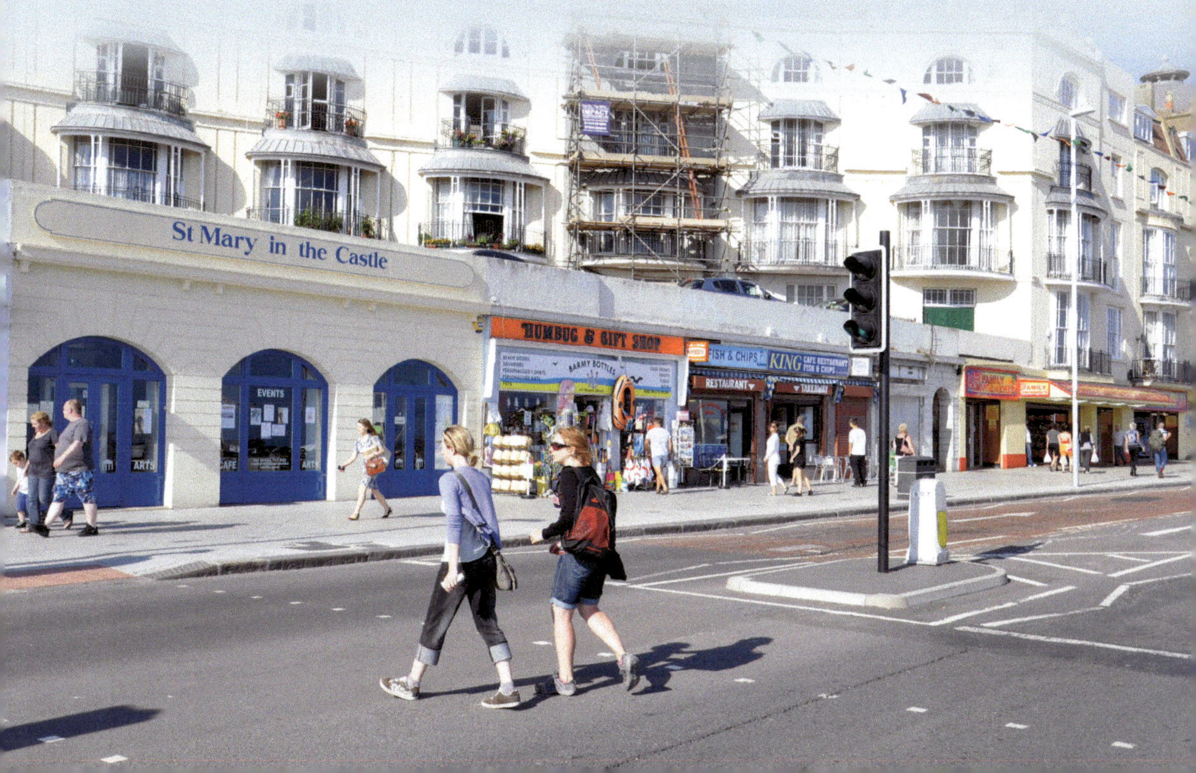

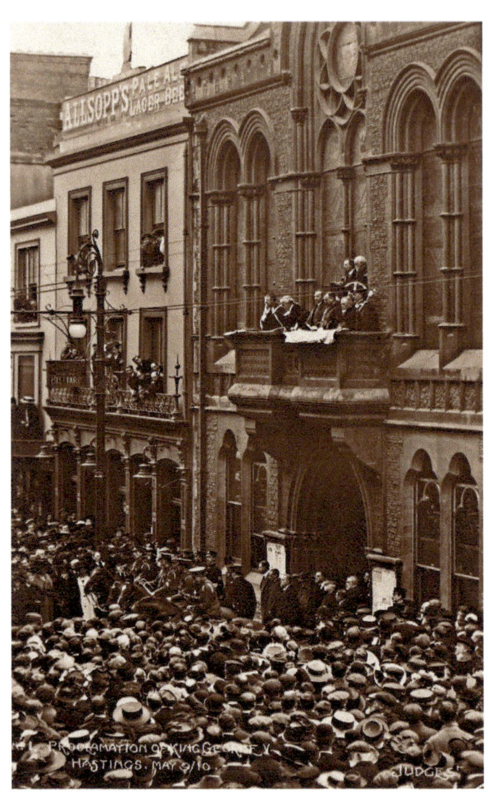

God Save The King

The short-lived Edwardian era ended abruptly with the death of King Edward VII on 6 May 1910. Three days later, Edward's son was proclaimed King George V of Great Britain and Ireland as well as Emperor of India. The declaration was made at 2.30 p.m. from Hastings Town Hall by the Mayor, R. W. Mitchell. After the proclamation was read, three cheers for the new king were given followed by a verse of the national anthem. A procession of nine carriages then made its way around the borough repeating the proclamation, stopping at Warrior Square (under the auspicious statue of Queen Victoria), the Royal Victoria Hotel, Filsham Road, Silverhill Junction, Ore Village School, London Road, the Old Town and, finally, Wellington Square.

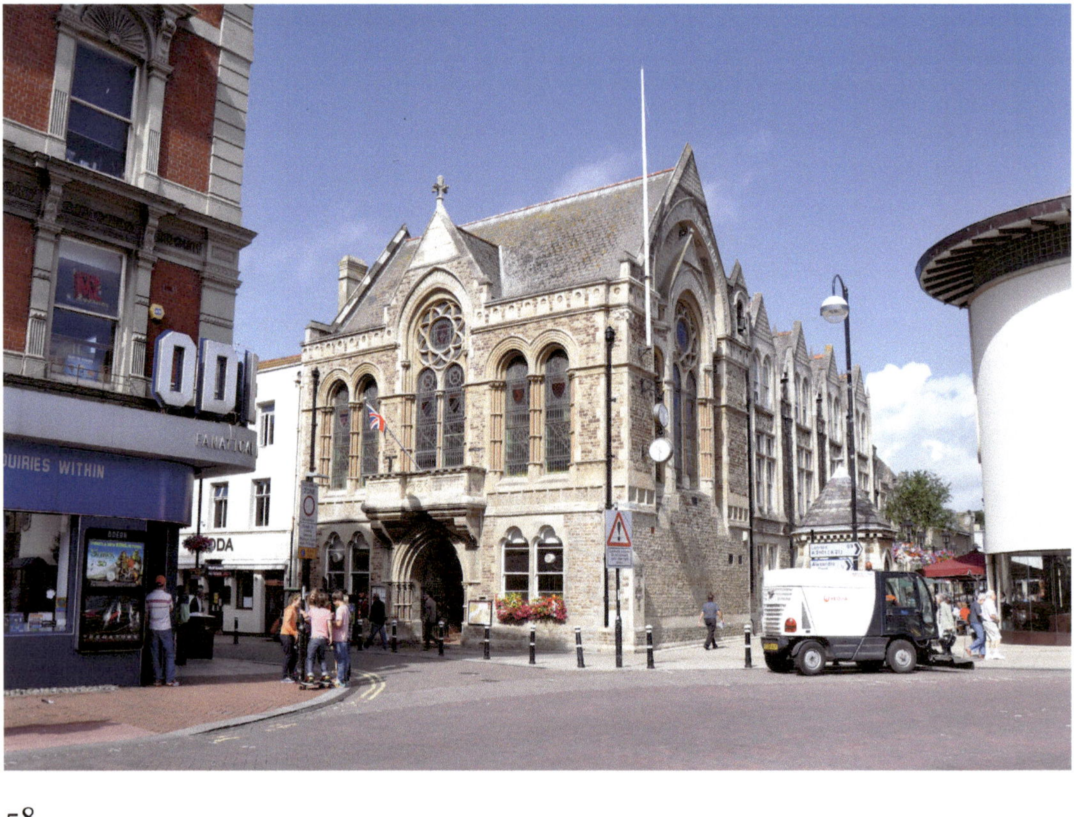

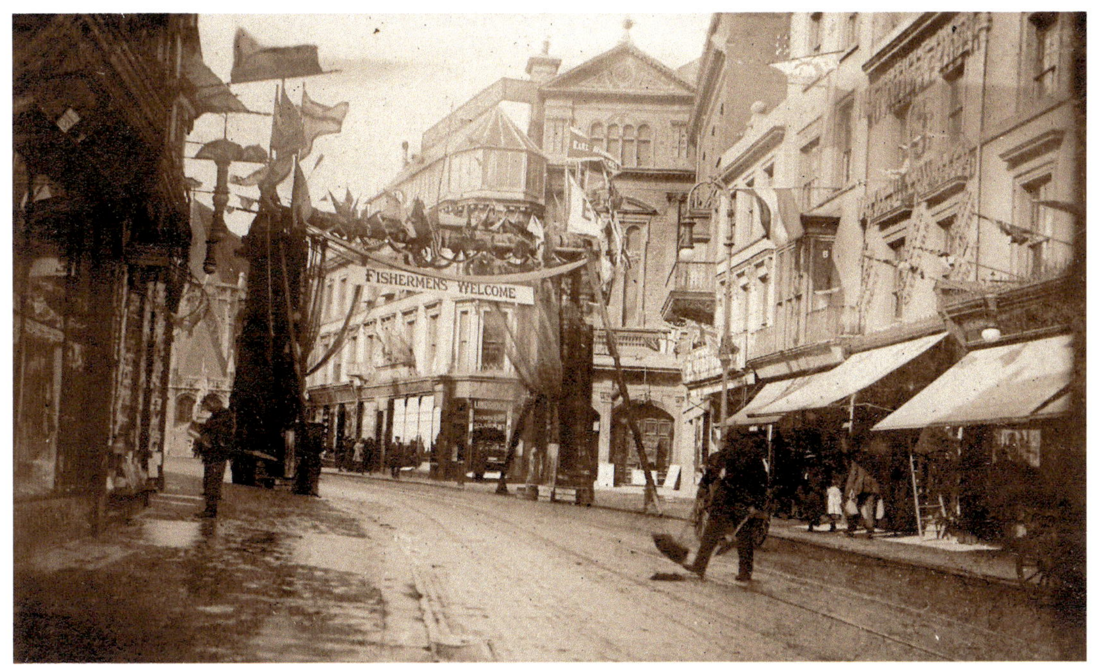

A Duchess Comes to Town

The Duchess of Albany paid a visit to Hastings on 1 April 1913 to open the King Edward Memorial Hospital Bazaar, a fund created in 1910 after the death of Edward VII (the Duchess' brother-in-law). The aim was to raise money so that the East Sussex Hospital could be moved from its location on the seafront to a new site on lands purchased from the Brisco estates. The new hospital, the Royal East Sussex, opened its doors in 1923.

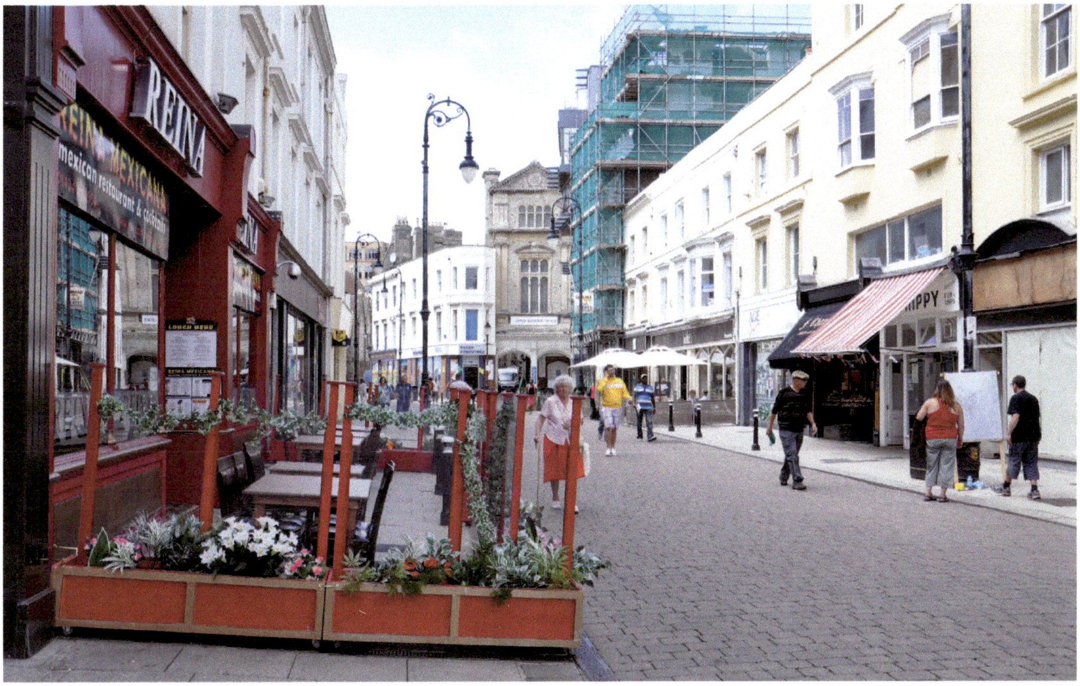

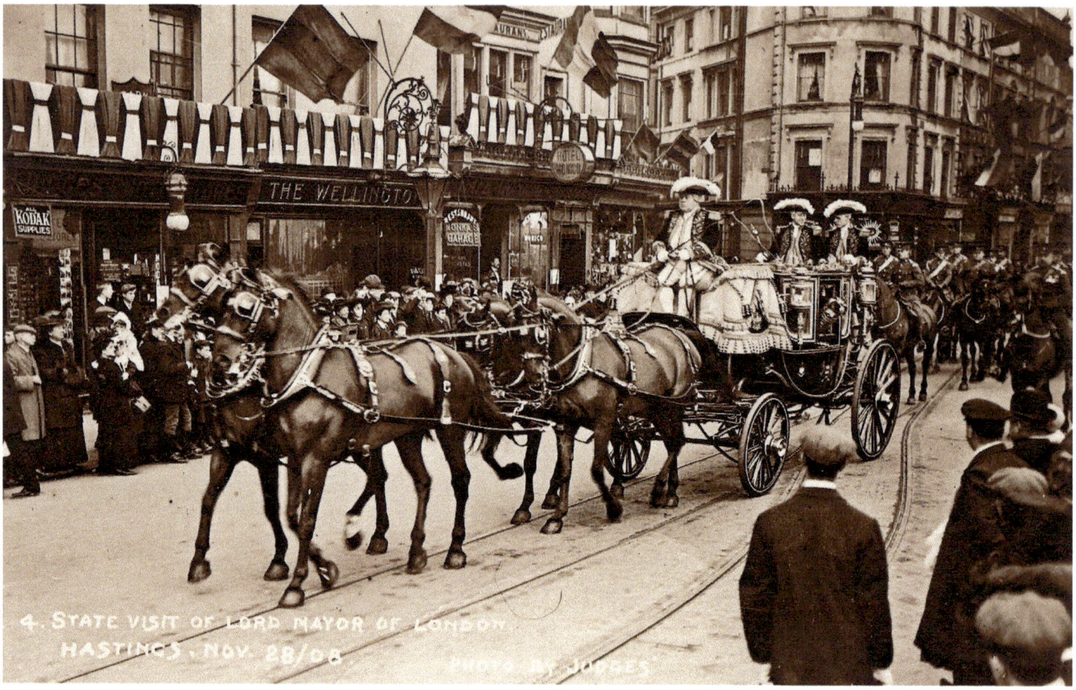

The Lord Mayor Comes to Town

The visit of the Lord Mayor of London, Sir George Wyatt Truscott, on 28 November 1908 attracted a large crowd to the town. The Lord Mayor travelled with the City Sword Bearer, the City Mace Bearer and a host of local dignitaries to the Buchanan Hospital where he opened a new children's wing. The Lord Mayor had once been a Burgess of Hastings and had a weekend house at 100 Marina.

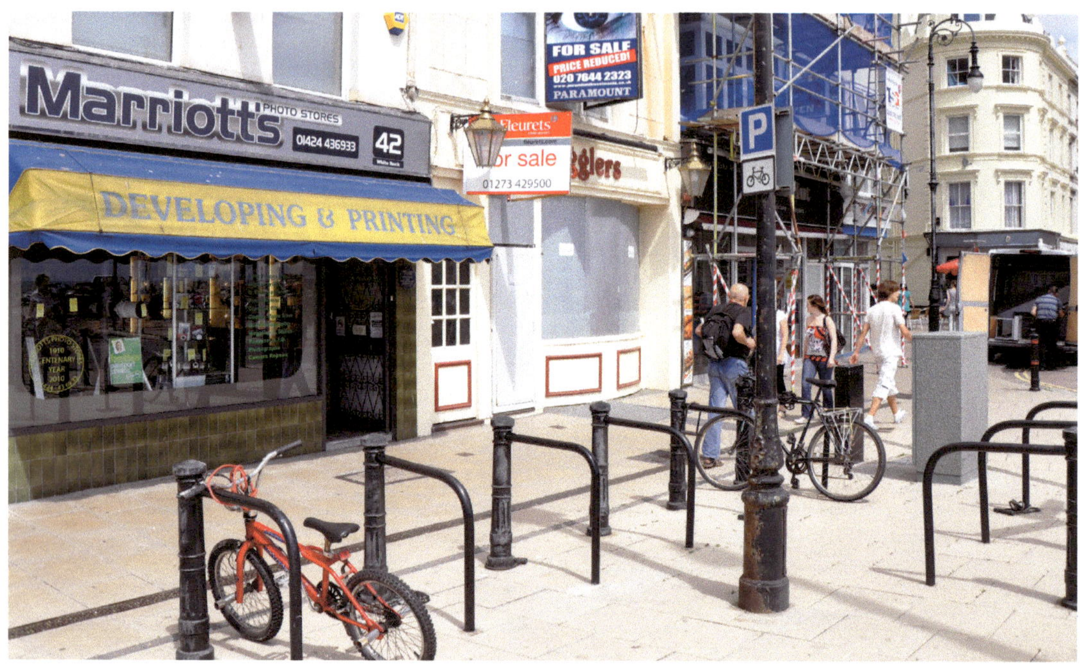

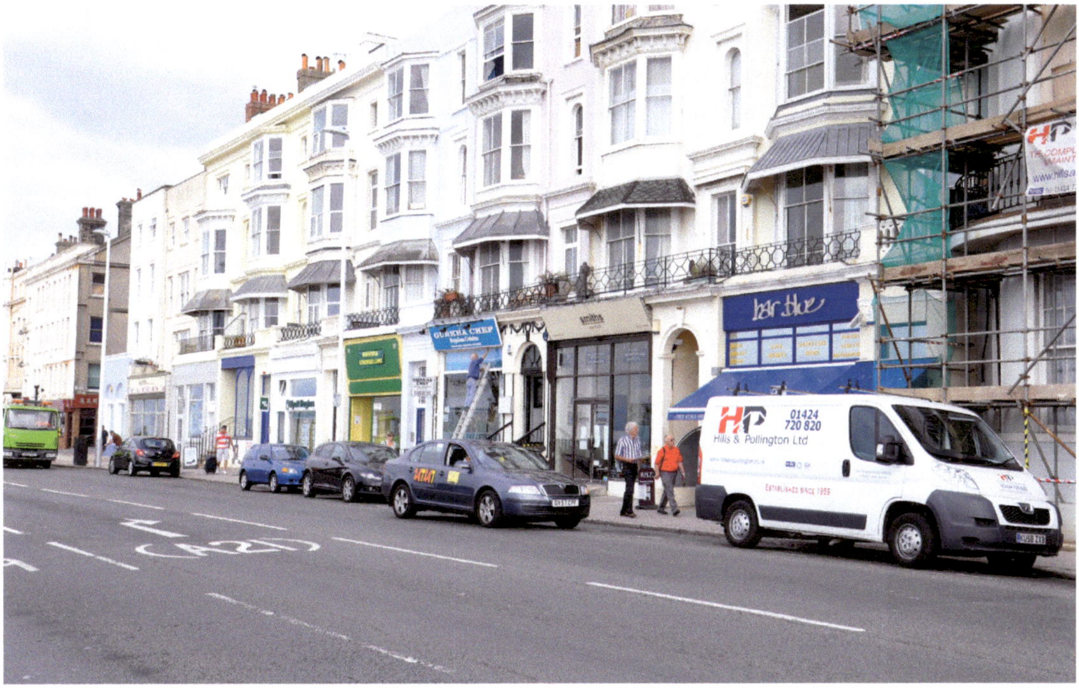

Invasion from London

On 17 March 1909 a large mock invasion of troops occurred in Hastings. The event, organised by the AA, pretended that a sea-borne enemy had taken control of the town. In response, troops were sent from London to counter the invasion. The first car, containing men from the Scots Guards, passed by the crowds at the Bo-Peep to a rapturous response. Car after car arrived, sometimes three abreast. The troops then marched to the Cricket Ground. The 'attack' was deemed to be a success and the group returned to London.

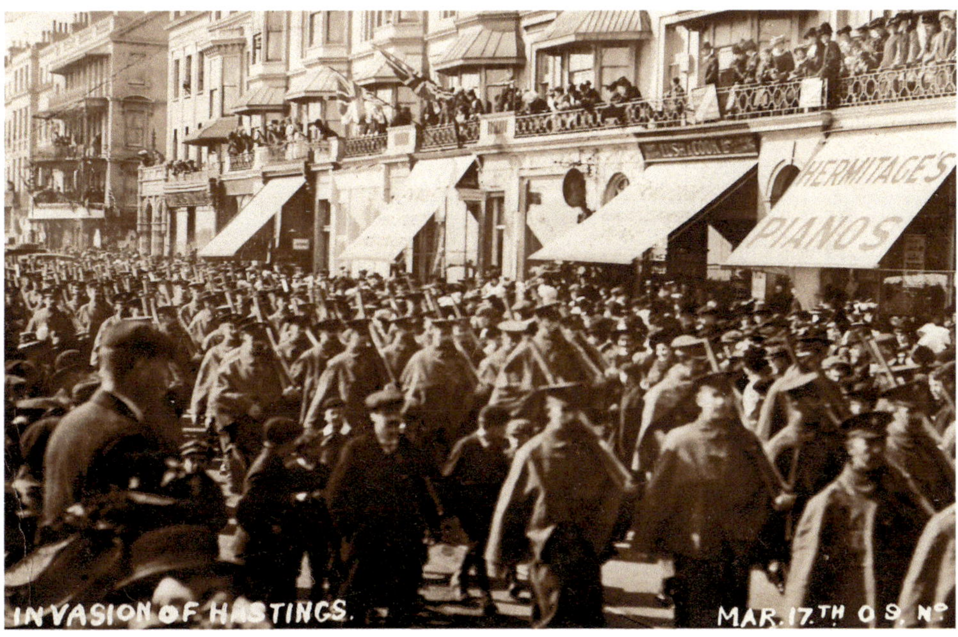

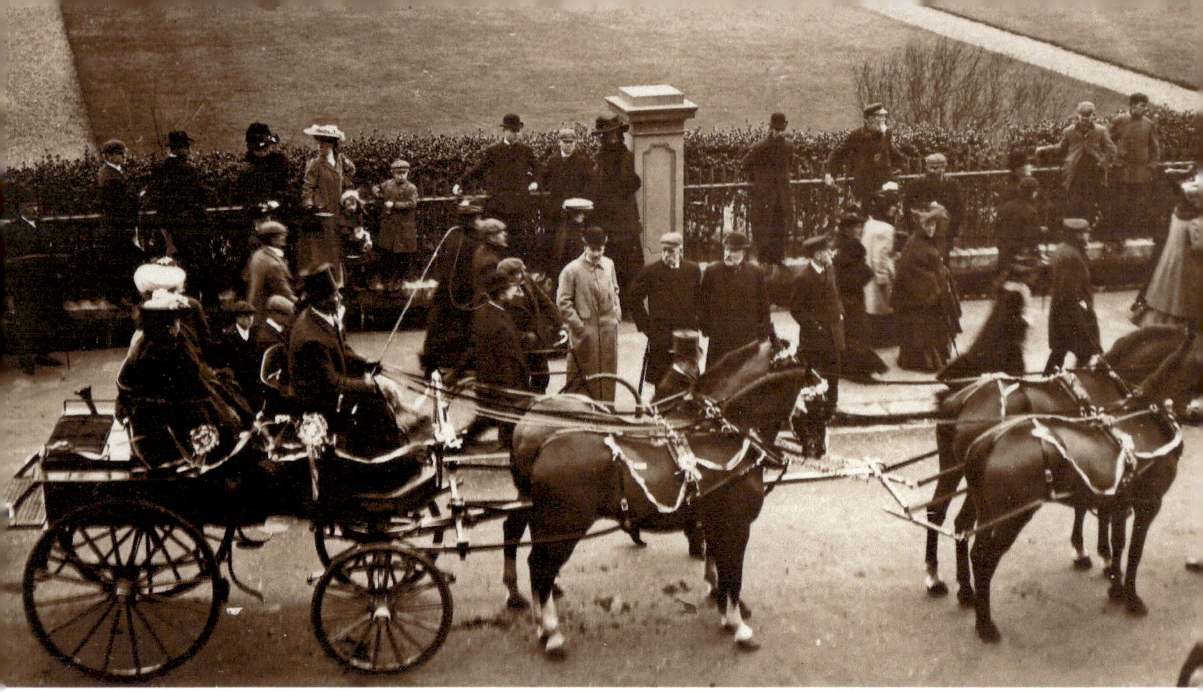

Conservative Celebrations

One week after his victory at the polls in January 1906, the Conservative victor, Harvey du Cros, led a procession of sixty carriages from Warrior Square to Bulverhythe, then along to the Old Town. Despite the pomp and ceremony, the local paper reported that there was 'very little enthusiasm' for the new MP (Hastings was one of only a handful of boroughs around the country to deliver a Tory victory). He resigned two years later and his son Arthur took his seat as Conservative MP.

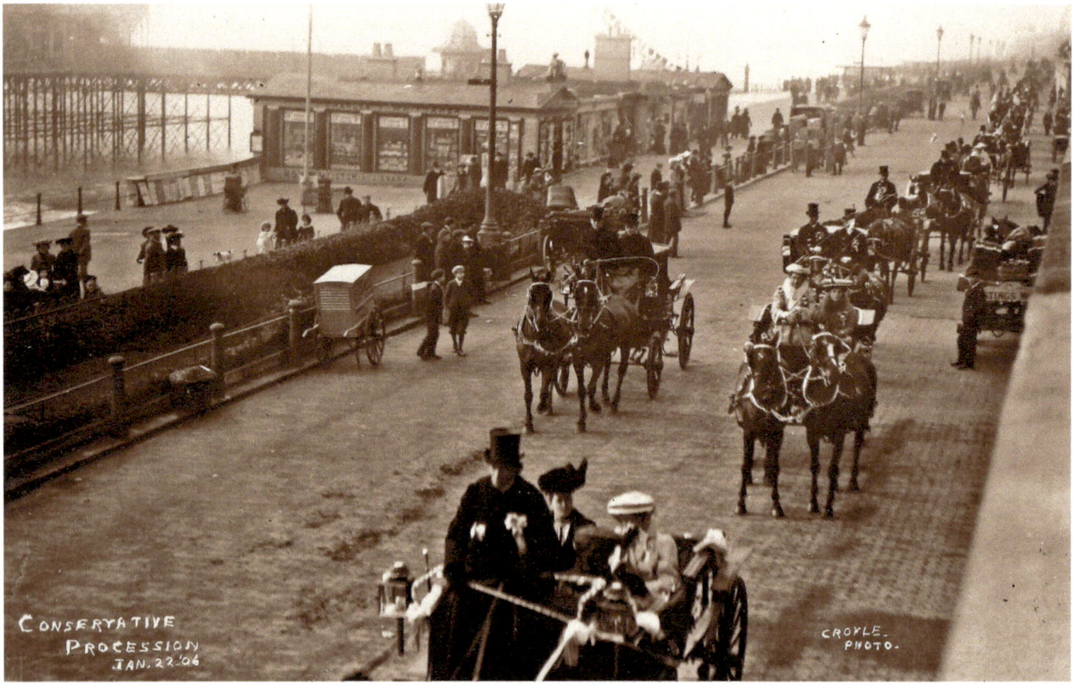

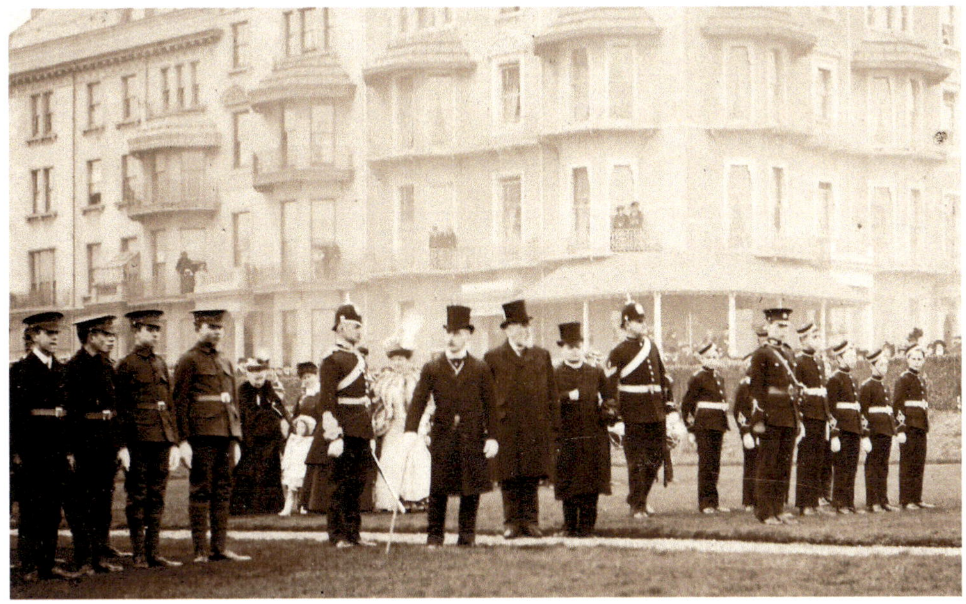

Britons Never Shall Be Slaves

On 23 February 1908 Hastings MP Harvey du Cros told the 'L' and 'M' companies of the 1st Sussex Royal Engineer Volunteers that it was a great privilege to inspect them. He told the troops in Warrior Square that, having inspected them, his privilege had turned to great pride, adding that their bearing had 'all the characteristics to freedom which proclaimed that Britons never shall be slaves'. At the end of the inspection the troops, with Harvey du Cros and Captain Holman at the helm, marched to St Peter's church where a service dedicated to the sick and poor took place. In attendance were the Battalion Band from Eastbourne, the Bugle Bands from the Hastings and Eastbourne Companies, and the Premier Cinque Port Military Band. Du Cros stepped down as the Conservative MP for Hastings the next day, citing ill health as the reason.

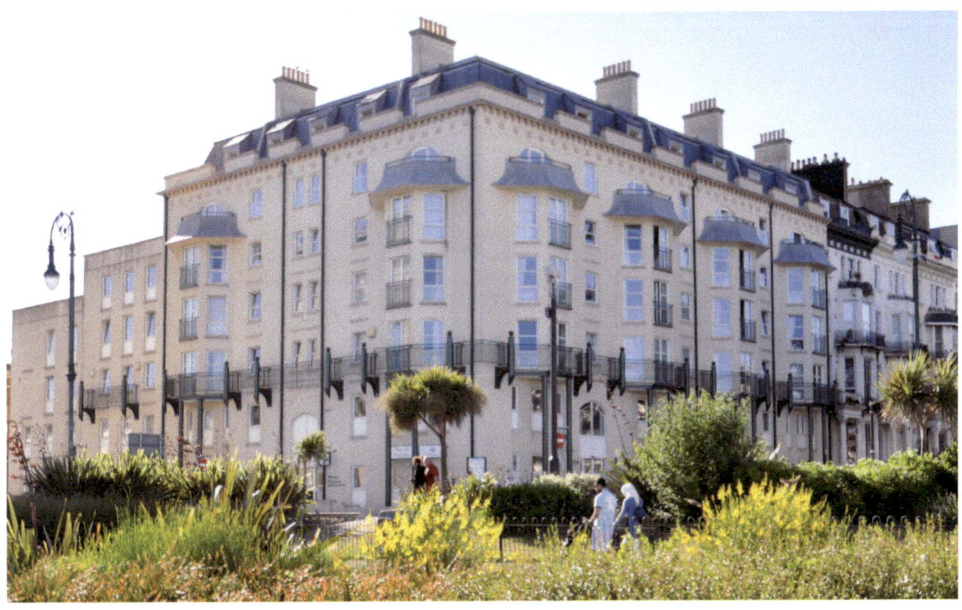

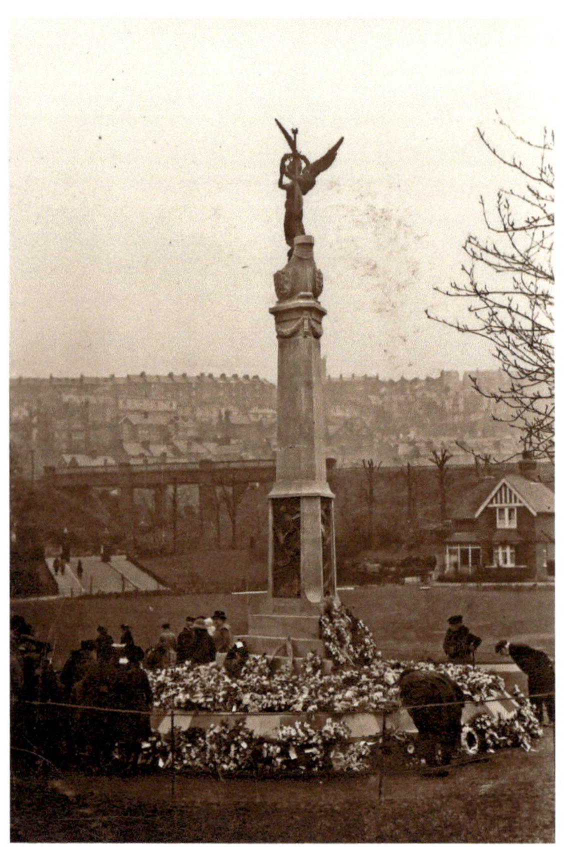

War Memorial, Alexandra Park

The Grade II listed monument to the town's war dead, created by Margaret Winser, was erected in 1922. It has recently undergone refurbishment worth £100,000. In a service on 27 March 2010 the revamped memorial was rededicated by Bishop Roger Jupp. The then mayor, Maureen Charlesworth, spearheaded charity efforts along with the British Legion to raise £26,000, the remaining funds being given by Hastings Borough Council. The memorial has had an additional five names added which had previously been omitted.

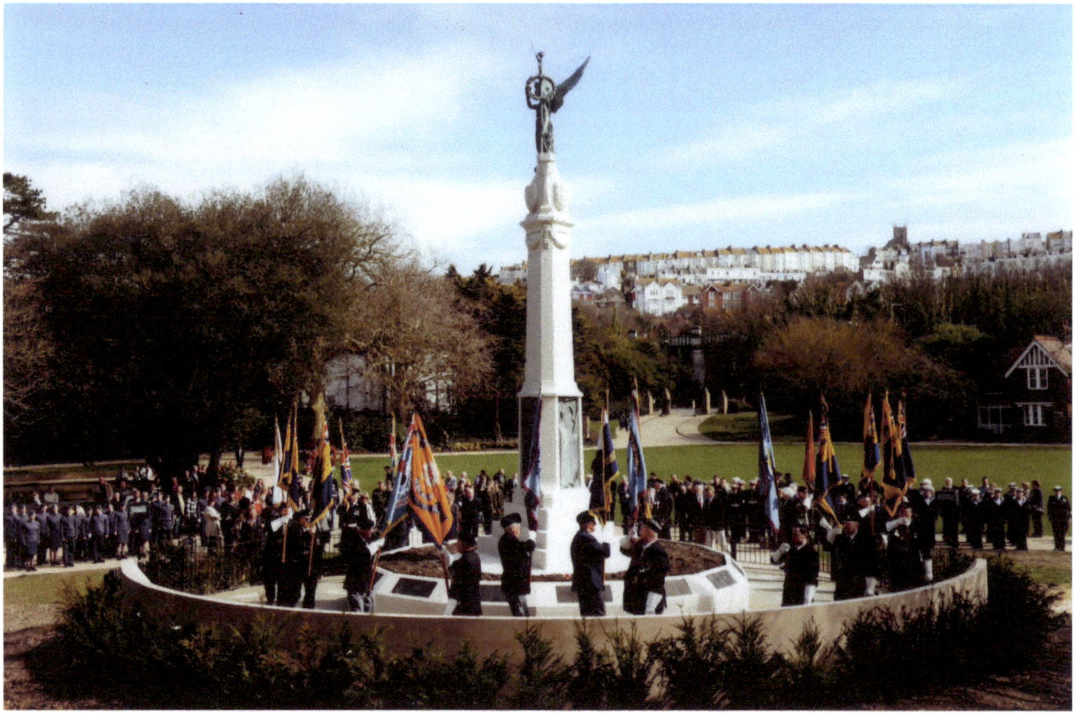

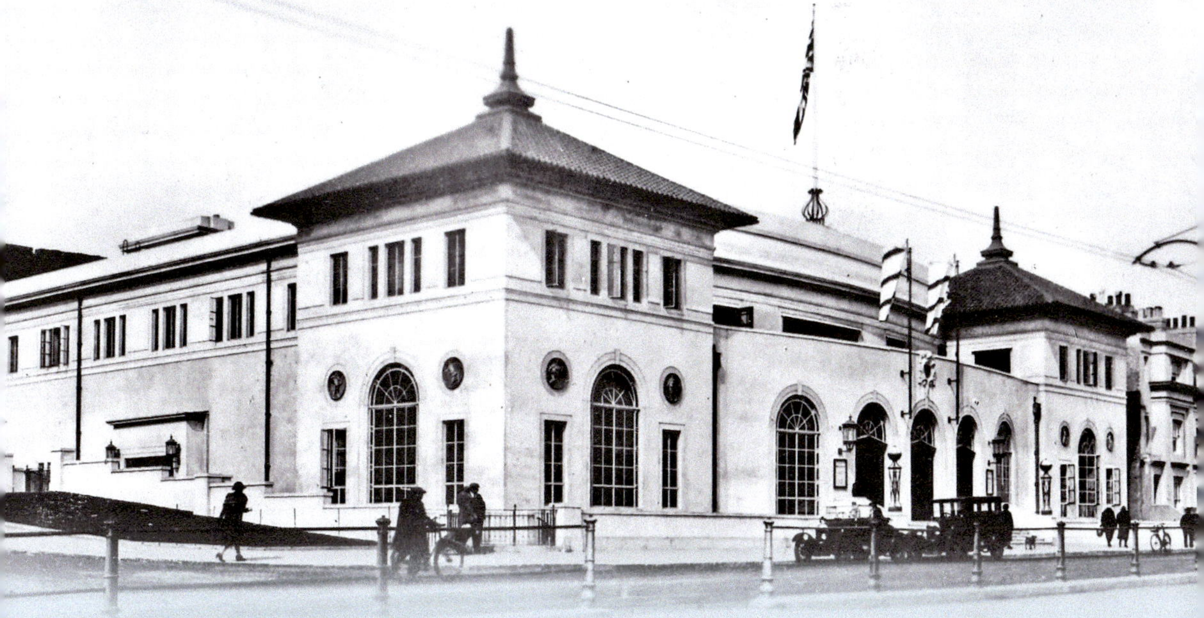

CHAPTER 6

Entertainment

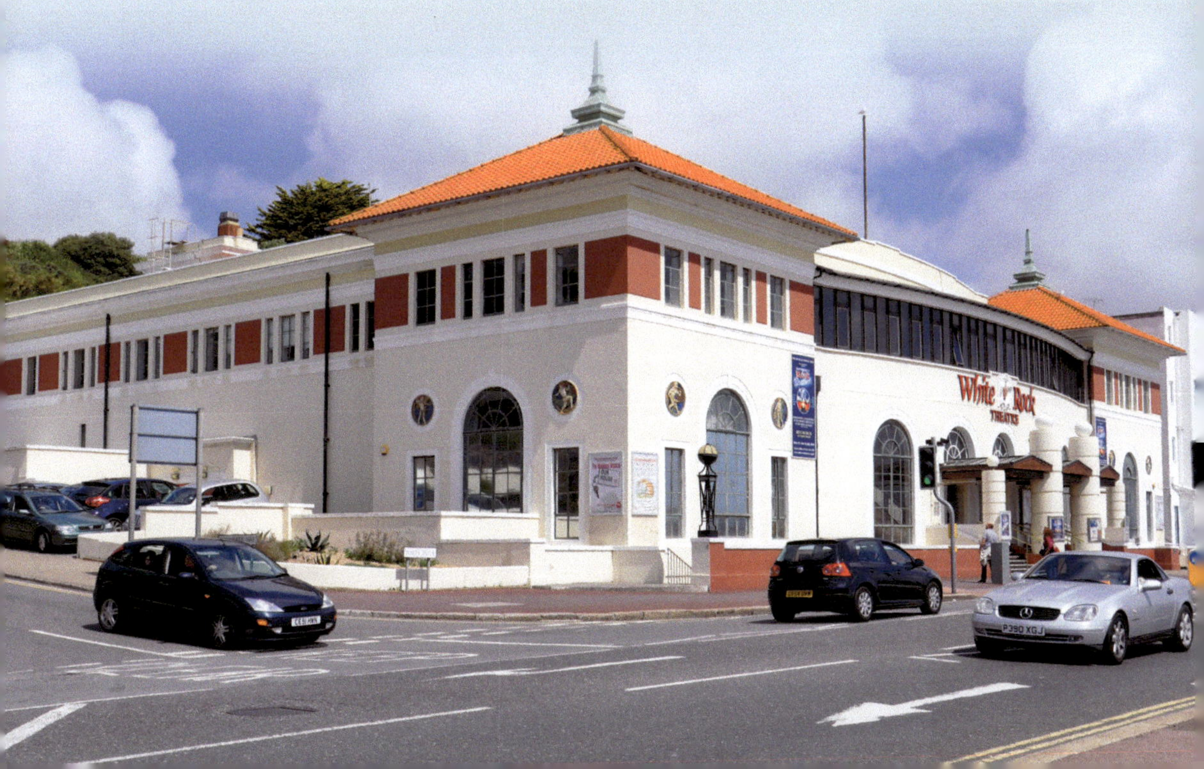

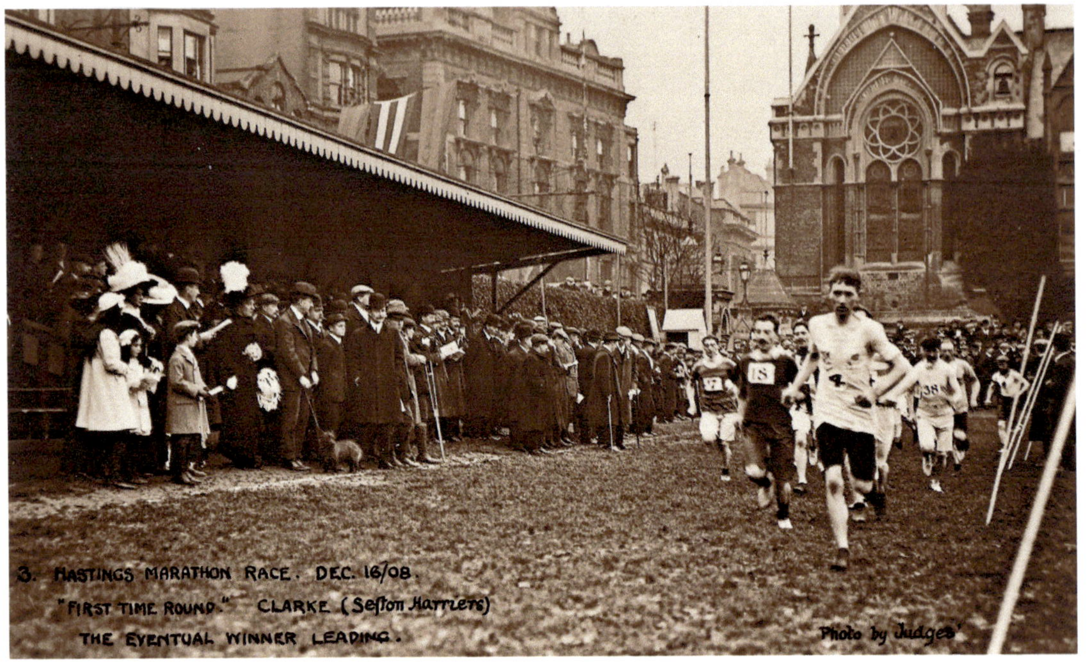

The Hastings Marathon

The route of the very first Hastings Marathon, which took place on 16 December 1908, was very different to the current one. It ran from the cricket ground out of the Station Road exit, up Bohemia Road through Battle, skirting Ashburnham Park through to Ninfield, then on to Sidley via Nazareth House, along the seafront past the Bull Inn, up Robertston Street and back into the cricket ground! The total route was 24.5 miles and attracted 51 competitors. The honour of first place in the inaugural Hastings Marathon was handed to W. T. Clarke, who completed the course in 2 hours and 38 minutes. The 2010 Hastings Half Marathon, which runs 13.1 miles, was won by Ben Fish in 1 hour and 7 minutes.

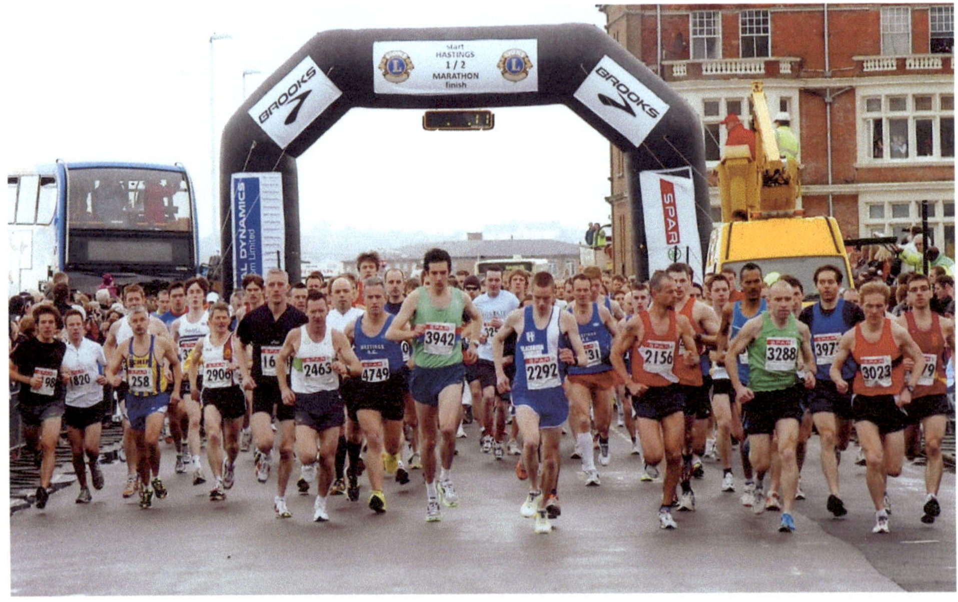

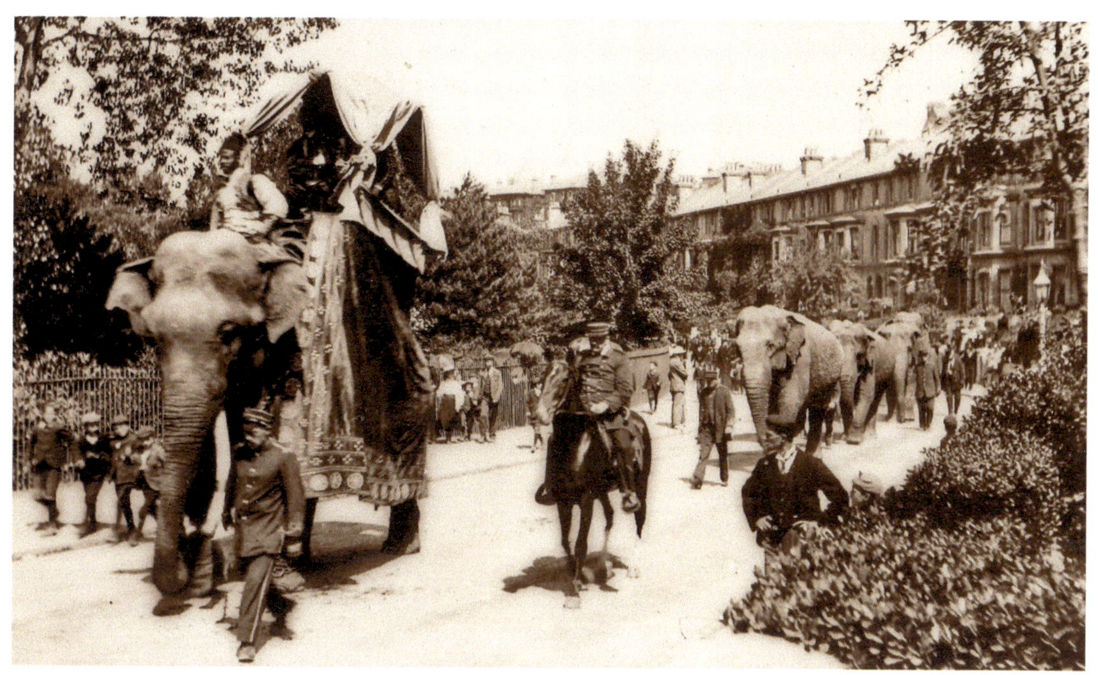

Elephants on St Helen's Road

Barnum and Bailey's Show visited Hastings in August 1898 and the spectacle attracted hundreds of visitors who watched the mile-long procession through the town, led by a chariot and forty horses. It was followed by carriages containing lions, tigers, panthers, wolves, leopards, bears and elephants. Completing the throng were brass bands, Roman chariots, cavaliers and roundheads, a bearded woman, a moss-haired girl, an elastic-skin man and a dog-faced boy, all culminating in a 15,000-person tent for the 'Greatest Show on Earth'.

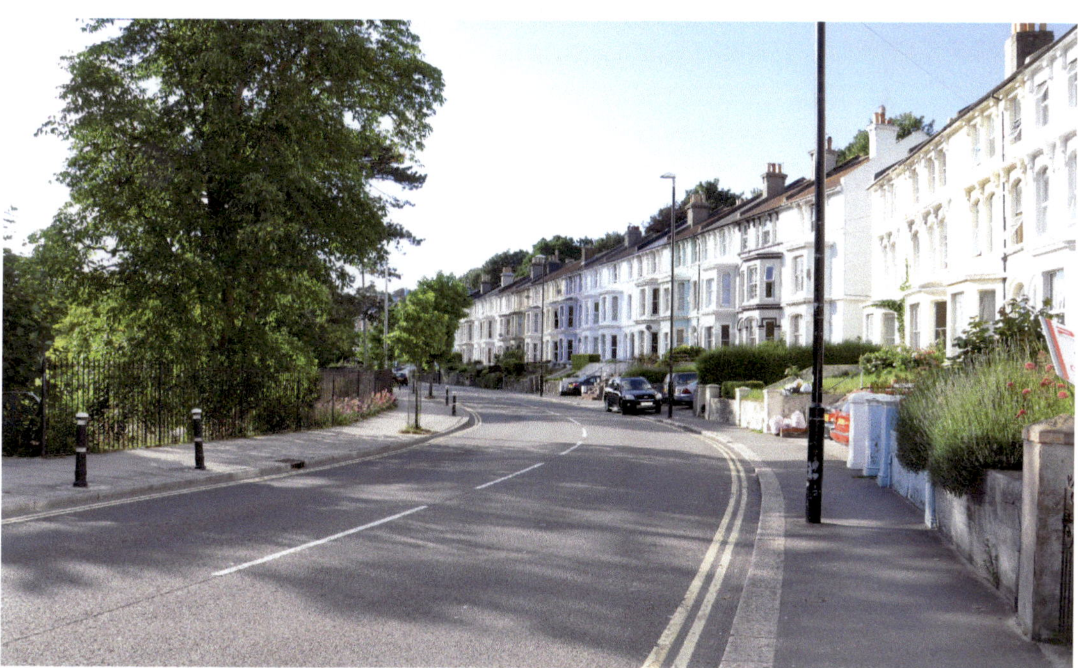

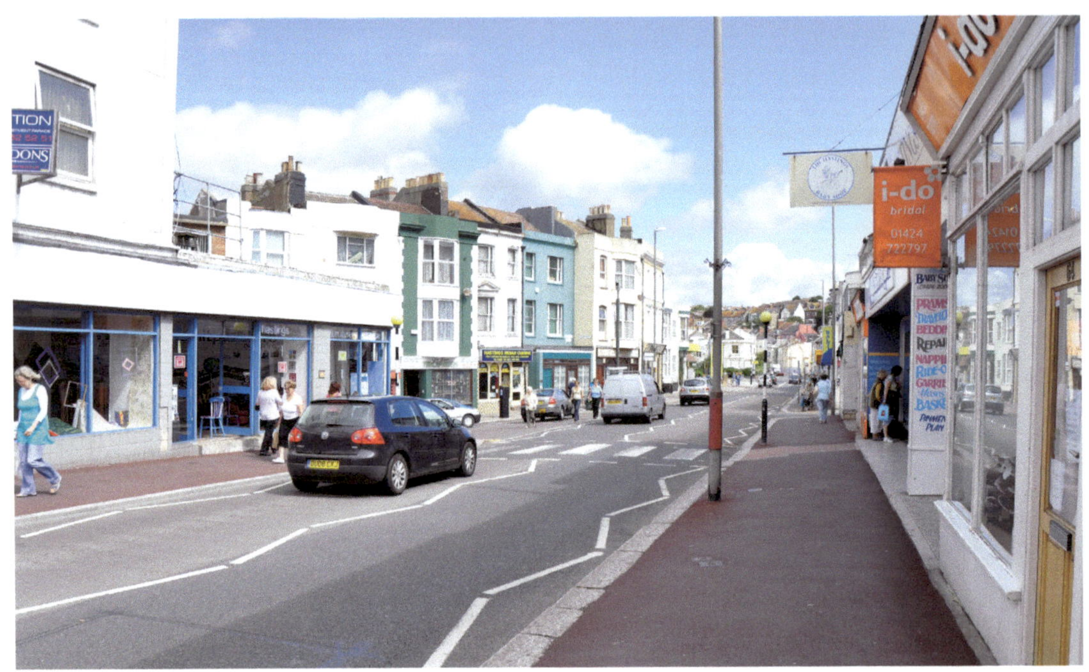

Queen's Road, Empire Day

The town's military and support services came together with most denominations of the town's churches on 28 May 1911 to celebrate Empire Day. The service was led by the Right Reverend Bishop Taylor-Smith and among those represented were the Royal Navy, Royal Naval Volunteers, 5th Battalion Royal Sussex Regiment, Special Reserve, Cadets, Boy Scouts, Imperial Scouts, Fire Brigade, and St John Ambulance Brigade, who had all marched from Warrior Square to Alexandra Park.

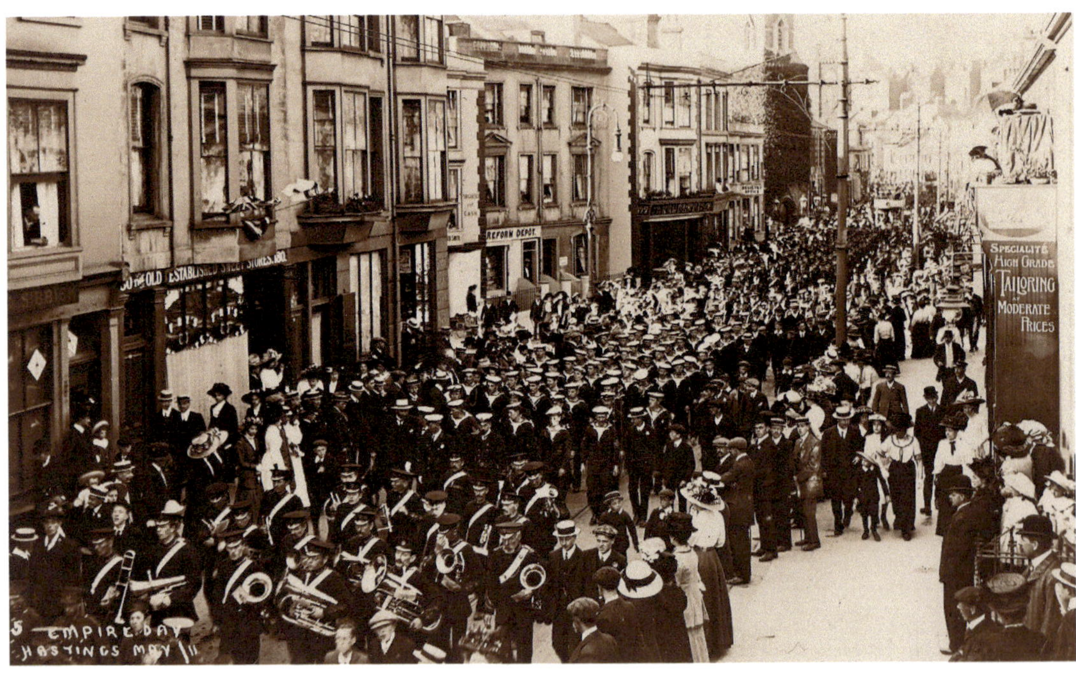

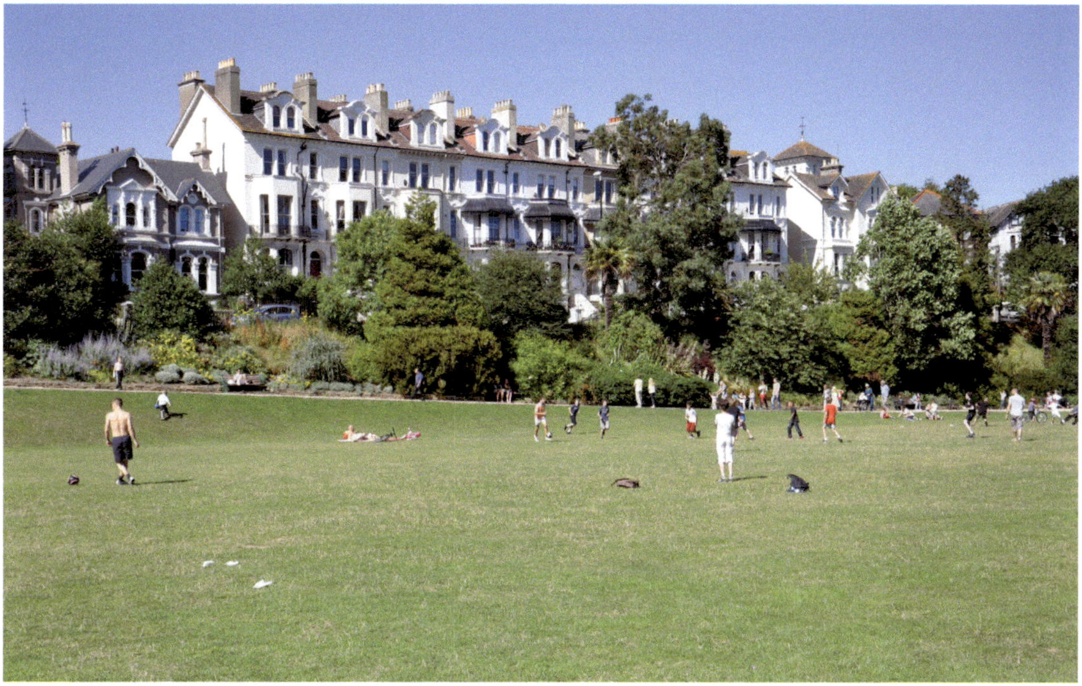

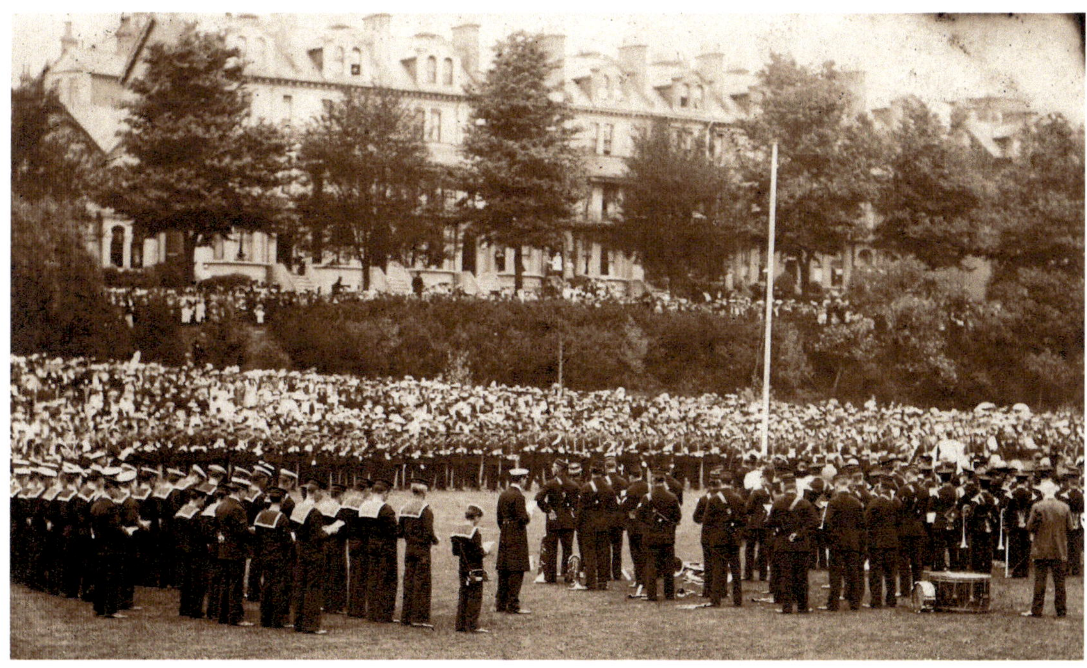

Drumhead Service

The second drumhead service to celebrate Empire Day was held in Alexandra Park on 26 May 1907. Seven hundred and ninety-four men from the volunteer forces marched to Alexandra Park for a religious service. The *Hastings & St Leonards Observer* described the event thus: 'They were there in order that they might realise the greatness, the vastness, and the responsibility of their Empire – an Empire so comprehensive … that upon her broad lands the glorious orb of day never set.'

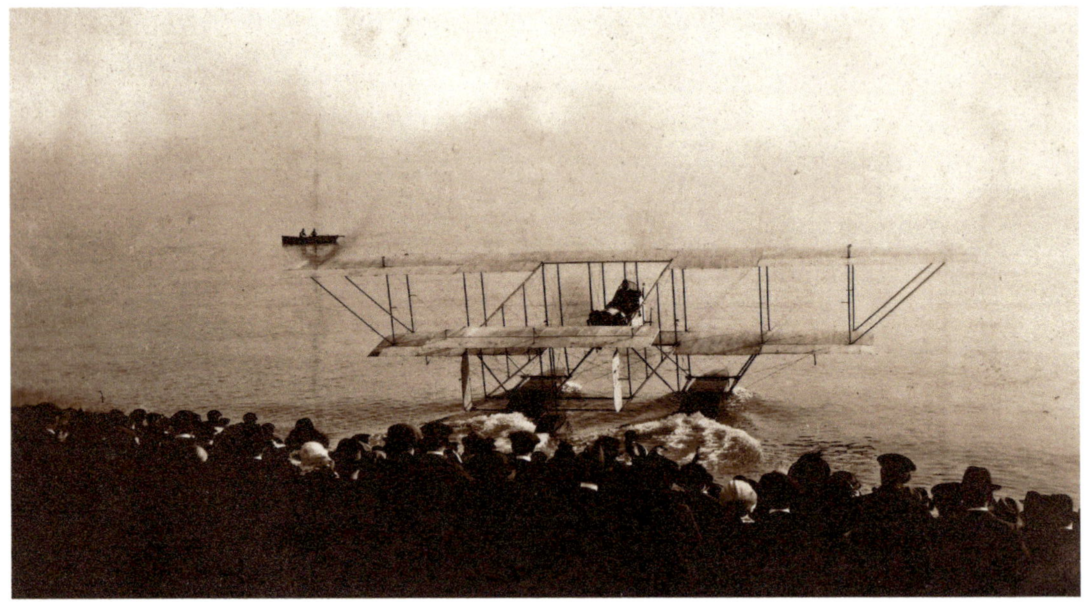

Entertainment Then

Alfred Stonham, or 'Biddy the Tubman' as he was better known, was a well-loved beach entertainer, delighting pre-Second World War audiences with his aquatic antics. His routine included performing a head stand on the tub rim with his feet waving wildly in the air before falling into the sea, then making an exaggerated climb back inside the tub. Another pre-war entertainment was the visit, on 27 February 1914, of a water plane, which came to a graceful landing in the sea just opposite Robertson Terrace so that pilot Lieutenant Ross could take luncheon at the Queen's Hotel. Ross left his plane in the care of the local coastguard as a voluminous crowd assembled at the water's edge. Since controlled, powered flight had only been possible in the preceding decade, this spectacle drew a captivated audience to the seafront, who let out a large cheer as Lieutenant Ross took to the skies for Sheerness.

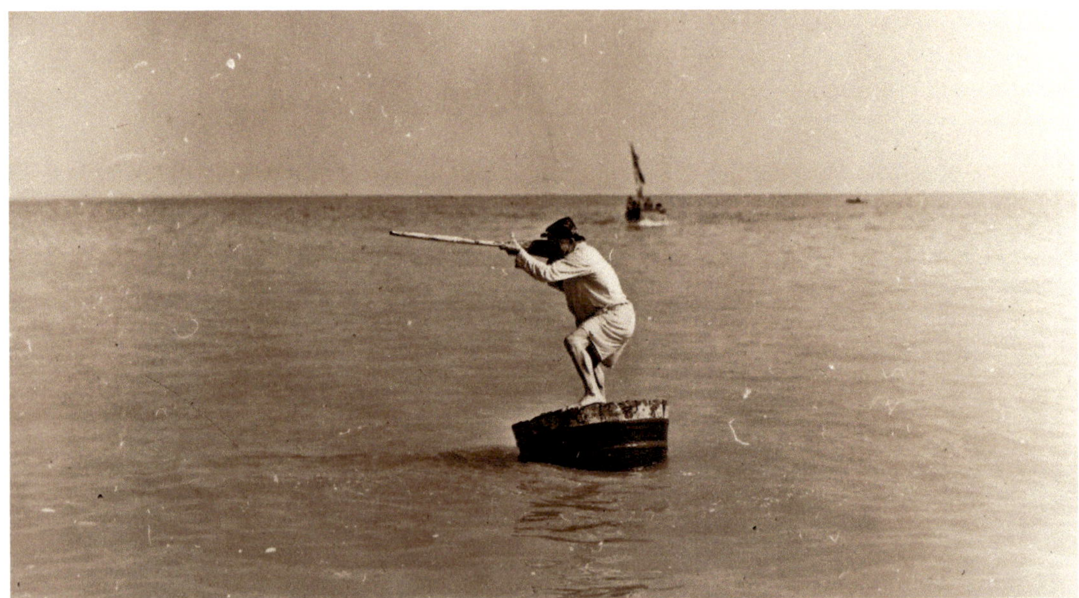

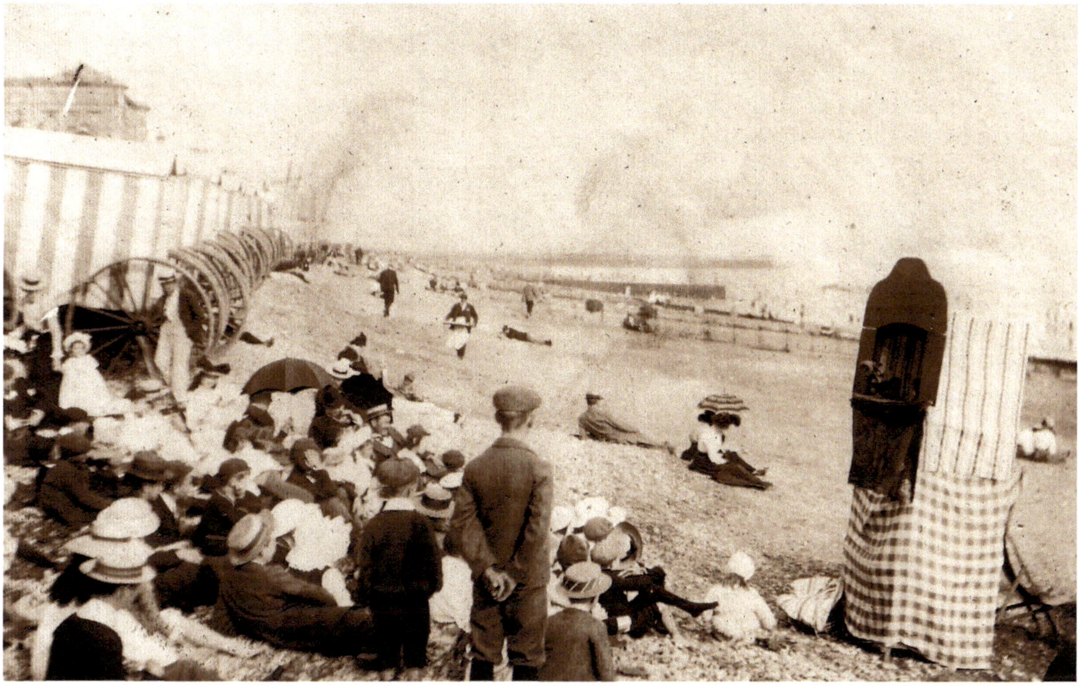

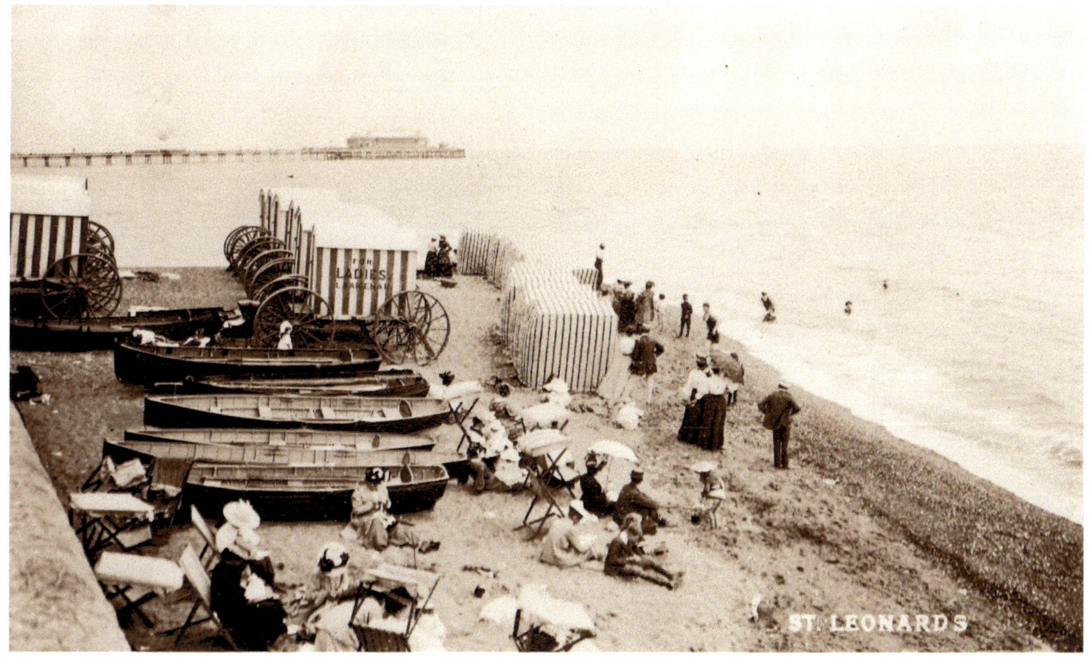

That's The Way To Do It: Victorian and Edwardian Entertainment

These two wonderfully evocative photographs epitomise Hastings as the superior seaside resort of the late Victorian and Edwardian eras. In both pictures are rows of the once-commonplace bathing huts; in the bottom photo they strictly state 'For Ladies' on the side. In the top photograph, a group of children and adults watch the popular Punch and Judy puppet show, a widespread form of beach entertainment during these periods.

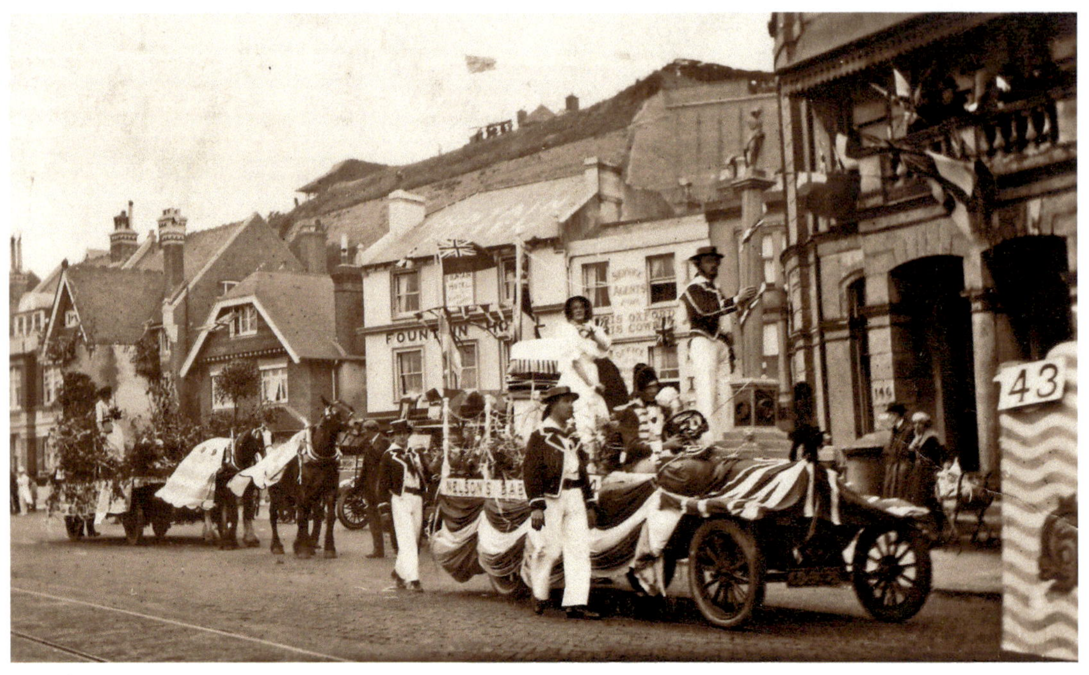

Whitsun Carnival, 1923

Prehistoric monsters, cars bedecked with streamers and flowers, kings and queens, Norman and Saxon soldiers, smugglers, stately ladies, bands, stone-age men, and barons of the Cinque Ports all took part in the Hastings Carnival, which lasted several days over the Whitsun weekend of 1923. Among the other highlights was a Battle of Hastings re-enactment, a pedestrian and cycle race on a new course on the Pilot Field, a children's carnival and sports activities.

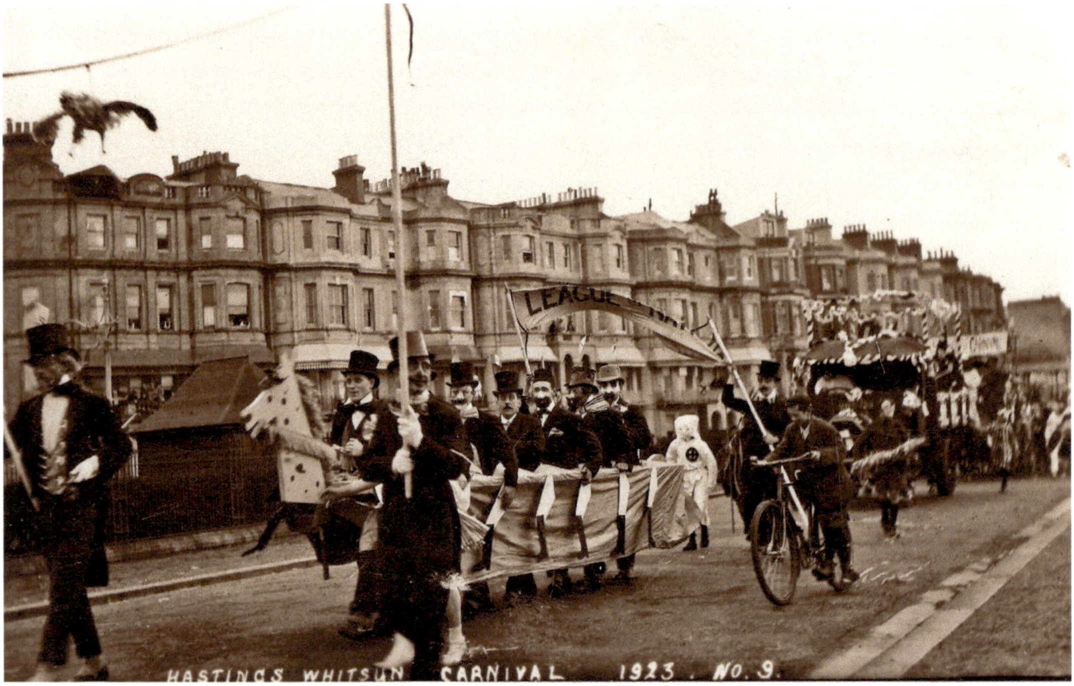

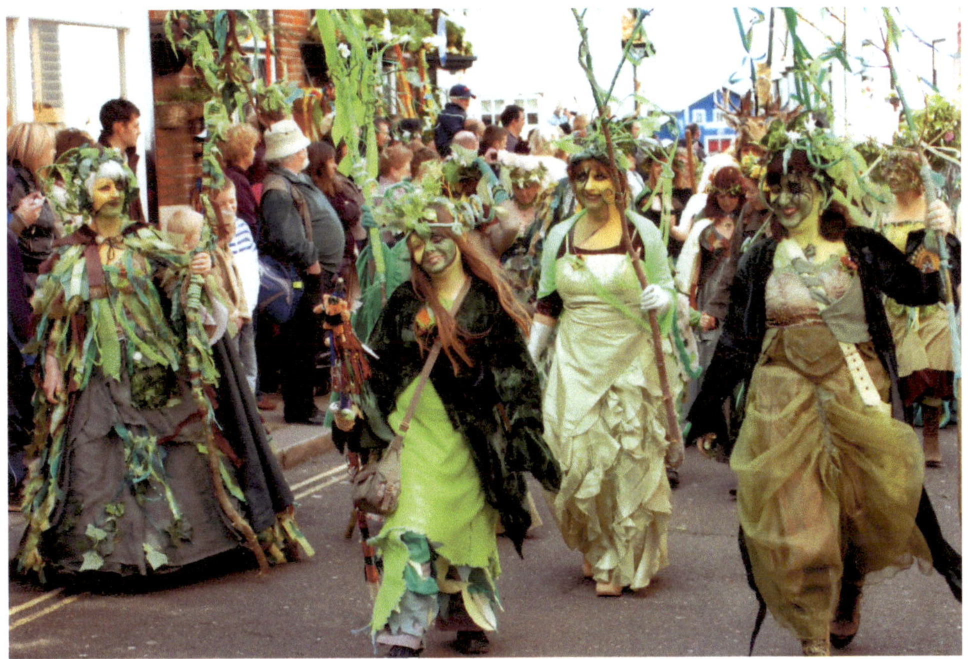

Entertainment Now

The Jack-in-the-Green festival (above) has been celebrating the start of summer in Hastings since 1983, although it had previously been a yearly event until around 1889, when Victorian society viewed such festivities unfavourably. They would have undoubtedly disapproved of another annual event in the town calendar: the Hastings Beer Festival (below). The 2010 festival attracted over 10,000 people and served 12,200 pints of ale, 9,700 pints of lager and 5,500 pints of cider. Who knows what Queen Victoria would have thought!

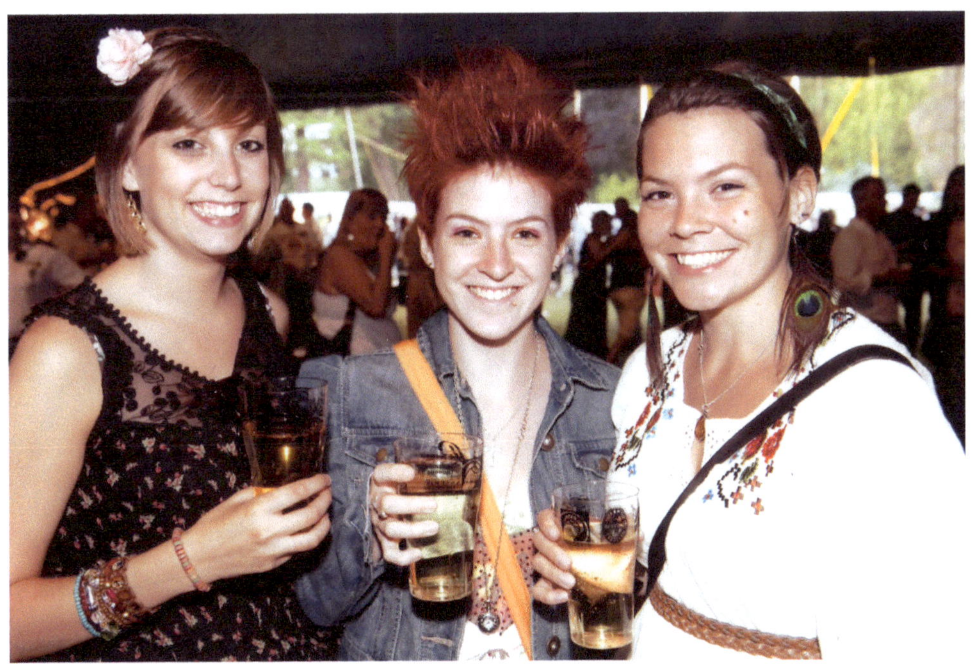

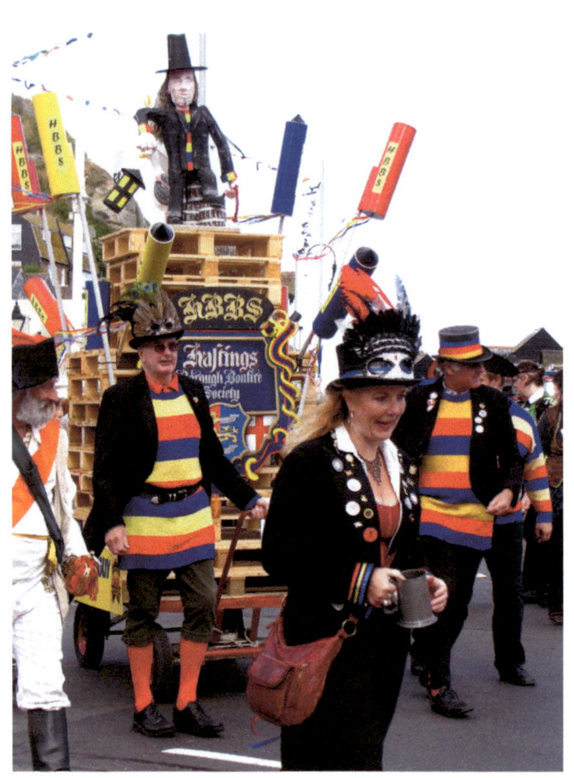

Hastings Carnival, 2010

The Grand Carnival Procession on 7 August 2010 rounded off an enjoyable Carnival Week with thousands of locals turning out to watch an assortment of weird and wonderful floats wind their way from Winkle Island along the seafront to Pelham Place and back to the Old Town. The Carnival Queen, Tamara Gates, and her three princesses were part of the procession, which included the Hastings Borough Bonfire Society (left) and a large Indian elephant that won first prize in the Best Motor Vehicle category. The day before the Grand Procession, Hastings smashed the Guinness World Record for the most pirates in one place! A record 6,166 pirates crowded onto the beach, snatching the title from a gathering of 1,670 in Portland, Oregon, USA.

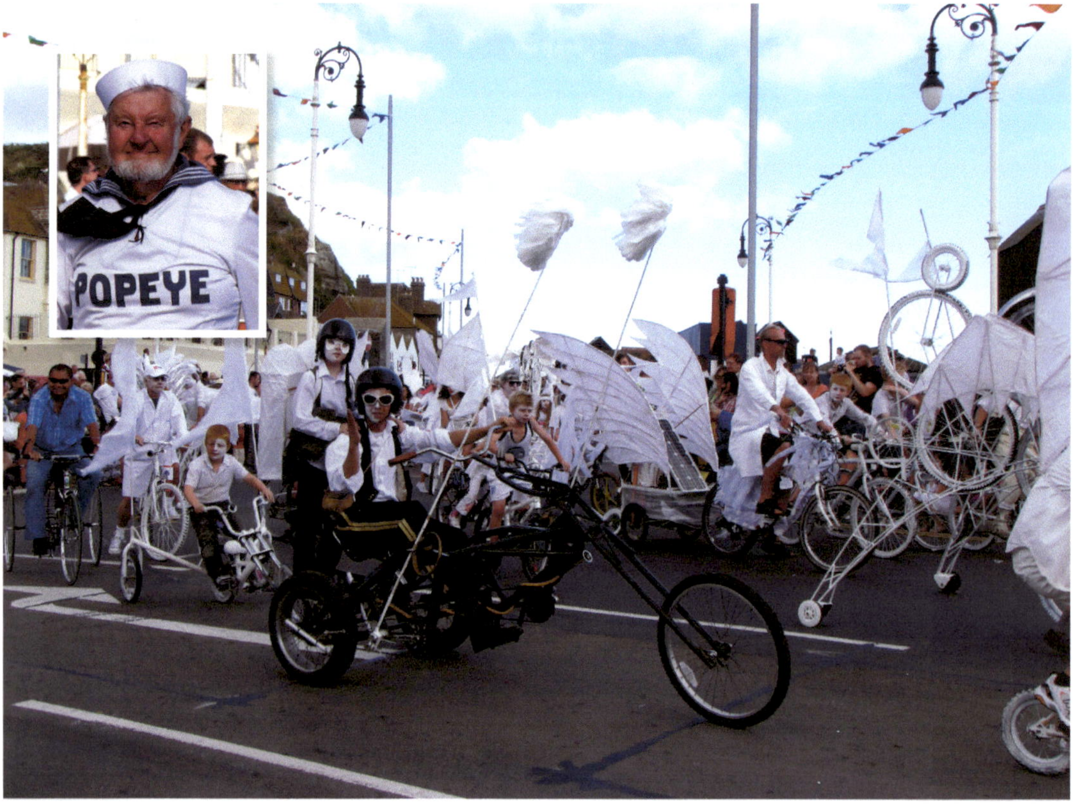

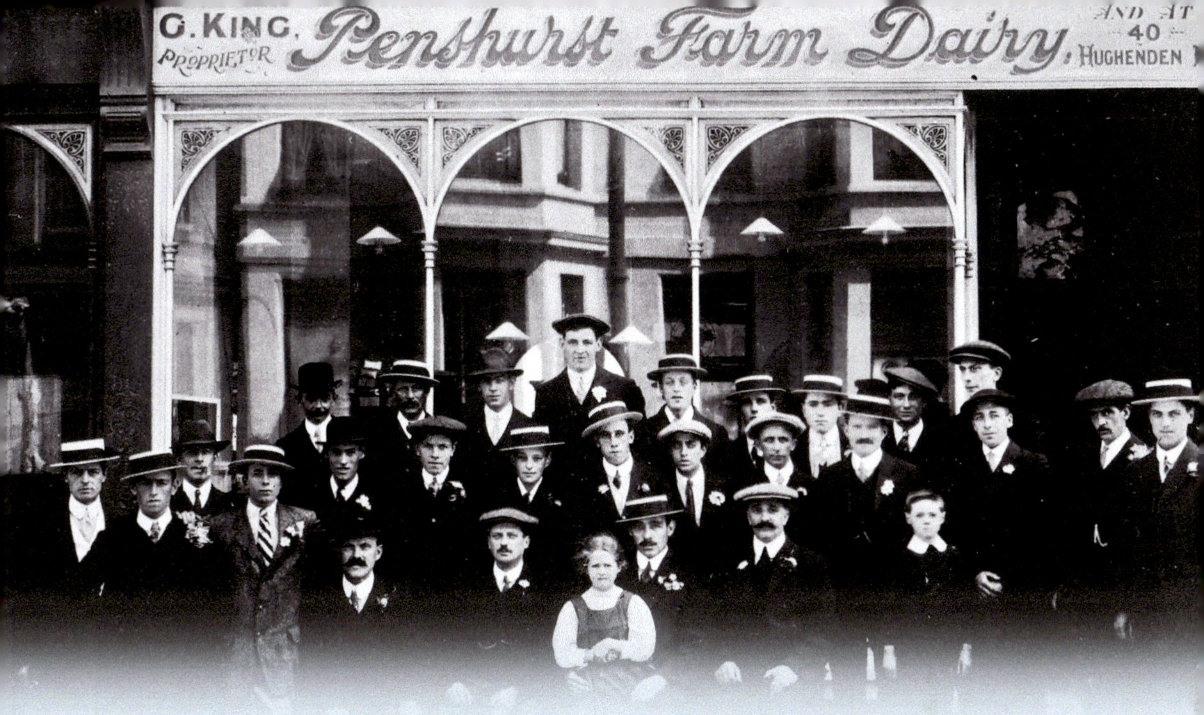

CHAPTER 7

Shops

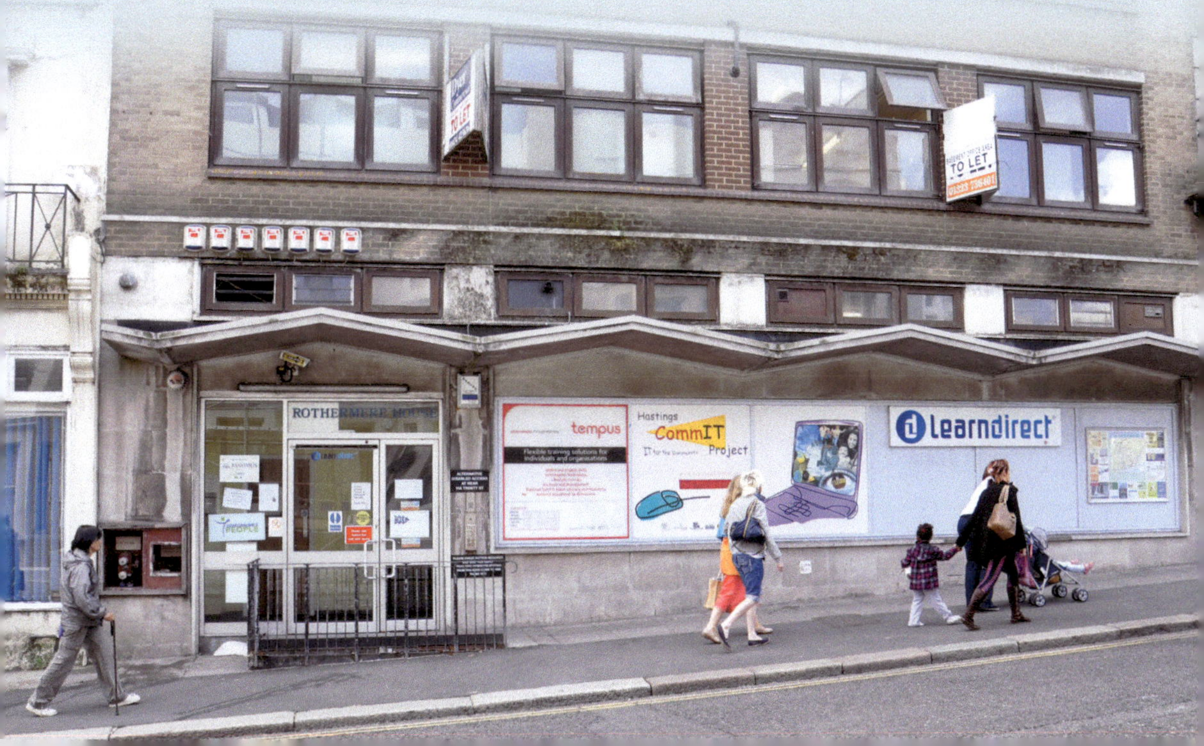

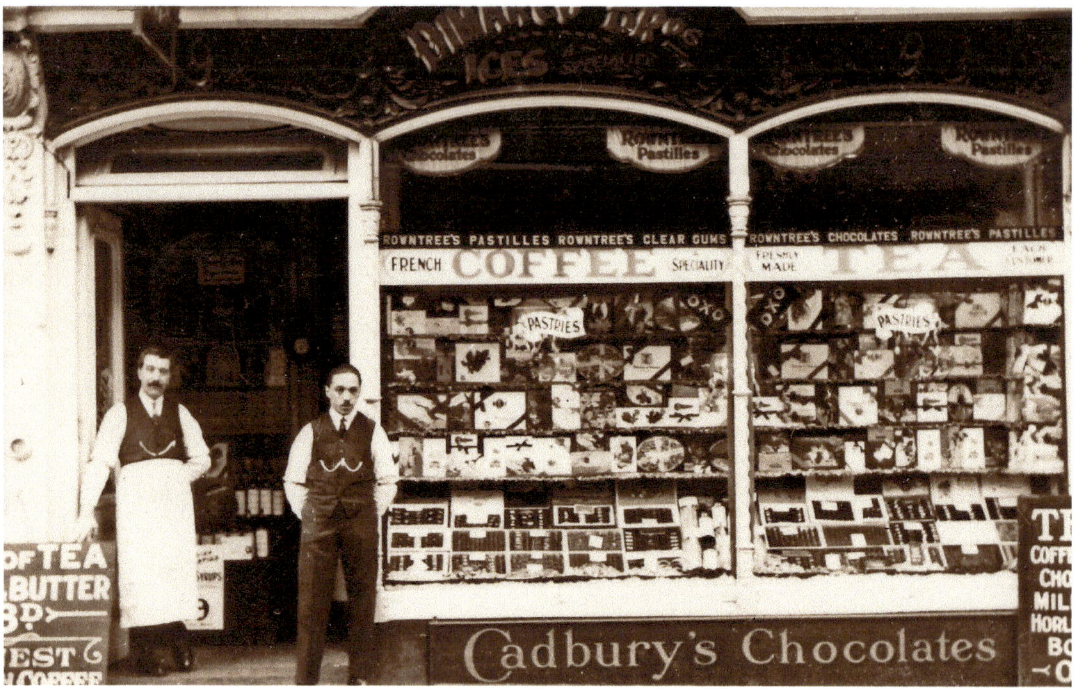

Dimarco Brothers' Café

The well-known Dimarco family ran an extremely successful ice cream shop and café in the town for many years. Their first shop (above) was opened in 1919 at 9 Wellington Place. It has been said that many Londoners would travel to the town principally to enjoy the delicious taste of their Italian ice cream. The firm closed its doors in 1985, bringing to an end the era of the family-run business. McDonalds opened a restaurant on the site in 1987.

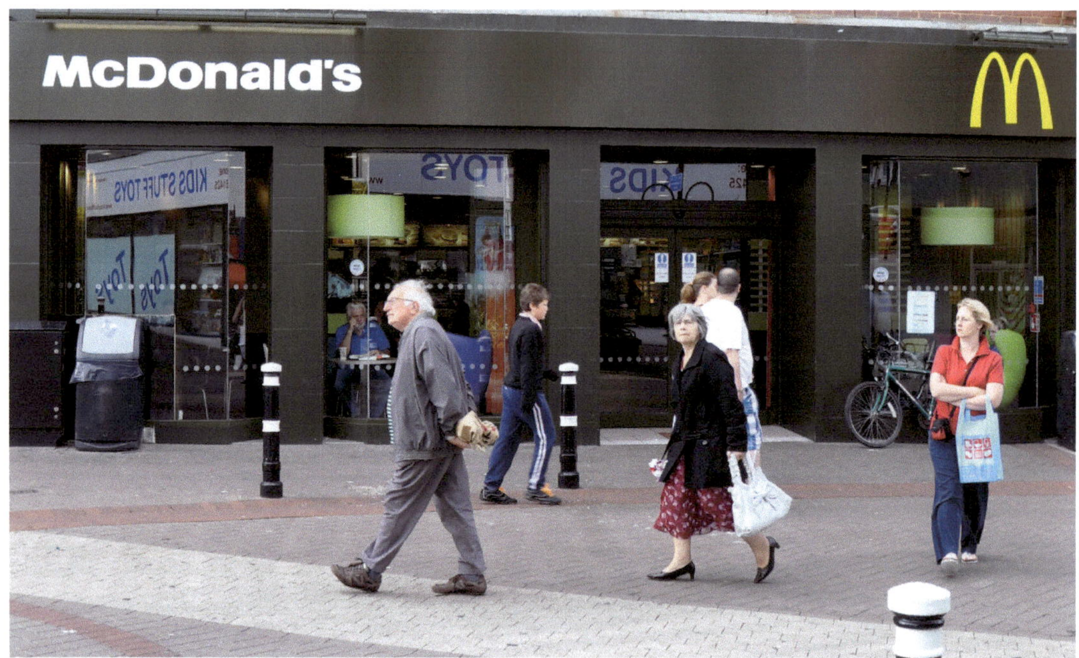

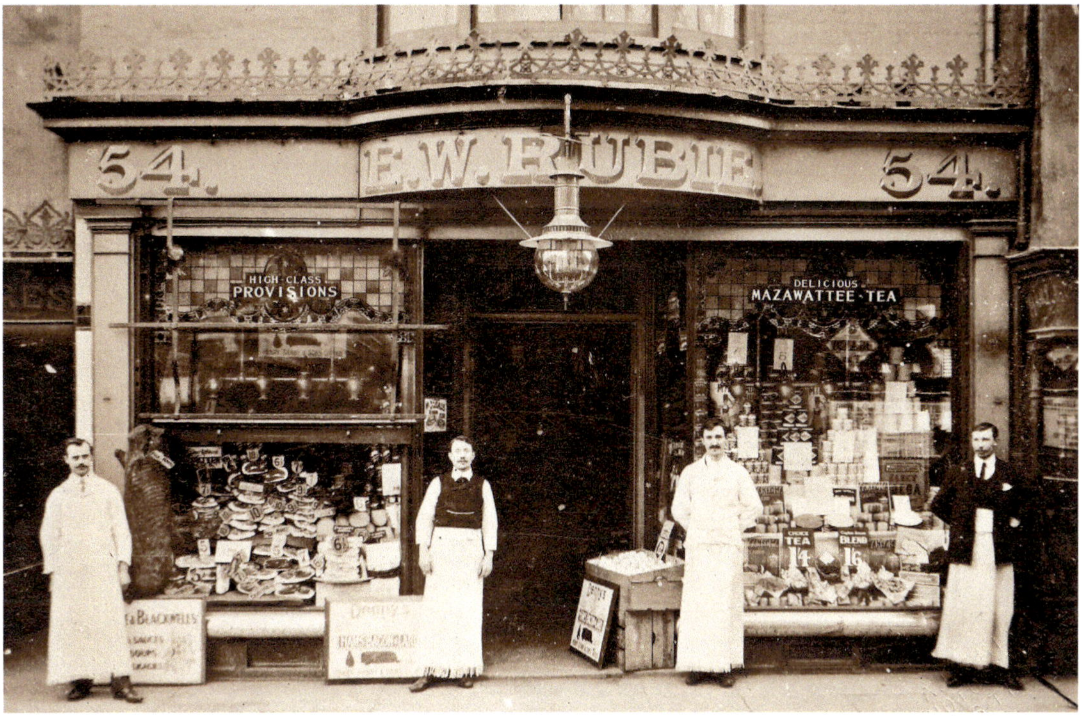

54 High Street

This is one of a minority of shops to have retained the original character and charm found in the older photograph, taken around 1905 – almost one hundred years after it was occupied by the Duke of Wellington, Major-General Sir Arthur Wellesley. He was posted to Hastings in February 1806 after returning from war in India and this property became his headquarters. Some of the troops he commanded were billeted around the area that is now the Stables Theatre.

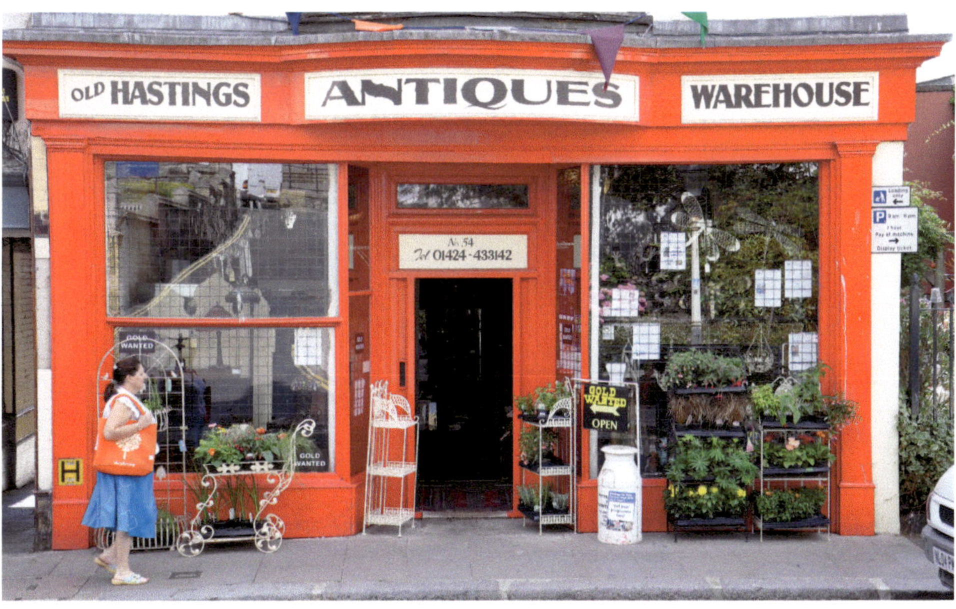

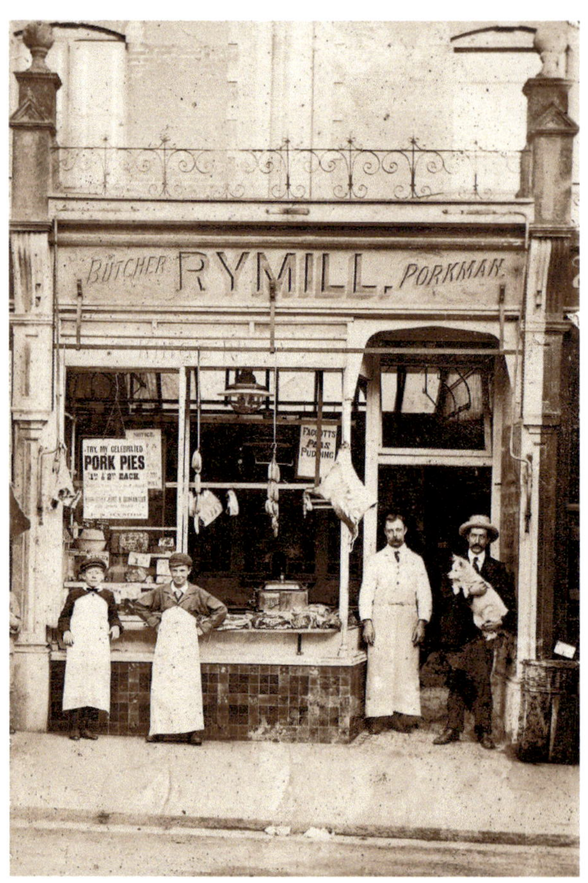

Butcher and a Baker

Rymill's butcher's shop formed a part of the run of shops on Silverhill Junction shown on page 83 which were destroyed in the Second World War. It was owned by Bert Rymill, an alderman and later mayor of the town; Rymill Road in St Leonards is named after him. The delightful bakery shop below was situated at 75 Manor Road; the owner was Oliver J. Kyle, a baker from Dublin.

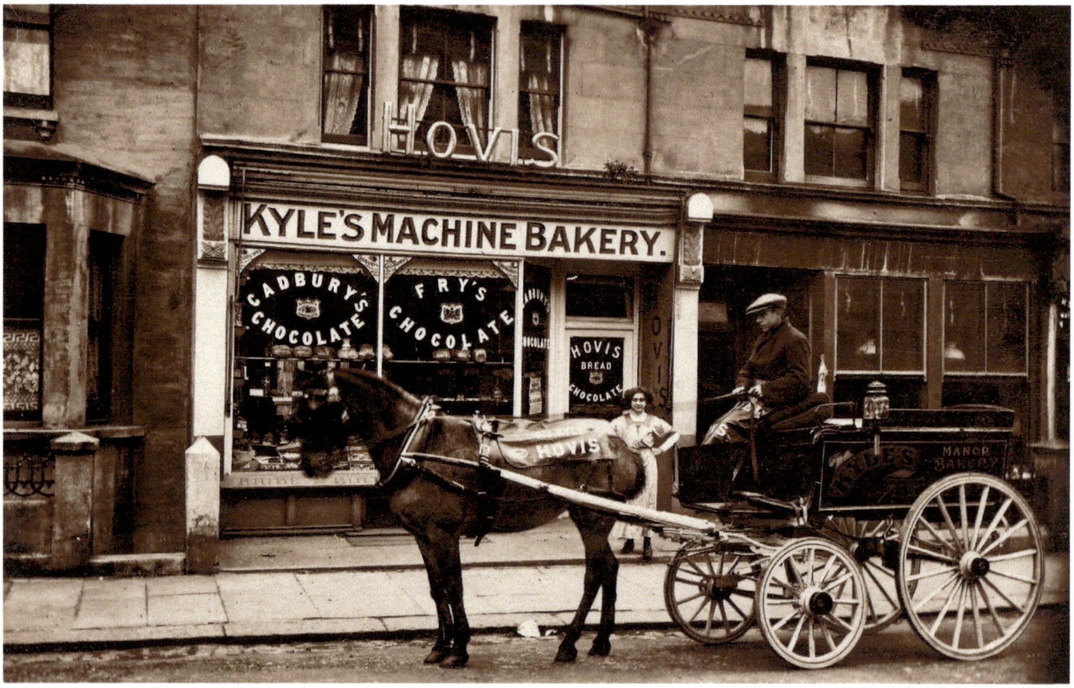

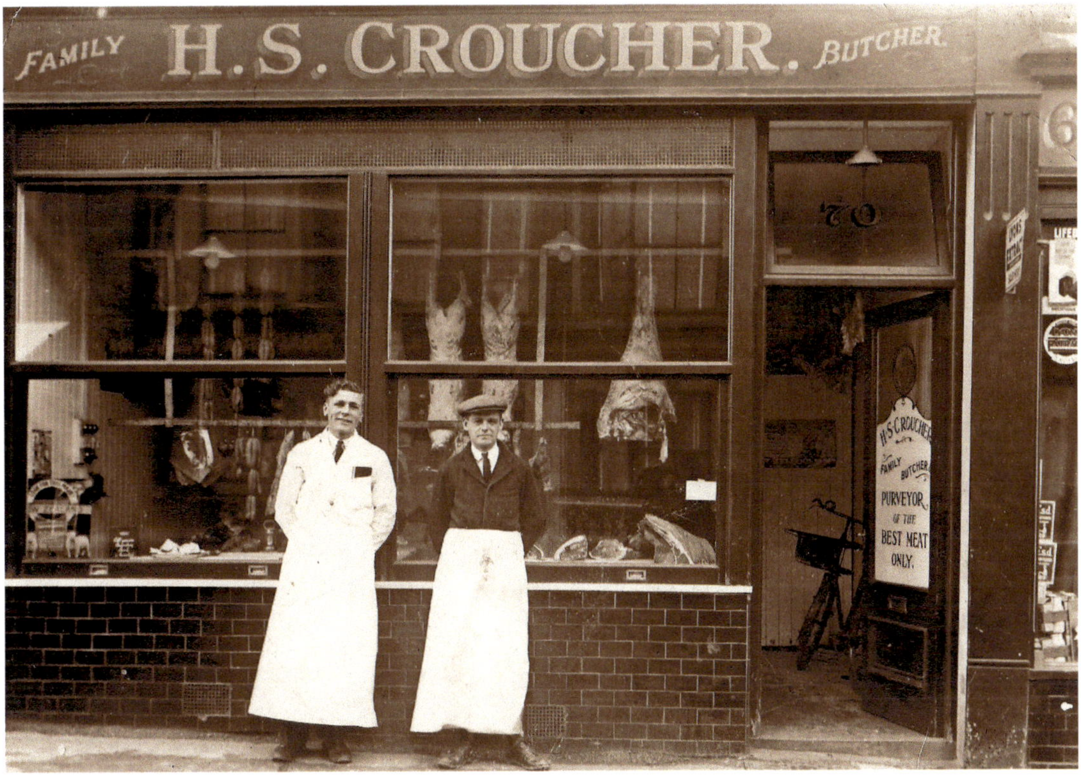

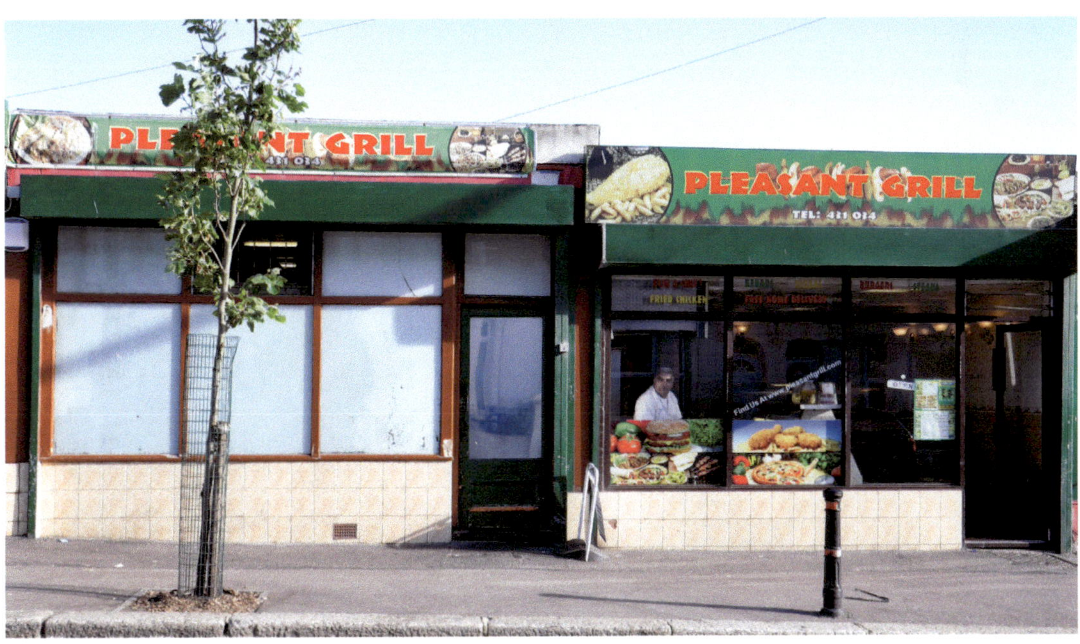

A Pleasant Shop

Henry Croucher stands outside his butcher's shop at 70 Mount Pleasant Road. The building has been through many guises and is currently the kitchen half of Pleasant Grill – a kebab takeaway shop.

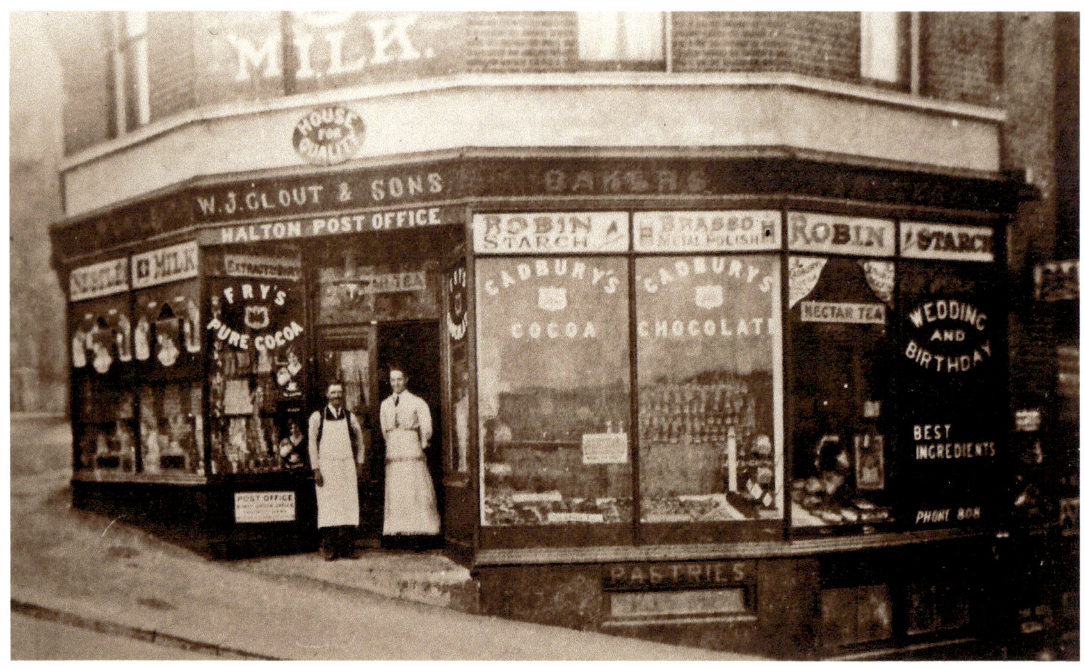

Halton Post Office

For many younger Hastings residents, the corner of Priory Road and Mount Pleasant Road has always appeared sadly as the unsightly and long-neglected building shown below, while older locals recall the shop in more gentrified times, when it functioned for the residents of the Halton area as a general shop, baker's and post office, and later as a sweet factory.

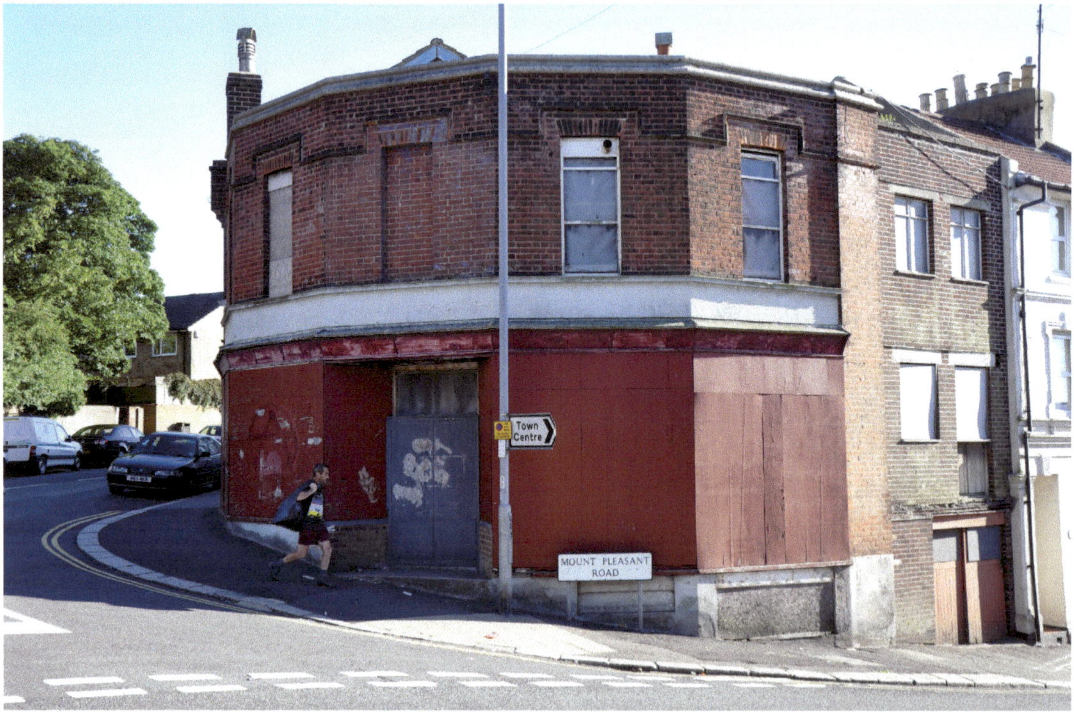

Battle Road Merchants

These two fascinating shops on Battle
Road have long been demolished and
replaced by an unsightly block of flats.
Until the arrival of the large Tesco on
Churchwood Drive, Battle Road was
the main shopping area for Hollington.
The workers of A. Vigor (No. 301)
stand proudly outside their grocer's
shop in 1913, while outside Pilgrim's
the watchmakers (No. 315) stand Mrs
Hodges and Miss Pilbeam.

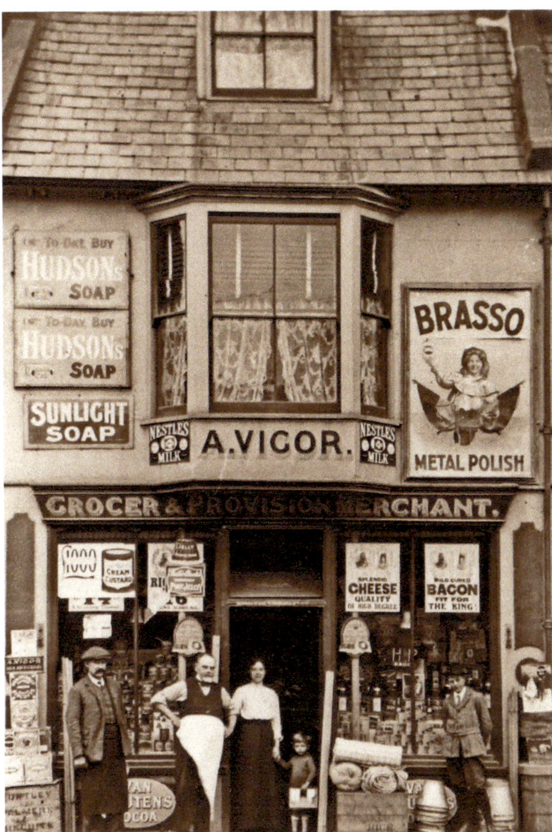

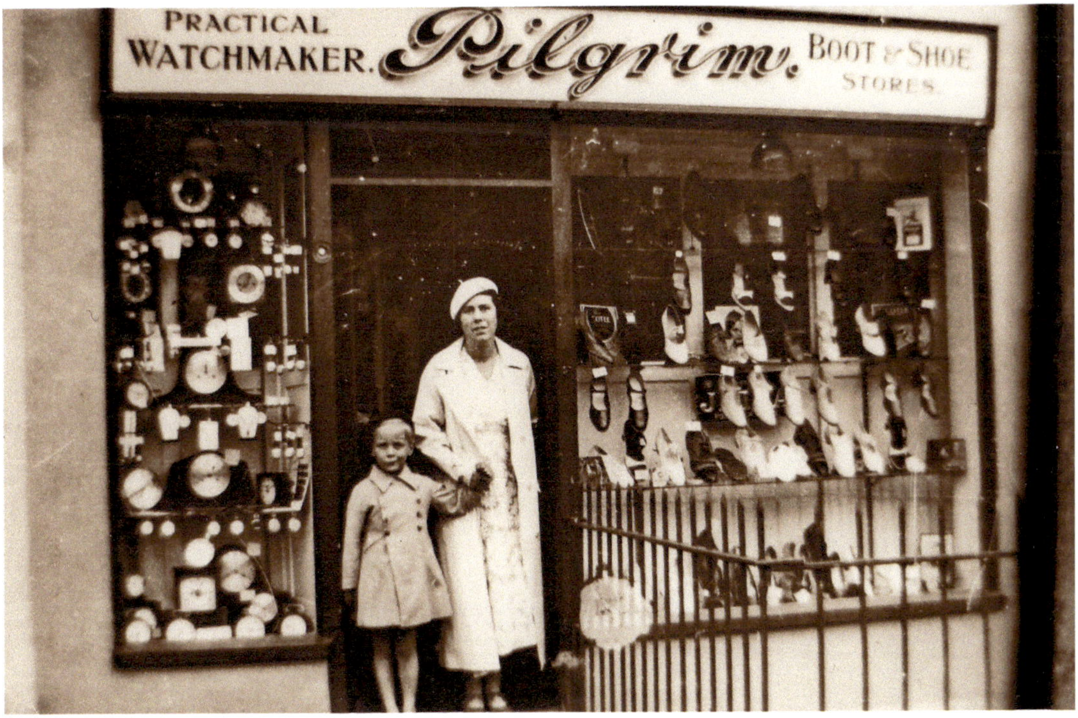

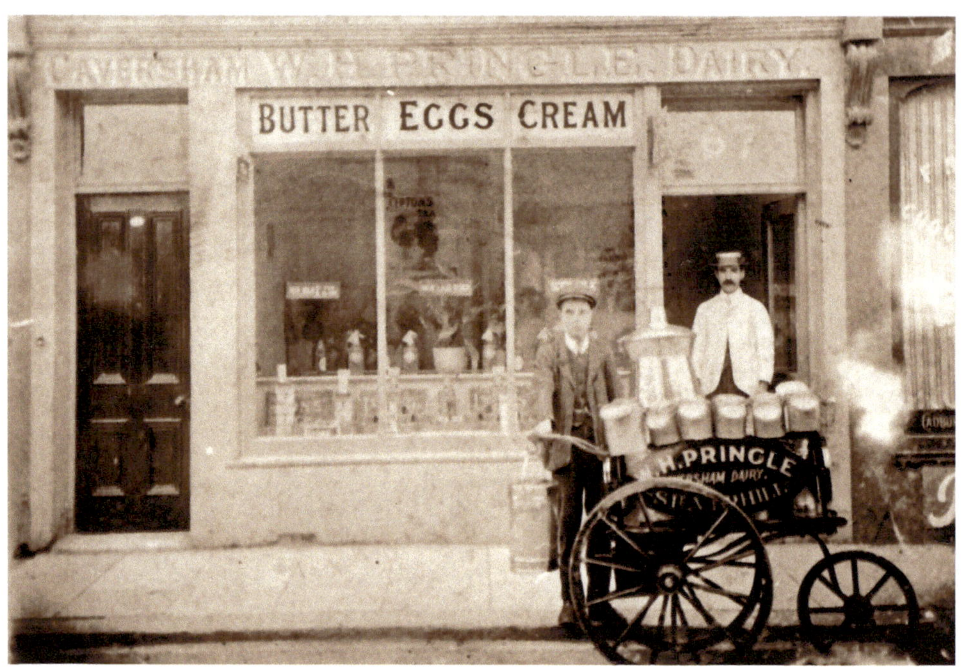

Sedlescombe Road North Merchants

These two shops once stood almost directly opposite each other between Alma Villas and Alma Terrace on Sedlescombe Road North. The Caversham Dairy was located at No. 67, opposite Cox's Dining Rooms at No. 58. Both shops have been converted into houses, but neither is aesthetically pleasing enough to warrant reproduction.

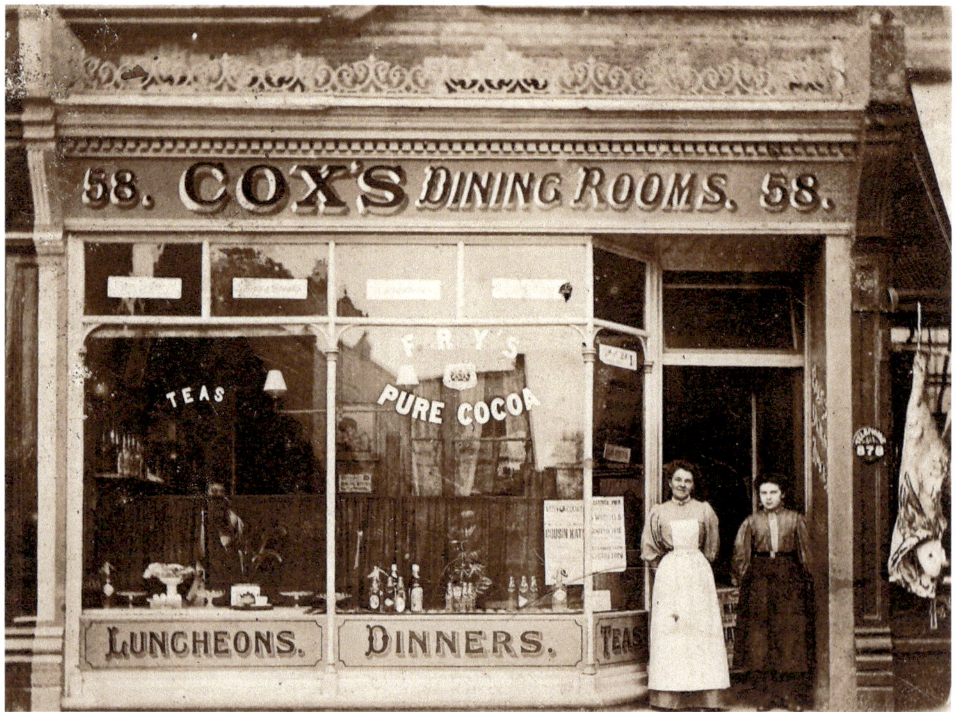

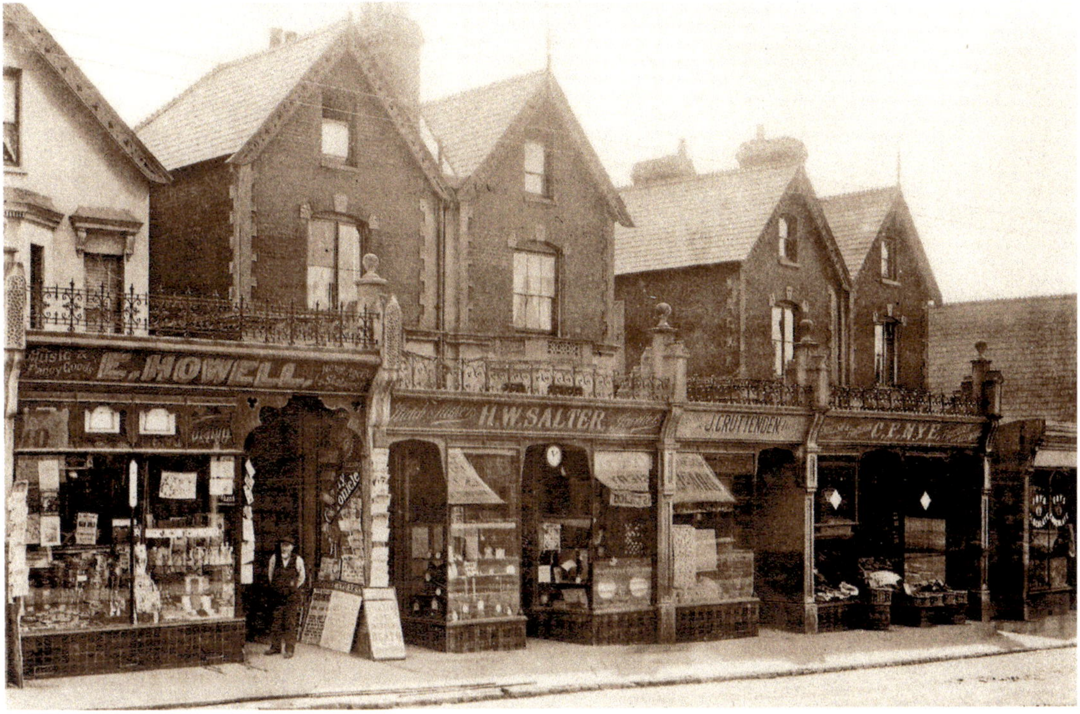

Sedlescombe Road North Merchants II

This attractive run of shops on Silverhill Junction was destroyed on 11 March 1943 when twenty Focke-Wulf 190s dropped a salvo of twenty-five powerful high-explosive bombs on the town. Thirty-eight people were killed during the raid, making it the worst air attack in the town's history. The buildings now standing in their place were hastily built with scant thought for design or appearance.

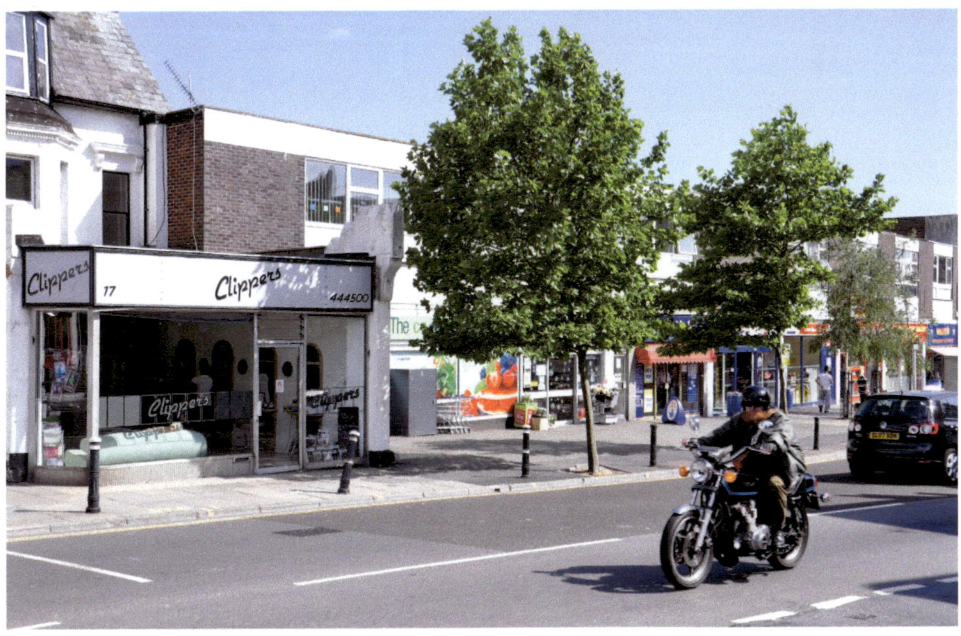

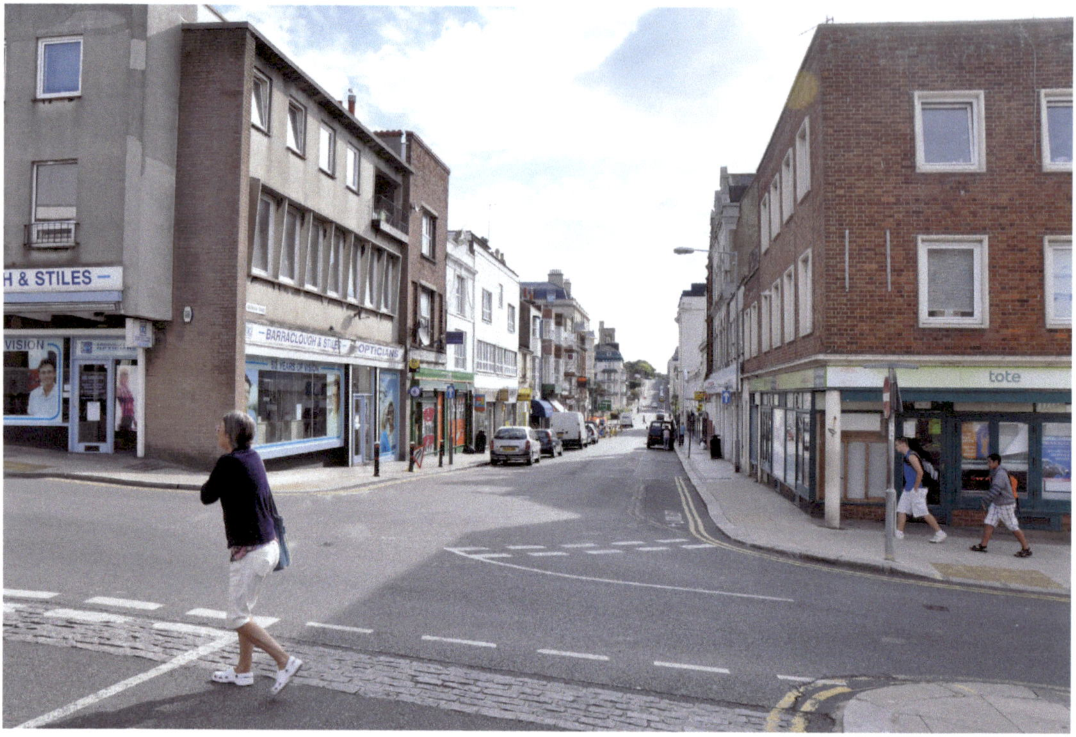

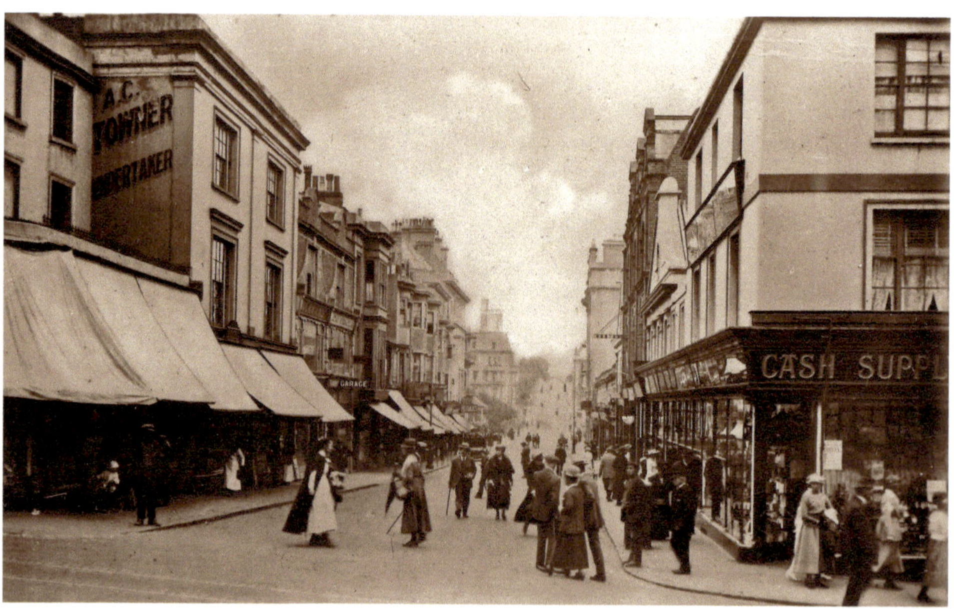

The Junction of Norman and London Road

This bustling run of shops in Norman Road has seen several architectural changes, largely owing to the Luftwaffe. On 23 May 1943, in what was the second worst raid on Hastings during the Second World War, Norman Road and London Road suffered heavily. As a direct result, many of the buildings that can be seen in the old photograph below are missing from the modern version, including 25 Norman Road, the premises of A. C. Towner, undertaker (on the left).

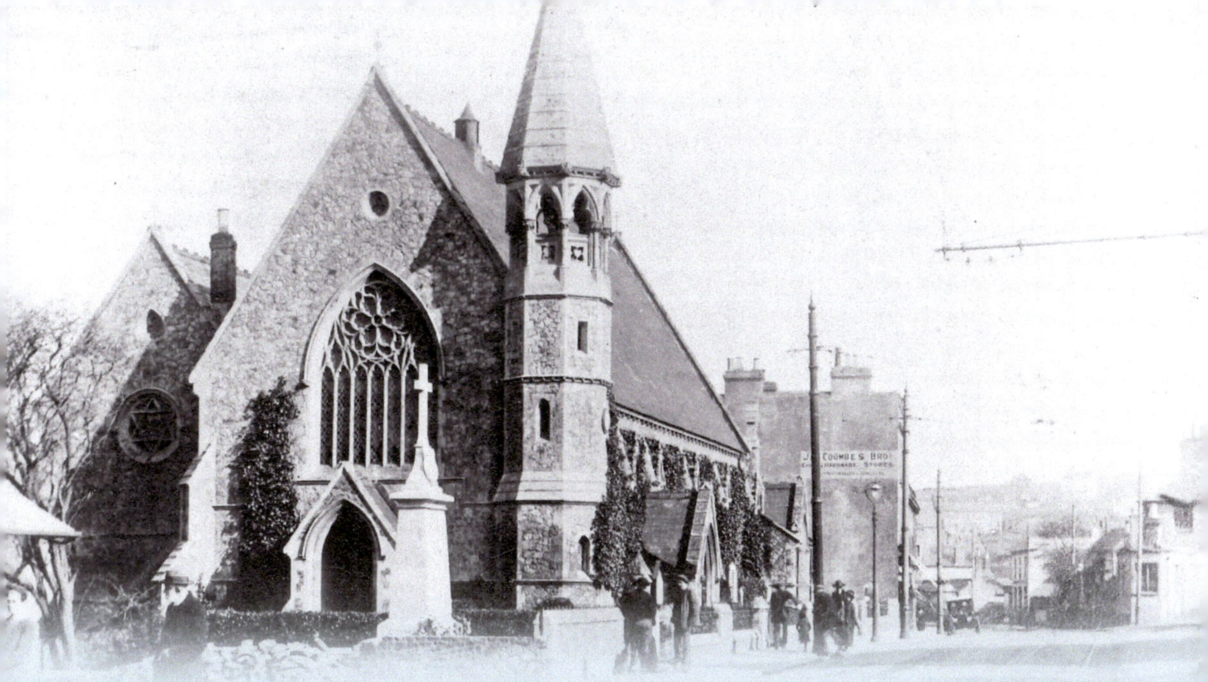

CHAPTER 8

Churches

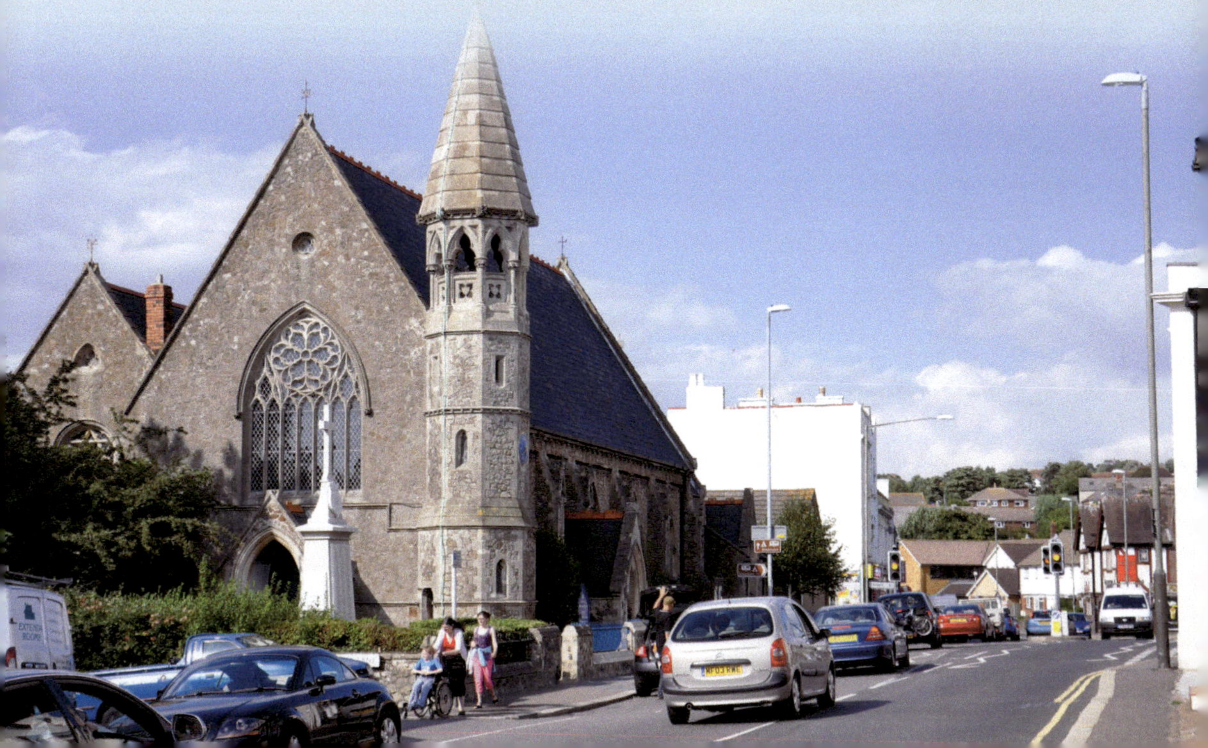

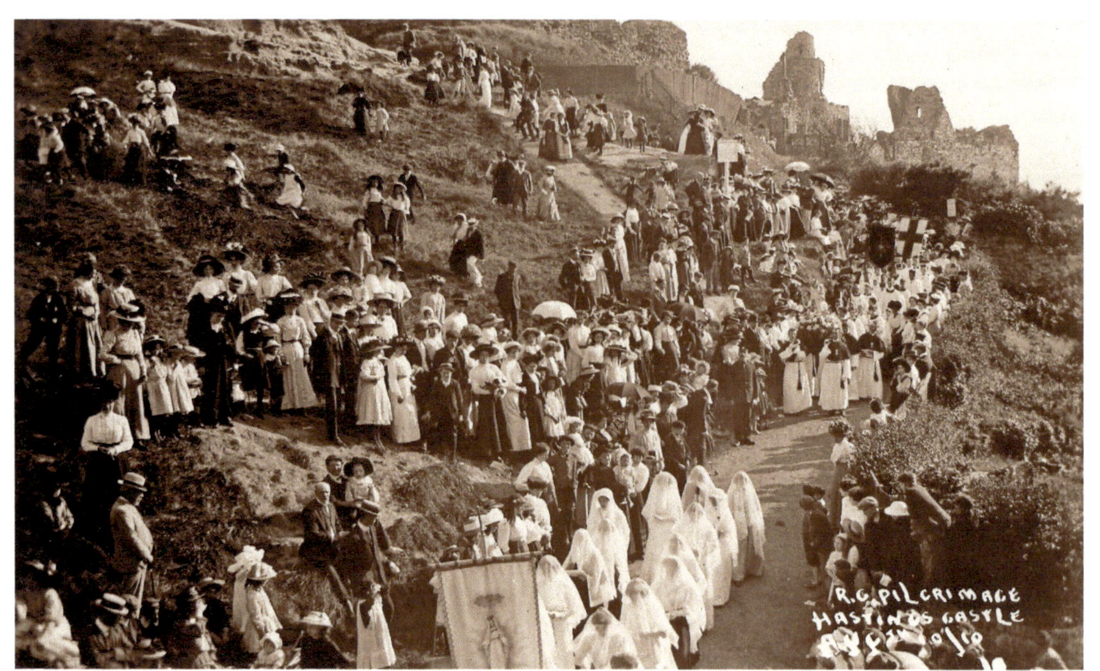

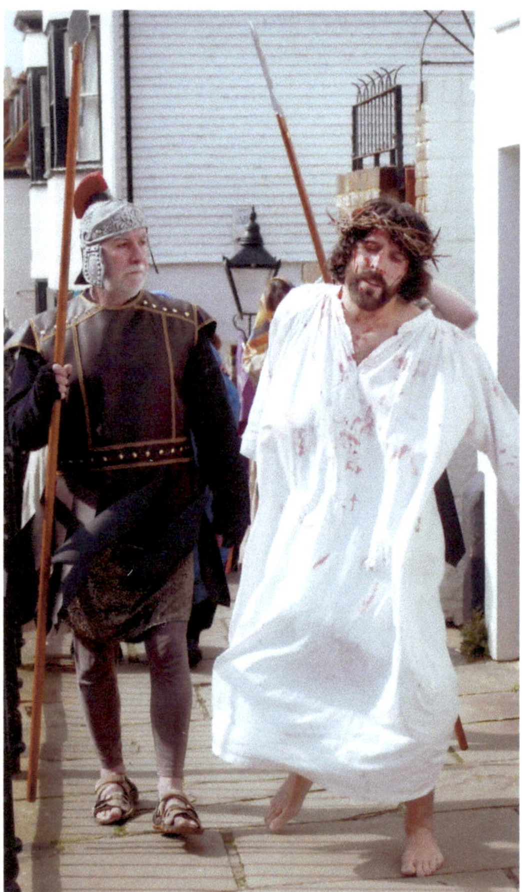

Processions from St Mary Star of the Sea

These two processions to St Mary Star of the Sea occurred almost a century apart. The first was Roman Catholic and took place on 16 August 1911, when hundreds of pilgrims from out of town joined local Catholics in marching from the Old Town over the West Hill to the ruins of St Mary's chapel in Hastings Castle. A service was held there before another was conducted at the church of St Mary Star of the Sea. Ninety-nine years later, on Good Friday 2010, a reconstruction of the crucifixion of Jesus took place. Five hundred people watched the annual 'Stations of the Cross' as Paul Dine, playing the part of Jesus during his final hours, and one hundred followers walked from St Clements church up the High Street to St Mary Star of the Sea before finishing at All Saints church.

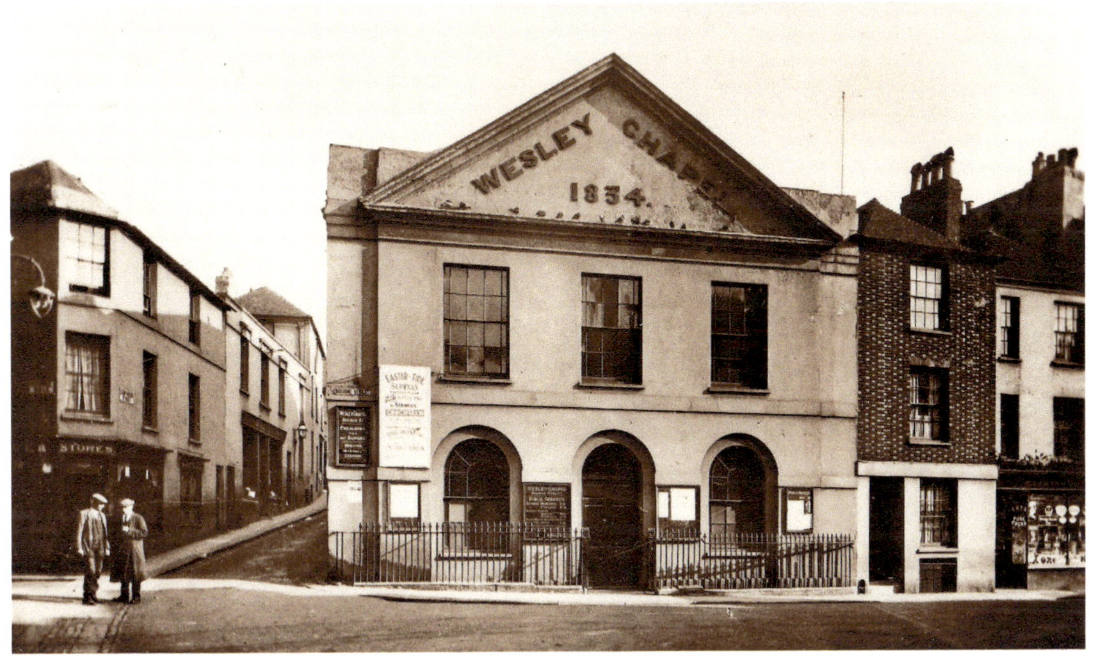

Wesleyan Chapel, Bourne Street

The local Wesleyans purchased the building in the above photograph in 1833 for the sum of £780. The building had, since 1825, been struggling as a theatre. According to Baines' *Historic Hastings*, the Wesleyans promptly burnt all the scenery and converted the building into a chapel, leaving Hastings without a theatre until the Gaiety opened in 1882. The chapel was demolished in January 1939 then rebuilt in 1940 as the building seen below.

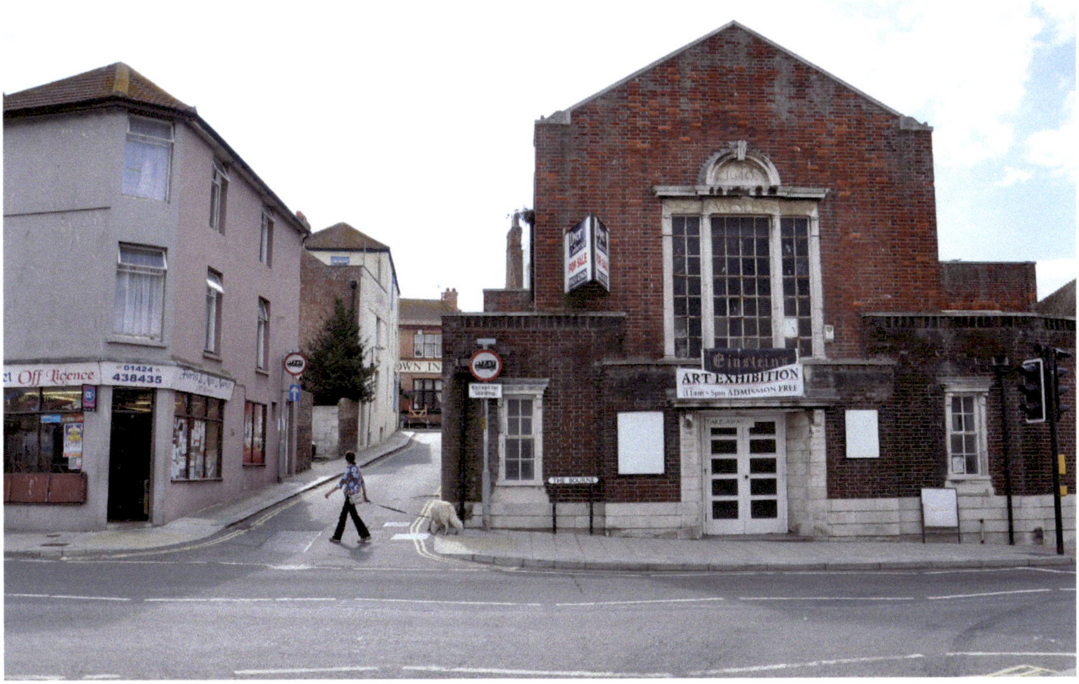

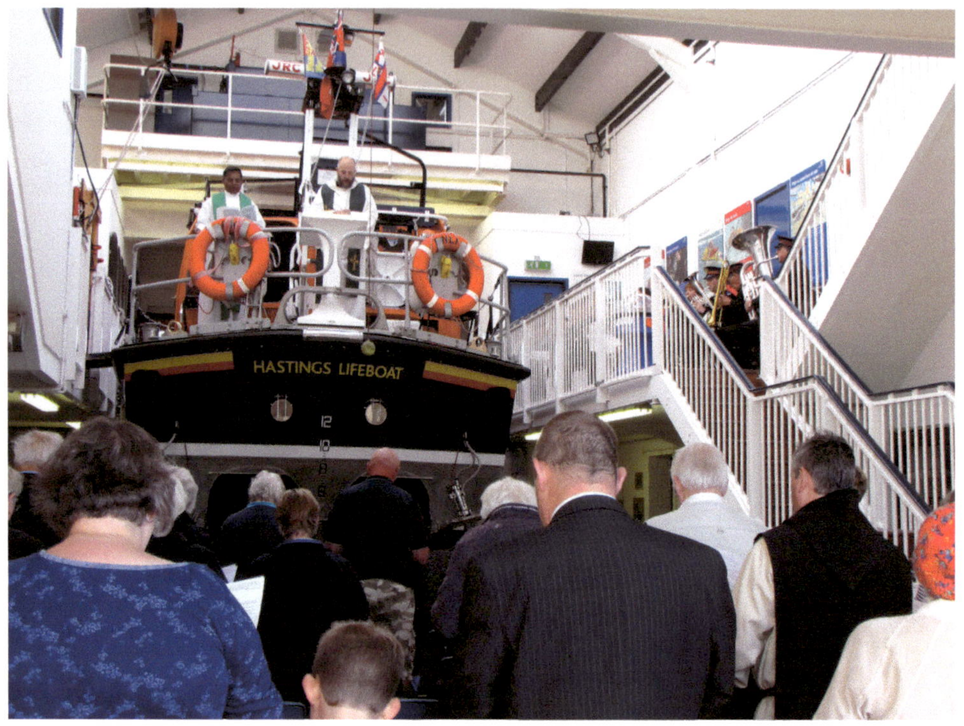

The Blessing of the Sea

'Year after year, from far back in the early youth of the ancient fishing town, pious men have invoked a benison on the harvest of the sea,' the local paper noted of this particular fishing tradition. In the photograph of the 1938 Blessing of the Sea, the vicar taking the service is standing inside the *Cyril and Lilian Bishop* lifeboat. The 2010 service was conducted by the Reverend Robert Featherstone on the *Hastings Lifeboat*.

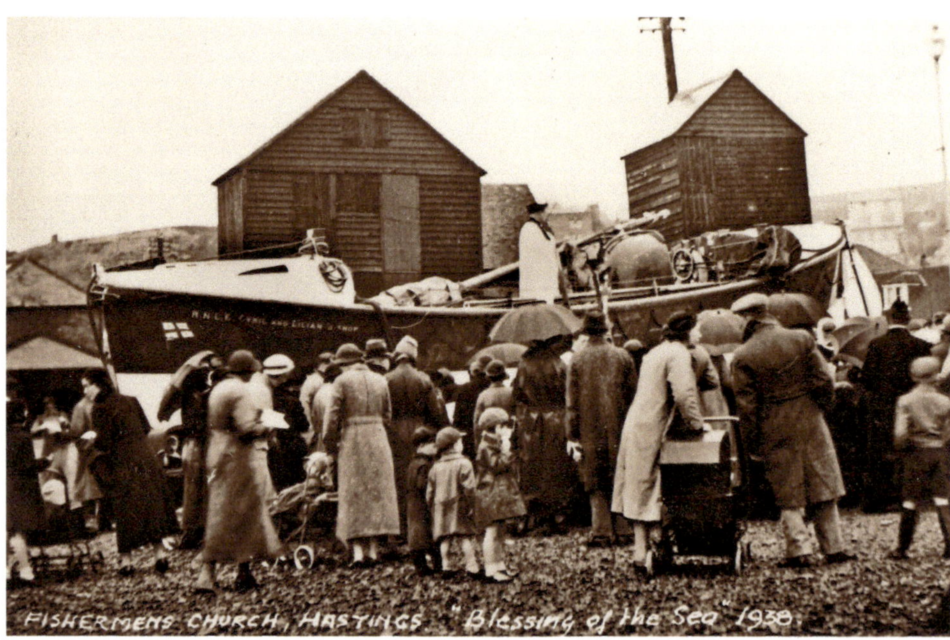

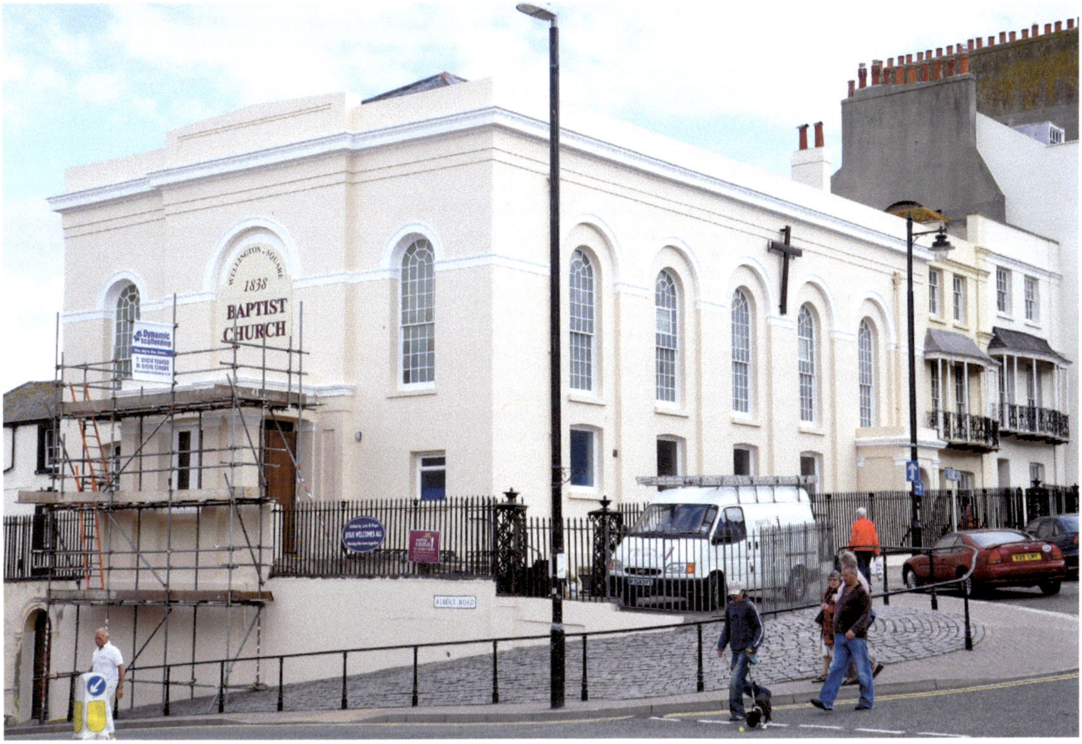

Wellington Square Baptist Church

The Baptist Chapel on the corner of Wellington Square was built in 1838 by a ship owner from Limehouse, East London. Just in front of the chapel stood one of the town's eighty-two gas lamps (seen in the photograph below) which were installed in 1830, replacing the oil lamps that had been in use for ten years. The lamps were only lit from September to April and not on the five nights before or after a full moon.

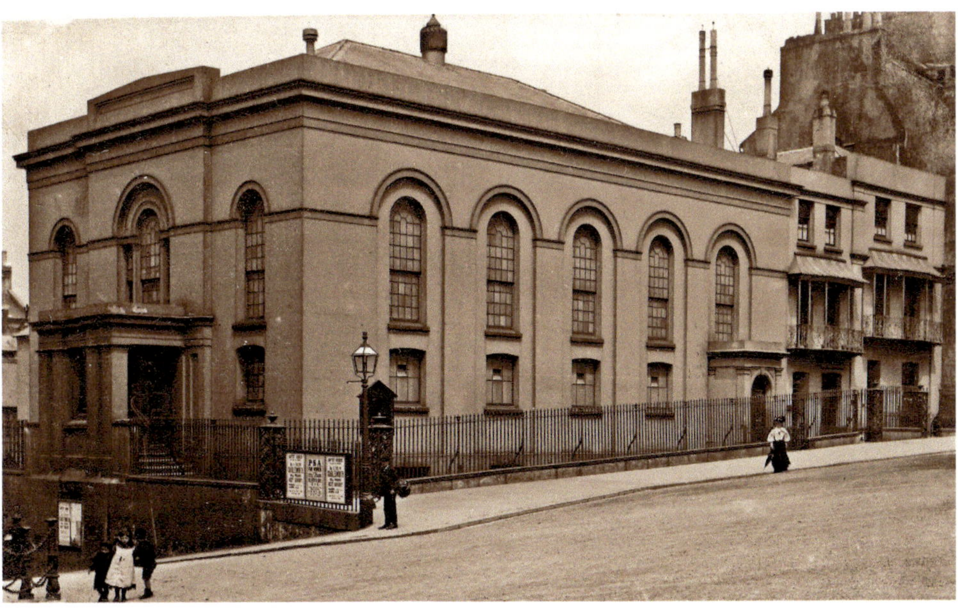

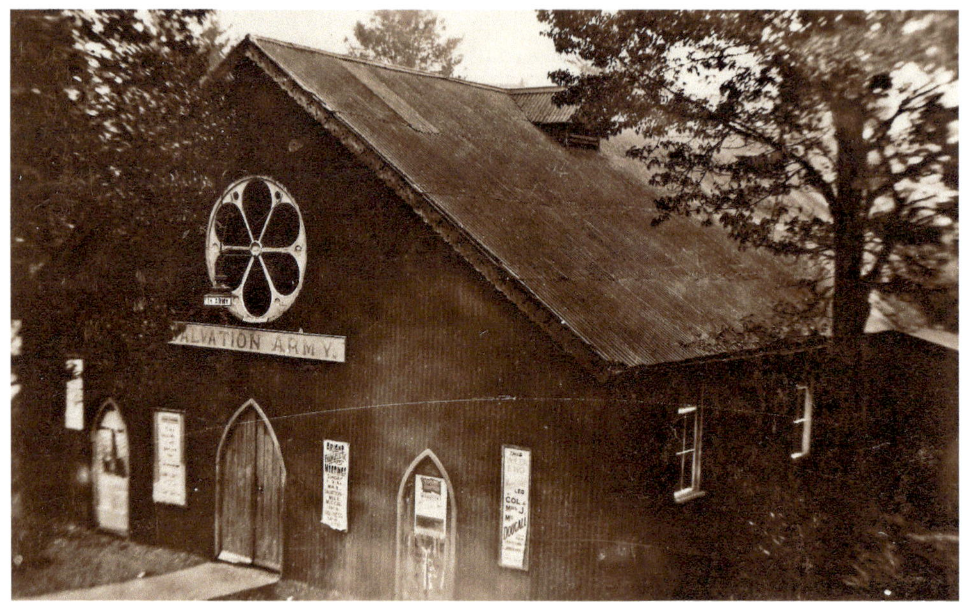

The Opening of the New Citadel

The Salvation Army's arrival in Hastings was not without its problems. It was here that the Salvation Army suffered its first martyr when, in 1883, many Salvationists were pelted with rocks and putrid fish after conducting an open-air service on the beach, as was commonplace during this period. During this particular skirmish, Susannah Beatty was knocked unconscious by the baying crowd and later died from her injuries. The first Salvation Army church in St Andrew's Square was named 'The Old Iron Fort' and remained the principal place of worship until the new halls were built on the same site and opened on 24 May 1930. Thankfully, the large crowds gathered to mark the occasion were not equipped with rocks and putrid fish.

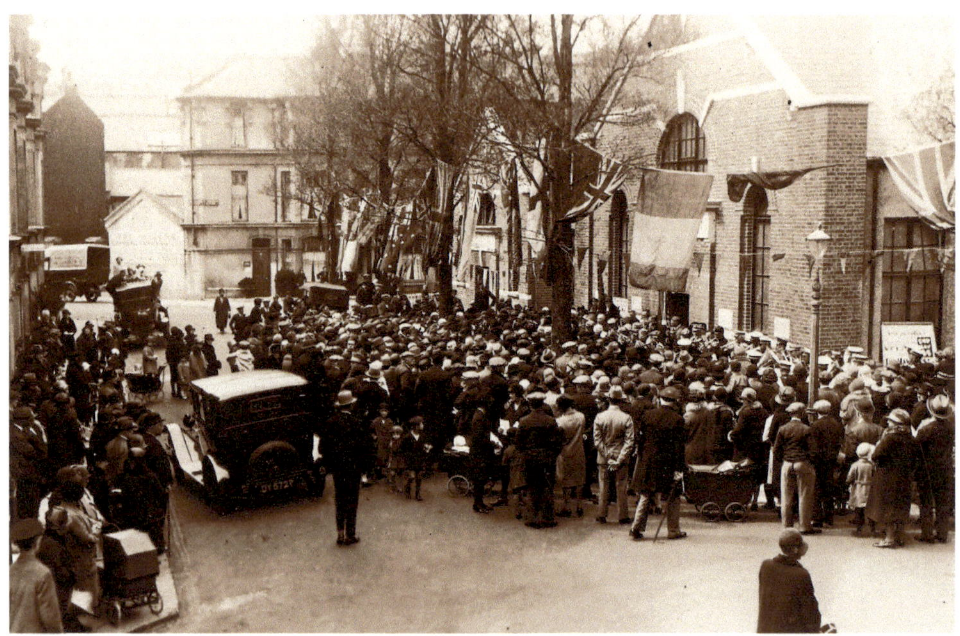

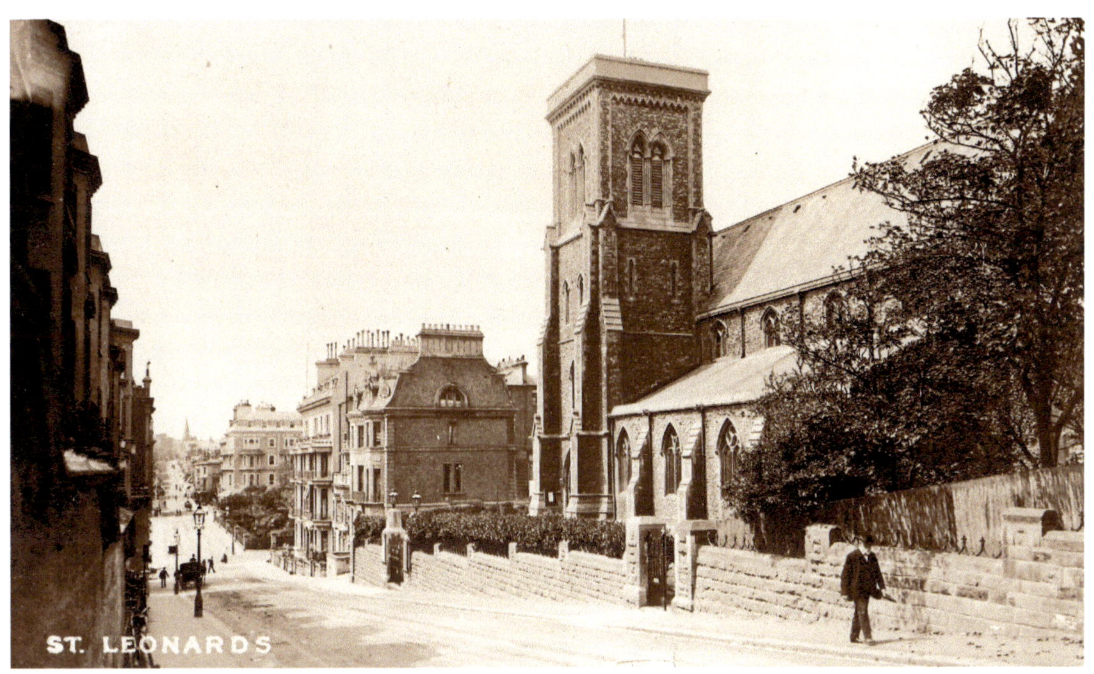

Greek Orthodox Church

This has been a Greek Orthodox church since 1982, prior to which date it was the parish church of St Mary Magdalen. The church was consecrated on 14 September 1852 and is notable as being a place in which the famous author Lewis Caroll occasionally preached under his real name, Reverend Charles Lutwidge Dodgson.

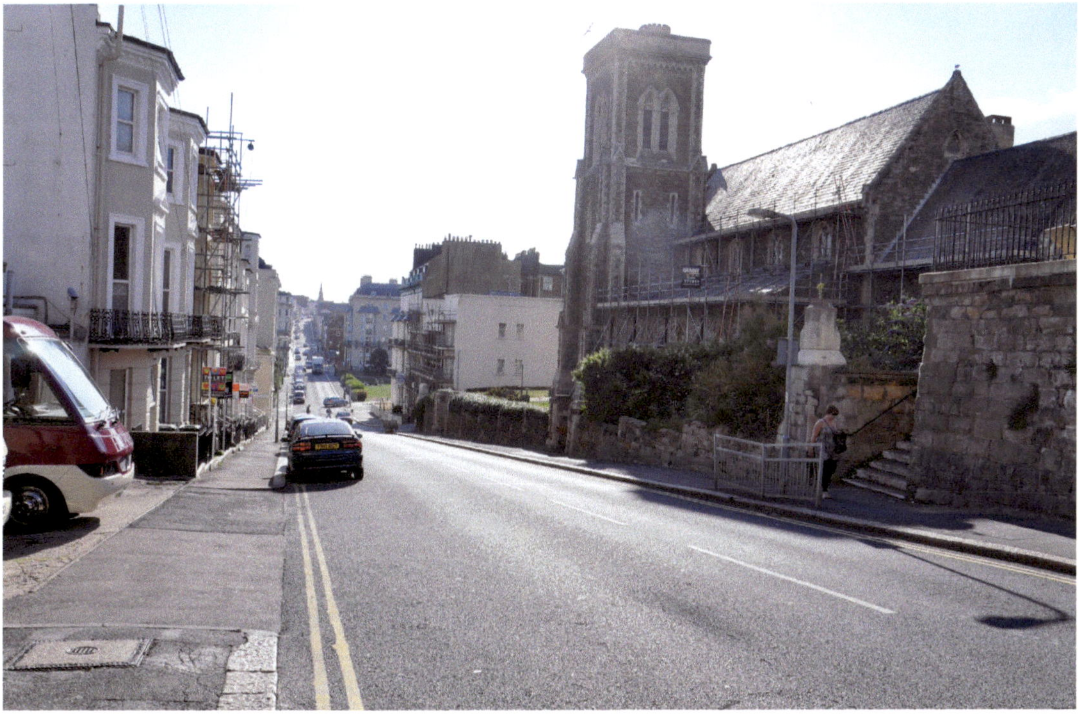

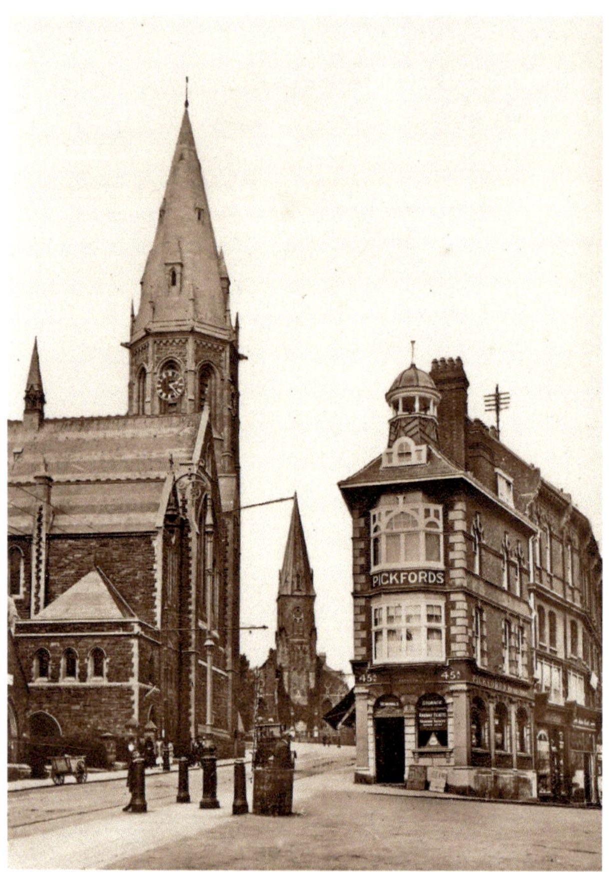

Tallest Building in the Town

When, in December 1894, the 189-feet-high Christ Church spire was completed on Silchester Road it made the building the tallest in the town at that time. The church had been opened in 1875 to serve the fast-rising population of St Leonards. On the south side of the building can be seen the original, much smaller church which was built in 1860 and is now used as community offices. In the modern view, the controversial widened pavements of Kings Road can be seen, giving greater pedestrian access to the shops and businesses.

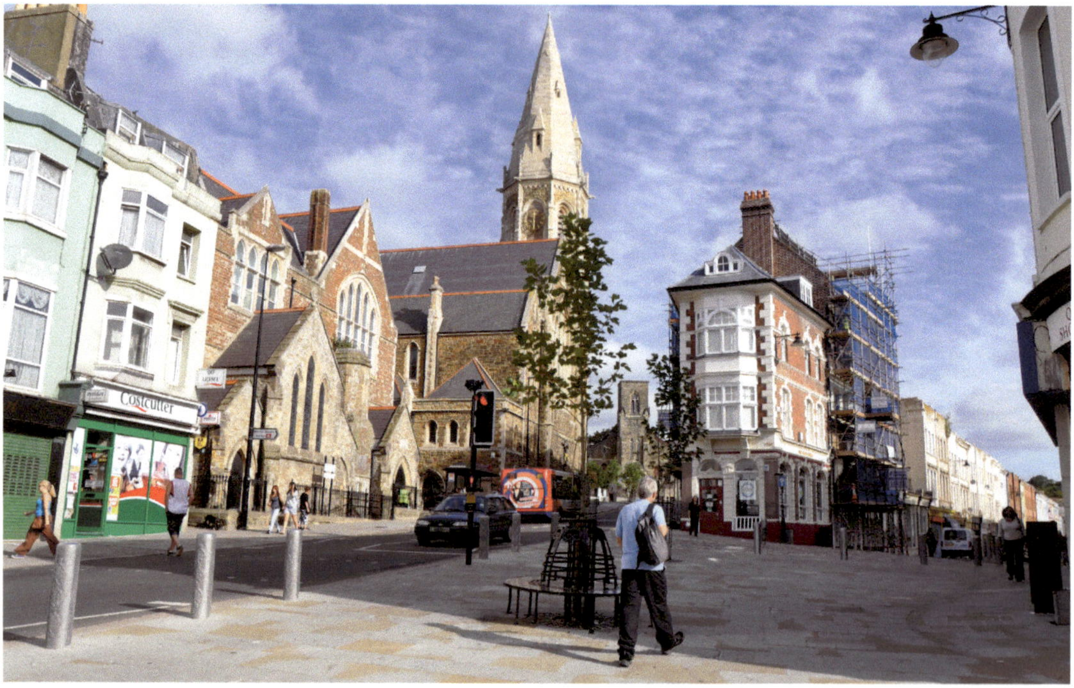

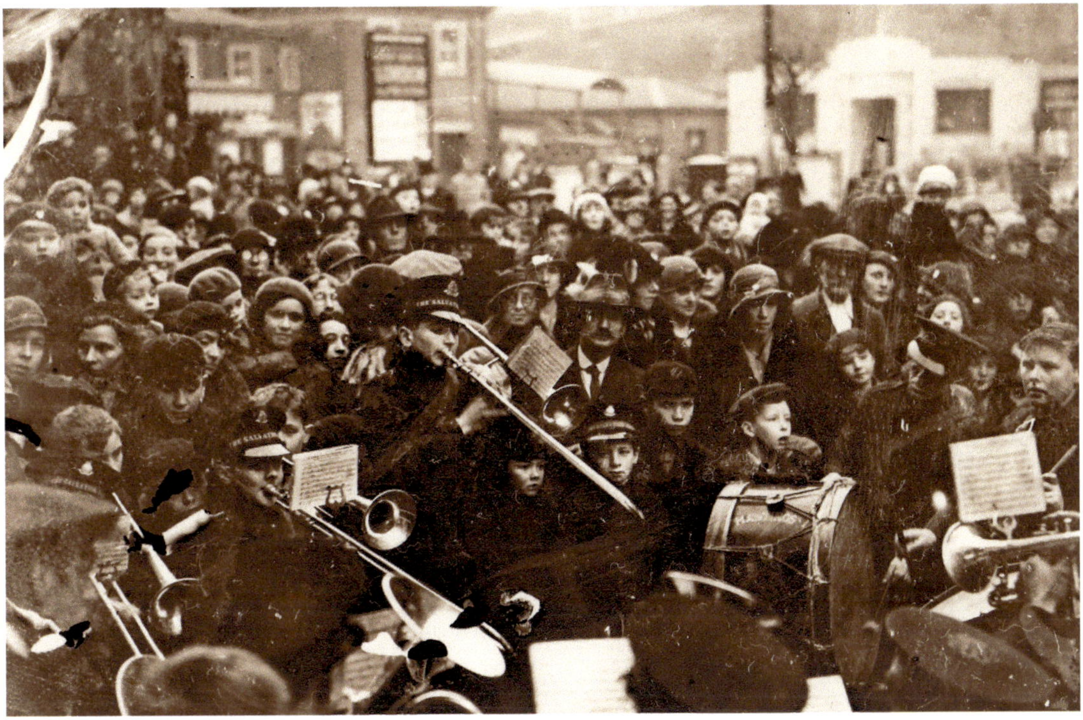

Christmas Carols on Kings Road

The old photograph, taken on 8 December 1934, is of the Hastings Citadel Young People's Band, who were out playing Christmas carols under the command of band leader Jack Glazier. Afterwards the band had tea at the Regal Cinema. Behind the large crowds is Warrior Square station, which opened in February 1851.

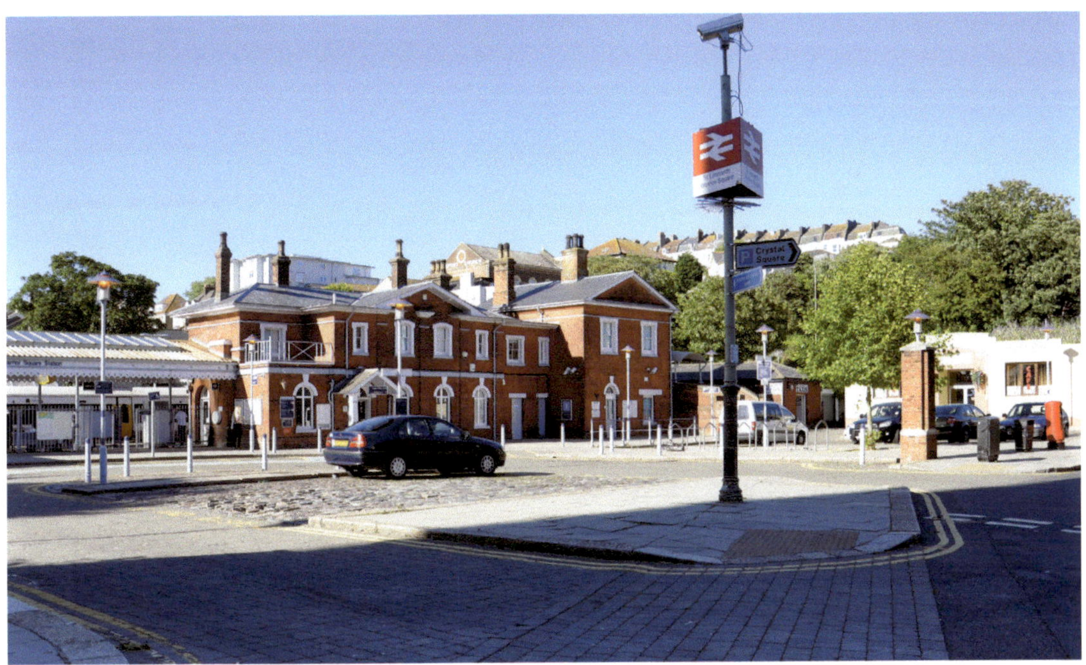

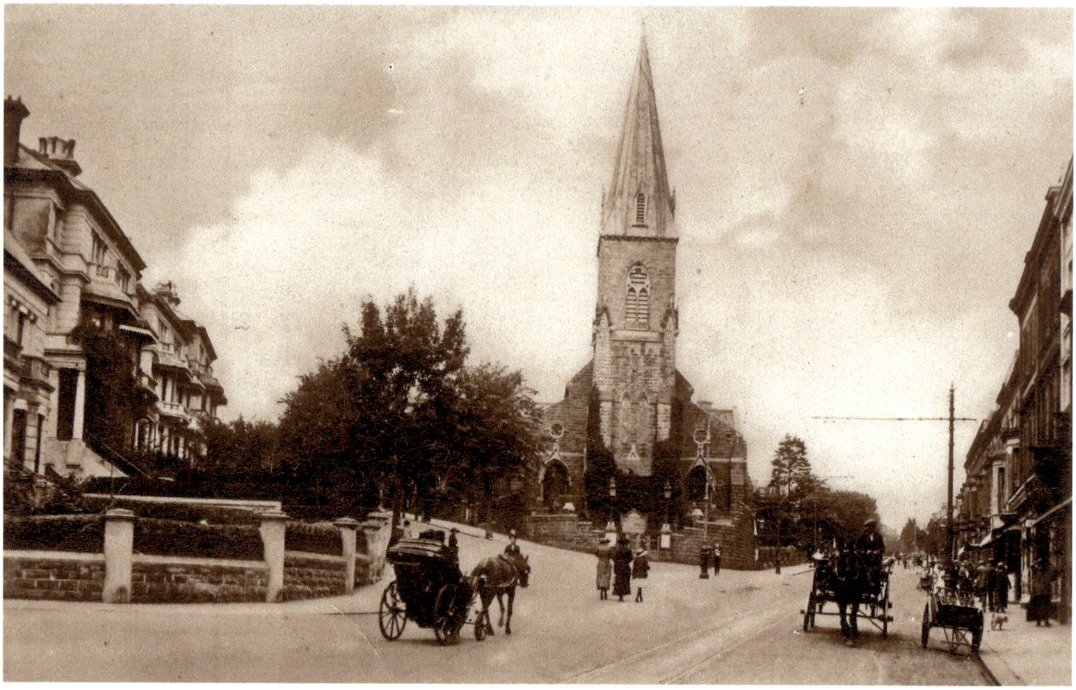

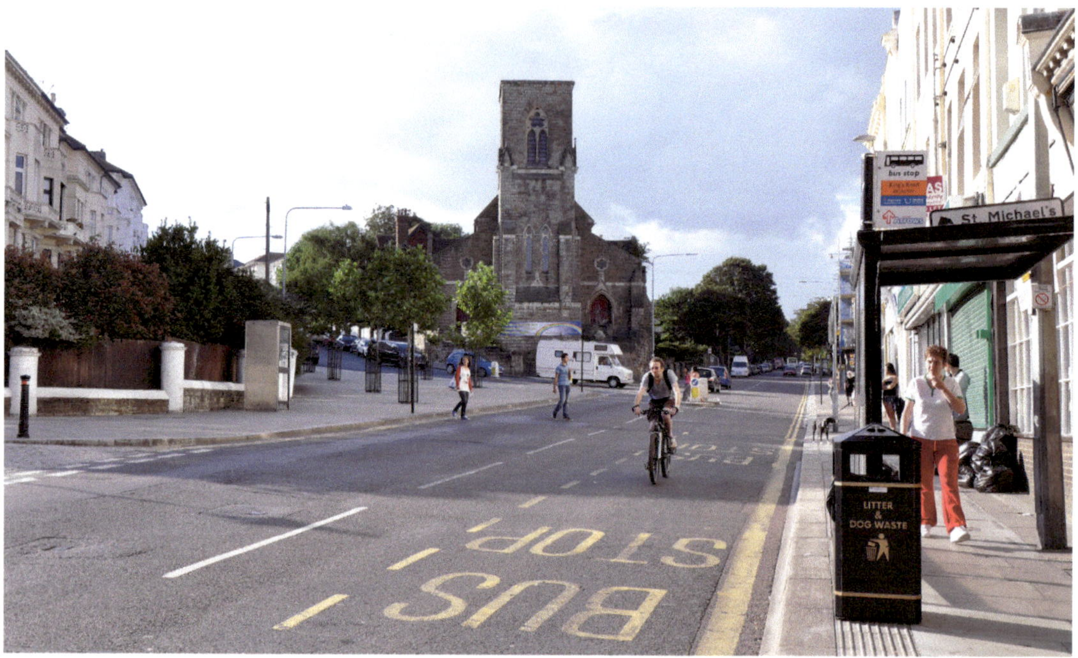

St Leonards-on-Sea United Reformed Church, London Road

Little has changed between these two photographs; the main difference is the loss of the copper church spire, which was damaged in the Great Storm of 1987. The church was founded in 1863 as a Congregational Church for the rising Nonconformist population of St Leonards. It joined with the United Reformed Church in 1972, but the building fell out of use and the last United Reformed service in the Grade II listed building took place in 2002.

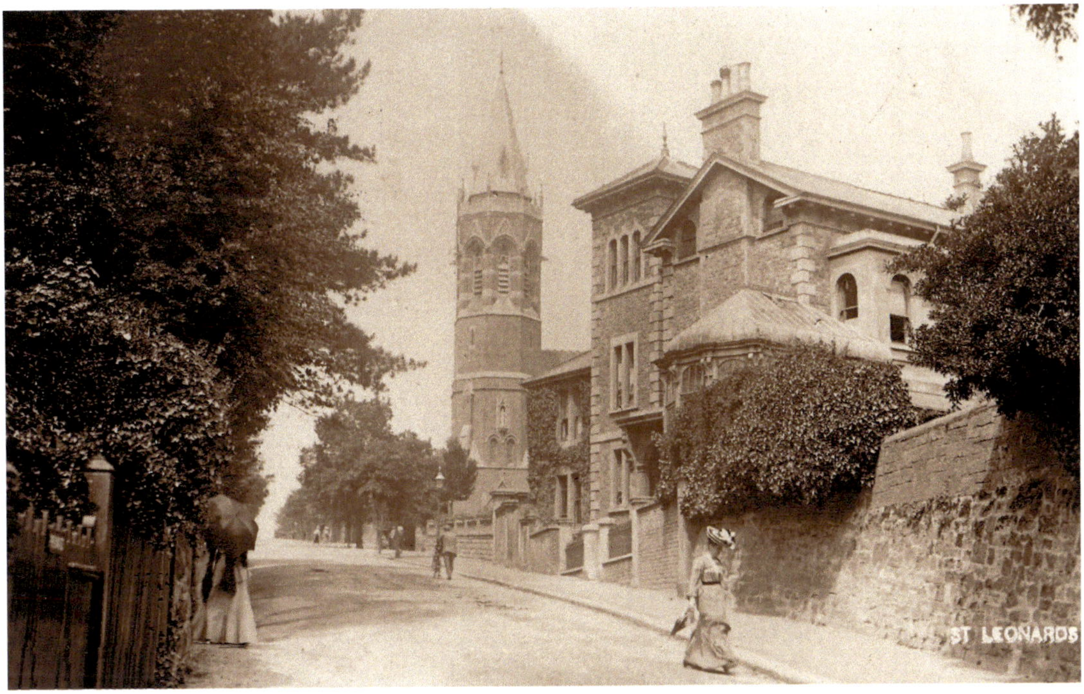

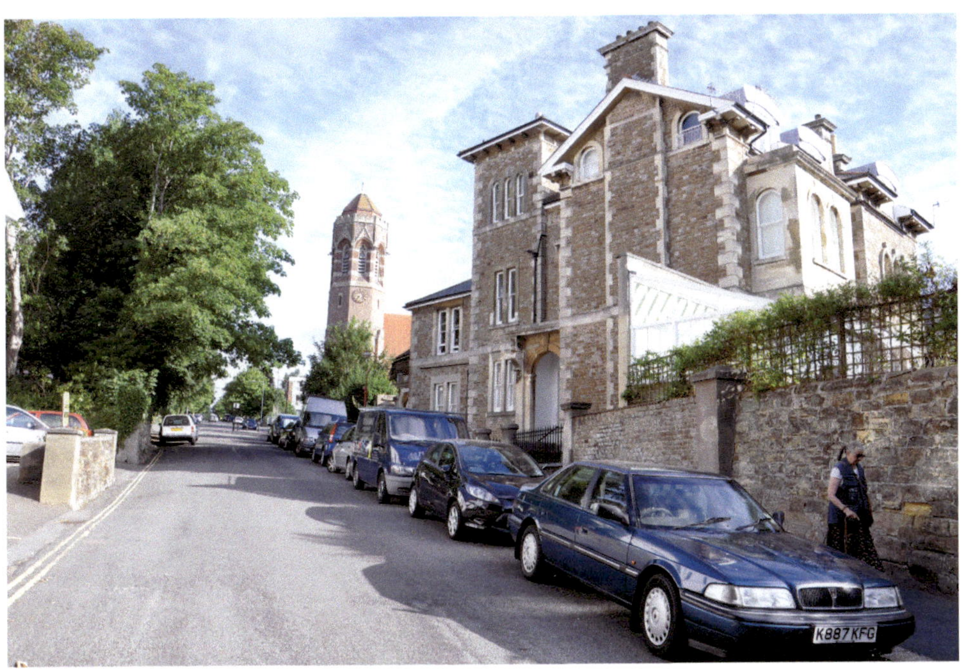

St John's Church: Fourth Version

The 2010 view of St John's church is the fourth church to be built on the site: the first blew down in 1866, just one year after completion; the second burnt down on 30 November 1878; the third was almost entirely destroyed by enemy bombing on 9 February 1943. Despite the spire being pierced by the bomb, it managed to survive the blast. The foundation stone of the current church was laid by HRH Princess Elizabeth on 18 May 1951.

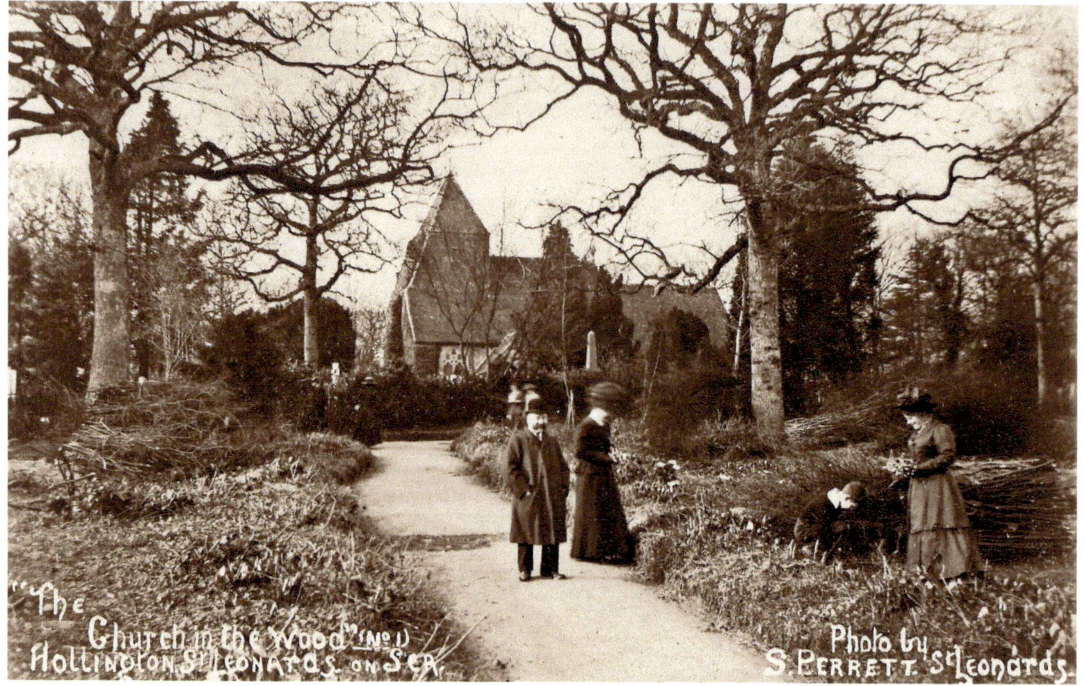

Built by the Evil One

Unfortunately, the older view of Church-in-the-Wood could not be replicated due to tree growth and the creation of a lychgate. Mary Howard described the church's location in the 1864 *Handbook for Hastings and St Leonards* thus: 'The peculiar situation of Hollington, "the Church in a Wood", often excites surprise, and has given occasion to the old legend of its having been built by the Evil One, pulling down and carrying off the materials of a fabric which was being erected in a more accessible spot...'

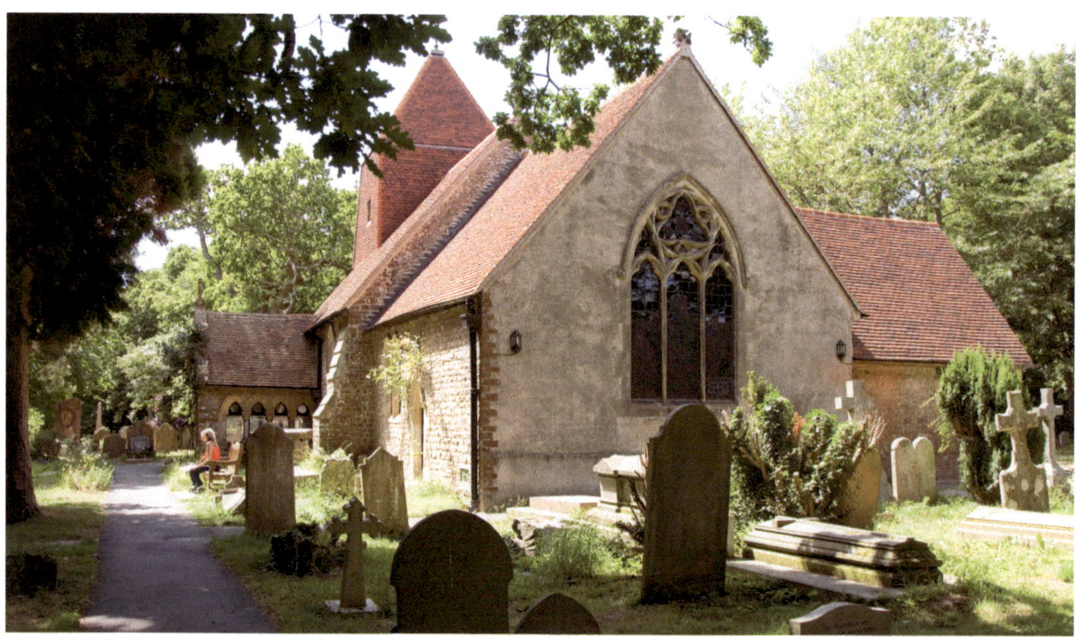